HUMAN RIGHTS *in* JUDAISM

HUMAN RIGHTS *in* JUDAISM

CULTURAL, RELIGIOUS, AND POLITICAL PERSPECTIVES

MICHAEL J. BROYDE
JOHN WITTE, Jr.

JASON ARONSON INC.
Northvale, New Jersey
Jerusalem

This book was set in 11 pt. Rockwell Light by Alpha Graphics of Pittsfield, New Hampshire.

Library of Congress Cataloging-in-Publication Data

Human rights in Judaism : cultural, religious and political
   perspectives / [edited by] Michael J. Broyde, John Witte, Jr.
      p. cm.
   Includes bibliographical references and index.
   ISBN 0–7657–9977–4
    1. Civil rights (Jewish law)   2. Human rights—Religious aspects—
Judaism.   3. Jews—Legal status, laws, etc.   4. Judaism and state.
I. Broyde, Michael J.   II. Witte, John, 1959–   .
LAW
296.3'82—DC21   97–27141
                                                    CIP

Manufactured in the United States of America. Jason Aronson Inc. offers books and cassettes. For information and catalog write to Jason Aronson Inc., 230 Livingston Street, Northvale, New Jersey 07647.

CONTENTS

ACKNOWLEDGMENTS

Earlier versions of several chapters in this volume were published in John Witte, Jr., and Johan D. van der Vyver, editors, *Religious Human Rights in Global Perspective: Religious Perspectives* (Martinus Nijhoff Publishers, 1996), pp. xvii–xxxv, 175–202, 203–234, 235–294, 295–322, and in Johan D. van der Vyver and John Witte, Jr., editors, *Religious Human Rights in Global Perspective: Legal Perspectives* (Martinus Nijhoff Publishers, 1996), 349–390. The editors would like to express their appreciation to Martinus Nijhoff Publishers for permission to print herein revised versions of these materials.

Portions of the Introduction are also drawn from John Witte, Jr., "Law, Religion, and Human Rights" in *Columbia Human Rights Law Review* 36 (1996) 1–31 and reprinted herein with the permission of the publisher.

The editors would also like to express their appreciation to Ms. Pamela Roth and Mr. Arthur Kurzweil of Jason Aronson Inc. for their sage editorial guidance in the preparation of this volume and to Ms. Louise Jackson for her help in preparing the manuscript.

Michael J. Broyde
John Witte, Jr.

INTRODUCTION

JOHN WITTE, JR.
EMORY UNIVERSITY

The world today is torn by a paradoxical crisis. On the one hand, we have been witnessing a democratic metamorphosis of almost apocalyptic alacrity. The Berlin Wall has fallen. The Soviet Empire is no more. African autocracies have crumbled. Apartheid has faded. Latin American dictators have ceded. More than thirty new democracies have been born since 1973. Democratic agitation has even reached Tiananmen Square.[1] On the other hand, the world is beset by tumult and tragedy of near diabolical dimensions. With the memories of the Holocaust, gulags, and world war still fresh in our minds, we see deadly explosions in Israel and the Middle East; bloody slaughter in Rwanda, Burundi, and the Sudan; tragic genocide in the Balkans; and massive unrest in Central America, Southern Asia, the Korean Peninsula, Chechenya, Azerbaijan, and other Eurasian republics. Every continent now faces opposing movements of incremental political unification versus radical balkanization, gentle religious ecumenism versus radical fundamentalism, sensible moral pluralization versus shocking moral relativism.[2] Even in the older, more stable democracies of

---

[1]See, for example, S. P. Huntington, *The Third Wave of Democracy: Democratization in the Late Twentieth Century* (Lincoln, Neb., 1991); J. Witte, Jr., ed., *Christianity and Democracy in Global Context* (Boulder/ San Francisco, 1993).

[2]See, for example, D. Horowitz, "The Challenge of Ethnic Conflict: Democracy in Divided Societies," *Journal of Democracy* 4:4 (1993): 18;

the West, bitter "culture wars" have aligned defenders of various old orders against an array of new deconstructionists. In America the abyss between city and country, ghetto and suburb, black and white, straight and gay, old and young, the monied and the maligned, the armed and their victims seems to grow constantly deeper.

Analyzing this paradox of the simultaneous democratization and destruction of the local and the world order presents one of the most pressing challenges of the twenty-first century. Meeting this challenge will certainly require the continued cultivation of worldwide science, commerce, technology, global literature, language, media, and the international environmental, health care, and conservation movements. These are matters beyond cavil—and beyond my ken.

My argument is at once simple and counterintuitive. The simple aspect is that any solution to the world crisis must be grounded in a regime of law and human rights. To prove this thesis would be to belabor the obvious. The counterintuitive part of the argument is that religion—in its Judaic, as well as every other form—must be seen as a vital dimension of any legal regime of human rights.

Modern human rights laws will provide no panacea to the world crisis in the next century, but they will be a critical part of any solution. The world's religions will not be easy allies to engage, but the struggle for human rights cannot be won without them, for human rights laws are inherently abstract ideals—universal statements about the good life and the good society. They depend upon the visions of human communities and institutions to give them content and coherence, to provide "the scale of values governing the[ir] exercise and concrete manifestation."[3] Religion is an in-

---

S. P. Huntington, "The Clash of Civilizations?" *Foreign Affairs* 22 (Summer 1993); M. Juergensmeyer, *The New Cold War: Religious Nationalism Confronts the Secular State* (Berehely, 1993); M. Marty and R. S. Appelby, eds., *Fundamentalisms and the State* (Chicago, 1993); and also their *Fundamentalisms Comprehended* (Chicago, 1995).

[3] J. Maritain, introduction to UNESCO, *Human Rights: Comments and Interpretations* (New York, 1949), 15–16, quoted and discussed in D. Hollenbach, "Human Rights and Religious Faith in the Middle East: Reflections of a Christian Theologian," *Human Rights Quarterly* 4 (1982): 94, 96.

eradicable condition of human lives and communities. Religions invariably provide universal sources and "scales of values" by which many persons and communities govern themselves. Religions must thus be seen as indispensable allies in the modern struggle for human rights.[4] Their faith and works must be adduced in order to give meaning and measure to the abstract claims of human rights norms and to give spirit and sanctity to the legal ideas and institutions of a human rights regime.

This Introduction will develop this argument in two parts. First, I shall argue that all laws, including human rights laws, have necessary religious sources, dimensions, and analogues. Second, I shall argue that the modern movement for human rights law has impoverished itself by its conventional deprecation of the roles and rights of religion, and that religious ideas and institutions need to be drawn into a healthy regime of law, democracy, and human rights.

The following chapters demonstrate the remarkable contributions that Judaism has made, and can make, to the theory, law, and activism of human rights.

LAW AND RELIGION

My first counterintuitive argument is that law and religion are two intermixed solvents of human living, two interlocking sources and systems of value and vision that exist in all human communities, regardless of time, place, and culture. Law and religion, Justice Harry Blackmun once wrote, "are an inherent part of the calculus of how a man should live" and how a society should run.[5] The

---

[4]M. Marty, "Religious Dimensions of Human Rights," in J. Witte, Jr., and J. D. van der Vyver, eds., *Religious Human Rights in Global Perspective: Religious Perspectives*, (Hague, 1996): 1:6–16; H. Cox and A. Sharma, "Positive Resources of Religion for Human Rights," in J. Kelsay and S. B. Twiss, eds., *Religion and Human Rights* (New York, 1994), 61–79.

[5]H. Blackmun, foreword in J. Witte, Jr., and F. S. Alexander, eds., *The Weightier Matters of the Law: Essays on Law and Religion* (Atlanta, 1988), ix.

contents of legal and religious systems, of course, can differ dramatically over time and across cultures; at points, they can converge or contradict each other. But these two systems are always present.[6]

To appreciate this interaction, one must move beyond the positivist concepts of law and the privatist concepts of religion that dominate the modern Western academy. Among many jurists today, law is considered to be simply a body of rules and statutes designed to govern society. Religion is conceived simply to be a body of doctrines and exercises designed to guide private conscience and the voluntary religious society. By these definitions, law has no place in the realm of religion; religion has no place in the regime of law.

Such concepts of law and religion are too narrow to enable us to understand the relationship between these two spheres and the sciences. Viewed in its broadest terms, law consists of all norms that govern human conduct and all actions taken to formulate and respond to those norms. Such norms include moral commandments, state statutes, religious canons, family rules, commercial habits, communal customs, forms of etiquette, and various other social standards. Even when viewed in narrower institutional terms, law consists of more than simply the rules of the state. On the one hand, law is the social activity by which certain rules or norms are formulated by legitimate authorities and then actualized by persons subject to those authorities. The process of legal formulation involves legislating, adjudicating, administering, and other conduct by legitimate officials. The process of legal actualization involves obeying, negotiating, litigating, and other conduct by legal subjects in response to those norms.[7] Moreover, numerous institutions besides the state are often involved in this social activity of legal

---

[6]See, generally, ibid.; H. J. Berman, *Faith and Order: The Reconciliation of Law and Religion* (Atlanta, 1993); J. Witte, Jr., "A New Concordance of Discordant Canons: Harold J. Berman on Law and Religion," *Emory Law Journal* 42 (1993): 523.

[7]See H. J. Berman, *Law and Revolution: The Formation of the Western Legal Tradition* (Cambridge, 1983), 4–5; J. Hall, *Comparative Law and Social Theory* (Indianapolis, 1963), 78–82.

formulation and actualization. The rules, customs, and processes of churches, colleges, corporations, clubs, convents, and other non-state associations are just as much a part of a society's legal system as are those of the state.

Likewise, religion cannot simply be reduced to private belief or to the activities of religious leaders. Viewed in its broadest terms, religion embraces all beliefs and actions that concern the ultimate origin, meaning, and purpose of life, of existence. Religion involves the responses of the human heart, soul, and mind to revelation, to transcendent values, to what Rudolf Otto once called the "idea of the holy."[8] Viewed in narrower institutional terms, religion embraces creeds, cults, codes of conduct, and confessional communities.[9] A creed defines the accepted cadre of beliefs and values concerning the ultimate origin, meaning, and purpose of life. A cult defines the appropriate rites, rituals, and patterns of worship and devotion that give expression to those beliefs. A code of conduct defines the appropriate individual and social habits of those who profess the creed and practice the cult. A confessional community defines the group of individuals who embrace and live out this creed, cult, and code of conduct, both on their own and with fellow believers. By this definition, a religion can be traditional or very new, closely confining or loosely structured, world-avertive or world-affirmative, atheistic, nontheistic, polytheistic, or monotheistic. It is critical to realize, however, that religion consists of both beliefs and the social articulation, implementation, and elaboration of those beliefs.

These broad functional definitions of law and religion provide no bright line tests to resolve penumbral cases. It is not always easy to distinguish between legal and nonlegal norms, between genuine and spurious religious claims. But these functional definitions of law and religion provide the principal means of differentiating between two distinct spheres of ideas and institutions and two distinct methods and forms of study—legal science and religious science, jurisprudence and theology.

---

[8]R. Otto, *The Idea of the Holy: An Inquiry into the Non-Rational Factor of the Idea of the Divine and Its Relation to the Rational*, 2d ed. (New York, 1950).

[9]L. W. Swidler, ed., *Religious Liberty and Human Rights in Nations and Religions* (Philadelphia, 1986), vii.

To be sure, the spheres and sciences of law and religion have, on occasion, both converged and contradicted each other. Every religious tradition has known both theonomism and antinomianism—the excessive legalization and the excessive spiritualization of religion. Every legal tradition has known both theocracy and totalitarianism—the excessive sacralization and the excessive secularization of law. But the dominant reality in most eras and cultures is that law and religion stand neither in monistic unity nor in dualistic antinomy, but in dialectical harmony. Every religious tradition strives to come to terms with law by striking a balance between the rational and the mystical, the prophetic and the priestly, the structural and the spiritual. Every legal tradition struggles to link its formal structures and processes with the beliefs and ideals of its people.[10] Law and religion are distinct spheres and sciences of human life, but they exist in dialectical interaction, constantly crossing over and cross-fertilizing each other.

Various modes of interaction between law and religion can be distinguished. For example, law and religion are *conceptually* related. Both disciplines draw upon the same underlying concepts about the nature of being and order, of the person and the community, and of knowledge and truth. Both law and religion embrace closely analogous concepts of sin and crime, covenant and contract, redemption and rehabilitation, righteousness and justice, which invariably combine in the mind of the legislator, judge, or juror. The modern legal concept of crime, for example, has been shaped by a Jewish and Christian theology of sin and penance. The modern legal concept of absolutely obligating contracts was forged in the crucible of early Jewish and later Puritan covenant theology.

Law and religion are *methodologically* related. Both disciplines have developed analogous hermeneutical methods, modes of interpreting their authoritative texts. Both have developed logical methods, modes of deducing precepts from principles, of reasoning from analogy and precedent. Both have developed ethical methods, modes of molding their deepest values and beliefs into prescribed or preferred habits of conduct. Both have developed

---

[10]See H. J. Berman, *The Interaction of Law and Religion* (New York, 1974), 133–142; Berman, Law and Revolution, x–xii.

forensic and rhetorical methods, modes of arranging and present-
ing arguments and data. Both have developed methods of adduc-
ing evidence and adjudicating disputes. Both have developed
methods of organizing, systematizing, and teaching their subject
matters.

Law and religion are *institutionally* related—principally in the
relationship between church and state, but also in the relationships
among sundry other religious and political groups. Jurists and theologians have worked hand-in-hand to define the proper relation
between these religious and political groups, to determine their
respective responsibilities, to facilitate their cooperation, to delimit
the forms of support and protection that each can afford the other.
Many of the great Western constitutional doctrines of church
and state—the "two cities theory" of Augustine, the "two powers
theory" of Gelasius, the "two swords theory" of the High Middle
Ages, the "two kingdoms theory" of the Reformation era—are
rooted in both civil law and canonical law, in theological jurisprudence and political theology. Much of American constitutional law
concerning religion and state is the product of both Enlightenment
legal and political doctrines and Christian theological and moral
dogma.

Law and religion are *professionally* related. In many earlier societies, and among certain groups even today, the legal profession and the religious profession are undifferentiated. Legal and
sacerdotal responsibilities are vested in one office or in one person, be one a rabbi, chieftain, oracle, or pontiff. Even when these
professions are differentiated, however, they remain closely related. The professions are similar in form. Both require extensive
doctrinal training and maintain stringent admissions policies. Both
have developed codes of professional ethics and internal structures of authority to enforce them. Both seek to promote cooperation, collegiality, and *esprit de corps.* The professions are also
parallel in function. There are close affinities between the media-
tion of the lawyer and the intercession of the cleric, between the
adjudication of the secular court and the arbitration of the religious
tribunal. Ideally, both professions serve and minister to society.
Both seek to exemplify the ideals of calling and community.

These and other forms of interaction have helped render the
spheres and sciences of law and religion to be dependent on—

and, indeed, dimensions of—each other. On the one hand, law gives religious lives and religious communities their *structure*— the order and orthodoxy that they need in order to survive and to flourish in society. Legal "habits of the heart" structure the inner spiritual life and discipline of religious believers, from the reclusive hermit to the aggressive zealot. Legal concepts of justice, order, atonement, restitution, responsibility, obligation, and many others, pervade the theological doctrines of many religious traditions. Legal structures and processes, such as the Jewish *halachah*, the Christian canon law, and the Muslim *shari'a*, define and govern religious communities and their distinctive beliefs and rituals, mores and morals. Without this legal structure, religion would readily decay into shallow spiritualism.

On the other hand, religion gives legal processes and norms their *spirit*—the sanctity and authority they need to command obedience and respect. Religion inspires the rituals of the courtroom, the decorum of the legislature, the pageantry of the executive office, all of which celebrate and confirm the ideal objectivity and uniformity, the truth and justice of the law. Religion gives law its ideal structural fairness, its "inner morality," as Lon Fuller once called it.[11] Legal rules and sanctions are publicly proclaimed and popularly known. They are uniform, stable, and understandable. They are prospectively applied and consistently enforced. Religion gives law its respect for tradition; for the continuity of institutions, language, and practice; for precedent and preservation. Just as religion has the Judaic tradition, the Christian tradition, and the Islamic tradition, so law has the common law tradition, the civil law tradition, and the constitutional tradition. As in religion, so in law— we abandon the time-tested practices of the past only with trepidation, only with explanation. Religion gives law its authority and legitimacy, by inducing in citizens and subjects a reverence for law and structures of authority, by producing what Harold Berman calls "a popular faith in a truth and a justice that transcends social utility."[12] As does religion, law has written or oral sources, texts, or oracles, which are considered to be decisive in themselves.

---

[11]L. Fuller, *The Morality of the Law*, rev. ed. (New Haven, 1964), 33–94.
[12]Berman, Faith and Order, 7

Religion has the Torah and the Bible and the rabbis and pastors who expound them. Law has the constitutions and the statutes and the judges and agencies that apply them. Without this religious spirit, law would readily decay into empty formalism.

Law and religion, therefore, are two great interlocking systems of value and belief. They have their own sources and structures of normativity and authority, their own methods and measures of enforcement and amendment, and their own rituals and habits of conceptualization and celebration of values. These spheres and sciences of law and religion exist in dialectical harmony. They share many elements, many concepts, and many methods. They also balance each other by counterpoising justice and mercy, rule and equity, orthodoxy and liberty, discipline and love. This dialectical harmony gives law and religion their vitality and their strength.

RELIGION AND HUMAN RIGHTS

My second counterintuitive argument is that religion, in all its denominational multiplicity, must be included within a legal regime of human rights. Many consider this a foolish argument. For even the great religions of the Book seem to be controversial candidates for any constructive role in the regime of human rights. None of these religious traditions speaks unequivocally about human rights, and none has amassed an exemplary human rights record over the centuries. Their sacred texts and canons say much more about commandments and obligations than about liberties and rights. Their theologians and jurists have resisted the importation of human rights as much as they have helped in their cultivation. Their internal policies and external advocacy have helped to perpetuate bigotry, chauvinism, and violence as much as they have served to propagate equality, liberty, and fraternity. "The blood of thousands" is at the doors of our churches, temples, and mosques. The bludgeons of pogroms, crusades, jihads, inquisitions, and ostracisms have been used to devastating effect within and among these great faiths.

Moreover, the modern cultivation of human rights (in the West, at least) began in earnest fifty years ago when Christianity and its

Enlightenment successors seemed incapable of delivering on their promises. In the middle of this century, there was no messianic return promised by Christians, no heavenly city of reason promised by enlightened libertarians, no withering away of the state promised by enlightened socialists. Instead, there was world war, gulags, and the Holocaust—a vile and evil fascism and irrationalism to which Christianity and the Enlightenment seemed to have no cogent response or effective deterrent.

The modern human rights movement was thus born out of desperation in the aftermath of World War II. It was an attempt to find a world faith to fill a spiritual void. It was an attempt to harvest from the Western religious traditions rudimentary elements of a new faith and a new law that would unite a badly broken world order. The proud claims of Article I of the 1948 Universal Declaration of Human Rights—"That all men are born free and equal in rights and dignity [and] are endowed with reason and conscience"—expounded the primitive truths of Christianity and the Enlightenment with little basis in post-war reality. Freedom and equality were hard to find anywhere. Reason and conscience had blatantly betrayed themselves in the previous decades.

Though conceived in desperation, the human rights movement grew precociously in the decades following World War II. Indeed, after the 1950s, a veritable "human rights revolution" erupted.[13] In America and Europe, this rights revolution yielded a powerful grassroots civil rights movement and a welter of landmark cases and statutes. In Africa and Latin America, it produced agitation, and eventually revolt, against colonial and autocratic rule. At the international level, the Universal Declaration of 1948 inspired new declarations, covenants, and conventions on more discrete rights, most notably the great 1966 Covenants. Academies throughout the world produced a prodigious amount of literature urging constant reform and the expansion of the human rights regime. Within a generation, human rights had become the "new civic or secular faith" of the post-war world order.[14]

––––––––––––––––––

[13]The phrase is from R. J. Vincent, *Human Rights and International Relations* (Cambridge, 1986), 93.

[14]J. Maritain, *Man and the State* (Chicago, 1951), 110–111. For a masterful survey, see N. Lerner, "Religious Human Rights under the United

Jewish and Christian communities participated actively as mid-wives in the birth of this modern rights revolution, and special religious rights protections were at first actively pursued. Individual religious groups issued bold confessional statements and manifestos on human rights shortly after World War II. Several denominations and the budding ecumenical church joined Jewish Non-Governmental Organizations (NGOs) in the cultivation of human rights at the international level. The Free Church tradition played a critical role in the civil rights movement in America and beyond, as did the social gospel and Christian democratic movements in Europe and Latin America.[15]

After expressing some initial interest, however, leaders of the rights revolution consigned religious groups and their distinctive religious rights and needs to a low priority. Freedom of speech and press, parity of race and gender, provision of work and welfare captured most of the energy and emoluments of the rights revolution. After the 1960s, academic inquiries and activist interventions into religious rights and their abuses became increasingly intermittent and isolated, inspired as much by parochial self-interest as by universal golden rules. The rights revolution seemed to be passing religion by.

This deprecation of the role and rights of religion was not simply the product of calculated agnosticism or callous apathy, though there was ample evidence of both. Leaders of the rights revolution were often forced, by reason of political pressure or limited resources, to address the most glaring rights abuses. Physical abuses—torture, rape, war crimes, false imprisonment, forced poverty—are easier to track and to treat than spiritual abuses and often demand more immediate attention. In desperate circumstances, it is better to be a Good Samaritan than a good preacher, to give food and comfort before sermons and catechisms.

Nations," in J. van der Vyver and J. Witte Jr., eds. *Religious Human Rights in Global Perspectives: Legal Perspectives*, (Hague, 1996), 79–134.

[15]See, generally, essay by Irwin Cotler and J. Bryan Hehir, "Religious Activism for Human Rights: A Christian Case Study," in Witte and Van der Vyver, *Religious Human Rights in Global Perspectives: Religious Perspectives*. 97–120; R. Papini, "Christianity and Democracy in Europe: The Christian Democratic Movement," in ibid., 47–64, note 2.

The relative silence of religious communities seemed to lend credence to this prioritization of effort. With some notable exceptions among Jewish and ecumenical Christian communities, religious groups after the 1960s made only modest contributions to the theory, law, and activism of human rights. The general principles set out in their post-war manifestos on rights were not converted to specific precepts or programs. Their general endorsement of human rights instruments was not followed by specific lobbying and litigation efforts. Whether most religious groups were content with their own condition, or intent on turning the other cheek or looking the other way in the face of religious rights abuses, their relative silence did considerable harm to the human rights revolution.

The deprecation of the special role and rights of religions from the early 1960s onward has introduced several distortions into the theory and law of human rights in vogue today. First, this deprecation has "impoverished" the general theory of human rights embraced by the rights revolution.[16] On the one hand, it has cut many rights from their roots. The right to religion, Georg Jellinek wrote, is "the mother of many other rights."[17] For the religious individual, the right to believe leads ineluctably to the rights to assemble, speak, worship, proselytize, educate, parent, travel, or to abstain from the same on the basis of one's beliefs. For the religious association, the right to exist invariably involves rights to corporate property, collective worship, organized charity, parochial education, freedom of press, and autonomy of governance. To ignore religious rights is to overlook the conceptual, if not historical, source of many other individual and associational rights. On the other hand, this deprecation of religious rights has abstracted rights from duties. The classic faiths of the Book adopt and advocate religious rights in order to protect religious duties. A religious individual or association has rights to exist and act, not in the abstract but in order to discharge discrete religious duties.

---

[16]Cf. M. Glendon, *Rights Talk: The Impoverishment of Political Discourse* (New York, 1991).

[17]G. Jellinek, *Die Erklärung der Menschen- und Bürgerrechte: Ein Beitrag zur modernen Verfassungsgeschichte* (Darmastadh, 1895), 42.

Religious rights provide the best example of the organic linkage between rights and responsibilities.[18] Without the example of religious rights readily at hand, leaders of the rights revolution have tended to lose sight of these organic connections and to treat rights as the abstract and seemingly limitless claims of individuals.

Second, this deprecation of religious rights has sharpened the divide between Western and non-Western theories of rights. Many non-Western traditions, particularly those of Islamic, Hindu, Buddhist, Taoist, and Traditional stock, can neither conceive of, nor accept, a system of rights that excludes religion. Religion is, for these traditions, inextricably integrated into every facet of life. Religious rights are thus an inherent aspect of the rights of speech, press, assembly, and other individual rights, as well as ethnic, cultural, linguistic, and similar associational rights. No system of rights that ignores or deprecates this cardinal role of religion can be respected or adopted. Since Western notions of rights dominate international law, many non-Western societies have neither accepted nor adopted the basic international declarations and covenants on human rights.

Third, this deprecation of religion has exaggerated the role of the state as the guarantor of human rights. The simple state vs. individual dialectic of modern human rights theories leaves it to the state to protect rights of all sorts—"first generation" civil and political rights, "second generation" social, cultural, and economic rights, and "third generation" environmental and developmental rights. In reality, the state is not, and cannot be, so omnicompetent—as the recently failed experiments in socialism have vividly shown. A vast plurality of "mediating structures" stand between the state and the individual, religious institutions prominently among them. Religious institutions, among others, play a vital role in the cultivation and realization of all rights, including religious rights. They create the conditions (if not the prototypes) for the realization of first generation civil and political rights. They pro-

---

[18]See, for example, D. Novak, "Religious Human Rights in Judaic Texts," in Witte and van der Vyver, eds., *Religious Human Rights in Global Perspectives: Religious Perspectives*, 175–202, note 4; A. An-Na'im, "Islamic Foundations of Religious Human Rights: *Religious Perspectives*" in ibid., 337–360.

vide a critical (and sometimes the principal) means to meet second generation rights of education, health care, child care, labor organizations, employment, and artistic opportunities, among others. Religious institutions offer some of the deepest insights into norms of creation, stewardship, and servanthood that lie at the heart of third generation rights.[19]

The challenge of the next century, therefore, will be to transform religious communities from "midwives" to "mothers" of human rights—from agents that assist in the birth of rights norms that were conceived elsewhere to associations that give birth and nurture to their own unique contributions to human rights norms and practices.

In the past few years, the great religions of the Book have begun this process of rights transformation.[20] The changes are awkward, incremental, controversial, and sometimes even fatal. But this rights transformation of religious communities around the world seems to be both inevitable and irreversible.

The chapters collected in this volume forcefully demonstrate the unique contributions of the Judaic tradition to the theory, law, and activism concerning human rights. Collectively, the chapters review both historical and current rights contributions of Judaism—within Israel and within Diaspora communities, within *halachah* and within secular national and international laws. The chapters concern not only the general human rights claims of the Jewish people as a whole, but also the unique plight of discrete groups within Judaism—women and the *agunah*, dissidents and the excommunicated, children and the destitute, pilgrims and the new emigres. The epilogue addresses the lingering tensions between rights and duties, liberties and commandments, within Jewish thought.

---

[19]See, for example, W. Huber, "Rights of Nature or Dignity of Nature?" *The Annual of the Society of Christian Ethics* (1991):43.

[20]See chapters and sources in Witte and van der Vyver, eds., *Religious Human Rights in Global Perspectives*, note 4.

1

RELIGIOUS HUMAN RIGHTS IN JUDAIC TEXTS

DAVID NOVAK
University of Toronto

RIGHTS OF RELIGION AND RELIGIOUS RIGHTS

In speaking of "religious human rights," two different ideas come to mind. First, there is the idea of what is commonly called "religious liberty," that is, the duty of society to respect and protect the right of every human person to worship any god of his or her choice or no god at all (as long as the exercise of that right is not disruptive of the secular order of that society, of course). In other words, one of the primary duties of society is the duty to protect the right of religious liberty along with other human rights. But, second, there is the idea of what one could call "the religious foundation of human rights," that is, religious rights as the source of all other rights.

These two separate ideas are not mutually exclusive or incapable of ever being connected. Both could be seen as aspects of the more general issue of the relation of religion and society, which is certainly a perennial political issue. Nevertheless, these being aspects of a larger issue does not resolve the tension I perceive between the two ideas. There is a considerable difference between a person who begins his or her reflection starting from the theme of religious rights *along with* other *human* rights, and another person who begins his or her reflection starting from the theme of the religious *source of* rights, which must consider the question of rights from more than merely a human perspective. Judaism, Christianity, and Islam, which are religions of revelation, see their own truth as coming from God, not man. Indeed, that stipulation is the only cogent distinction that can be made between a religion and a philosophy. Therefore, the distinction between beginning from one idea or the other involves real differences in terms of the way we approach the whole issue of religion and society.

In fact, the difference between these two ideas is the subject of one of the great constitutional debates of our time, namely, the debate over the meaning of the so-called "religion clauses" of the First Amendment to the Constitution of the United States. It is to be recalled that there is not one clause of the First Amendment pertaining to religion but two. "Congress shall [1] make no law respecting an establishment of religion or [2] prohibiting the free exercise thereof." The question under great debate today is whether the clause dealing with free exercise of religion derives from the disestablishment clause or vice versa.[1] It is much more than an issue of syntactical analysis. Rather, the question is whether the exercise of religion is something the secular political authority, having the power of lawmaking, *subsequently entitles* the citizens of the polity to, or whether the citizens of the polity *already have the right* to exercise (that is, practice) their religion *before* the secular political authority makes any laws at all. In both options, the state is not to become the arbiter of which *one* religion is to be favored above all others. The difference here is that in the first option, religion might very well be something *beneath* the domain of the state because it is too trivial for the state to want to legislate, whereas in the second option religion is something *beyond* the domain of the state because it is too important for the state to be able to legislate.

The difference between these two approaches to the First Amendment is nothing less than a political debate about whether

---

[1]See Michael W. McConnell, "The Origins and Historical Understanding of the Free Exercise of Religion," *Harvard Law Review* 103 (1990): 1410ff.; Mary Ann Glendon and Raul F. Yanes, "Structural Free Exercise," *Michigan Law Review* 90 (1991): 477ff.; Michael Sandel, "Freedom of Conscience or Freedom of Choice?" in Os Guiness and James Davison Hunter, eds., *Articles of Faith, Articles of Peace* (Washington, 1990), 72ff.

religion requires secular justification or whether the secular realm requires religious justification. For religious people, it would seem that the practice of their religions must be the source of all other practices, including those practices involved in interhuman relationships that, in and of themselves, are not distinctly religious.[2] For secularists, though, religion can at best be a matter of tolerated taste. There is hardly an issue of political–moral dispute today—be it over abortion, euthanasia, criminal punishment, or war—into which this basic religious–secular dispute is not ultimately to be found at its core.[3] And, certainly, this is not the first time in human history when conflicting interpretations of an opaque text have been the locus of a great political debate.

Without placing the presentations of texts from religious traditions in this political context, such presentations can be little more than "background music" for discussions of the real questions at hand in all their gravity. Thus, some theoretical prolegomenon is a necessary condition for making the highly selective presentation of these texts an integral participant in the political discussion of rights today. This discussion is much too important theoretically and practically to bother with obscurantist scholarship. Only scholarship that truly *engages* is worthy of our political efforts here and now. And since my religious engagement is existentially prior to my engagement in any polity (the two only being identical when the Kingdom of God finally comes), in good faith I can only approach the question of religious human rights from the second standpoint, namely, religion as the source of *all* other rights.

THE BASIC HERMENEUTICAL QUESTION

A generation ago, in his introduction to an important volume of essays entitled *Judaism and Human Rights*, the Jewish political theorist Milton R. Konvitz correctly noted, "There is no word or phrase

---

[2]See Thomas Aquinas, *Summa Theologiae*, 2/1, q. 94, art. 4, ad 1.

[3]For a full discussion of the ramifications of this *Kulturkampf*, see James Davison Hunter, *Culture Wars* (New York, 1991).

for 'human rights' in the Hebrew Scriptures or in any other ancient Jewish text. . . . Yet . . . the absence of these and related words and phrases does not mean the nonexistence of the ideals and values for which they stand or to which they point."[4] Konvitz was, of course, arguing against the kind of historicist reduction that would dismiss the question addressed in his volume and this volume by severing any connection between the issues of the present and the teachings of the past. Nevertheless, the other extreme to be avoided is simply to assume that ancient religious texts—in our case, ancient Judaic texts—can function as precedents for moral principles that are already formulated fully in and for the present. For when this is done, the continuing moral necessity of rereading these texts becomes lost because the principles of which these texts are precedents are assumed to be true in and of themselves, here and now. They are taken to be self-sufficient even if not always self-evident. And, indeed, anything but tangential concern with these ancient precedents might actually be counterproductive by diverting attention away from the real and pressing concerns to which moral principles are always to be addressed.

A good example of this latter fallacy, what might be called the "fallacy of immediate relevance," is the simple location in the Jewish tradition of precedents for democracy. Now certainly, all of us who wish to strengthen the cause of religious liberty are well aware of the historical fact that religious liberty can only function in some sort of democratic polity today, especially where minority and individual (the greatest minority) rights are affirmed. And I cannot imagine any rational person wanting to live in anything but a democracy in the world today. The real alternatives are too horrible to entertain seriously. Jews, especially, have very good historical reasons for being in favor of democracy, even enthused by it. Jews have thrived in democracies and, conversely, they have frequently been major victims of the modern alternatives to democracy. This is why, in the volume previously mentioned, all the authors assume that Judaism is for democracy. However, without a critical role for Judaism in its relation to democracy in its current form—namely,

---

[4]Milton Konvitz, ed., *Judaism and Human Rights* (New York, 1972), 13.

a role in which it attempts to re-think democracy as to what it is-to-be and not just to confirm it as-it-is—without that critical role I do not see how Judaism would not be quickly turned into a matter of ultimately antiquarian interest, which is irrelevant when moral principles are practically *directed toward* the future and not just *traced from* the past parenthetically. In other words, unless Judaism can provide a basis for judging democracy and its espousal of human rights, it becomes, in the words of the great German Jewish philosopher of the early twentieth century, Hermann Cohen, only a historical origin (*Anfang*) of facts rather than a philosophical source (*Ursprung*) of concepts (*Begriffe*).[5] The task, then, is to look for a definition of rights that can bridge the gap between our modern limitation of that idea to *human* rights, that is, to the realm of intrapersonal and interpersonal relationships, and the ancient Judaic inclusion of that idea into the relationship between God and humans.[6] When this is done, we will be in a better position to see the Jewish tradition in a critical relationship to the reality of democracy and its concern for human rights—namely, the manner in which the Jewish tradition can provide an intelligent viewpoint from which to not merely follow contemporary democracy and at best to be patronized by its adherents, but to judge and re-direct it. By so doing, we might actually find in contemporary democracy those practices that are indispensable for the conduct of a society worthy of the moral allegiance of rational human persons and concurrently reject those practices that make a society unworthy of such moral allegiance.

RIGHTS, DUTIES, AND ENTITLEMENTS

The concept of rights can only be understood in correlation to the concept of duty. For the sake of greater clarity, let us assume that rights are claims, and duties are obligations. In the case of benevo-

---

[5]Hermann Cohen, *Religion of Reason Out of the Sources of Judaism*, S. Kaplan, trans. (New York, 1972), 10, 63–64.

[6]See *Mishnah*, *Yoma* 8:9, and Babylonian Talmud, *Yoma* 87a, re: 1 Samuel 2:25, Isidore Epstein, trans. (London, 1987).

lence, which in the Jewish tradition is both a right of the less fortunate and a duty of the more fortunate (and hence does not have
the arbitrary meaning connoted by the usual word "charity"), it
makes no sense to speak of my right to your support unless it can
be assumed that you have a duty to support me.[7] Your duty is a
recognition of my right, just as my right is a recognition of your
duty. Without the correlative duty for you to be benevolent, my
claim is nothing but begging. And without my correlative right to
your benevolence, your duty is nothing but largesse. The difference between begging and a right, and the difference between a
duty and largesse, is that the former is justified whereas the latter
is unjustified by a third party. Both rights and duties require enforcement to be cogent. That is, rights and duties are only intelligible in a social context where there is the rule of law. Accordingly,
a right without a correlative duty has no socially sanctioned object for the exercise of its claim, and a duty without a correlative
right has no socially sanctioned object for the exercise of its obligation. Thus, it is the situation of claiming persons and obligated
persons in a society that gives their respective rights and duties
legal structure. Certainly in Judaism, rights and duties are the business of law.[8]

The question to be asked at this point is whether rights entail
duties or duties entail rights. In democratic societies, it is usually
assumed that rights entail duties. That is, human persons as individuals have inherent needs and powers. For the sake of the opti-
mal fulfillment of these inherent needs that only collective power
can opportune and protect, individuals contract over to society
some of their inherent powers in return for these opportunities and
protection. When this "social contract" is recognized, "natural
rights" are then retroactively seen as its source.[9] Outside of society, however, there are only natural needs and powers that are
sensed by individuals. "Rights" are constituted by reason, which
is a linguistic/social phenomenon. Thus, in this view, individuals
entitle the right of society to command its own duties in the form of

---

[7]See Babylonian Talmud, *Bava Batra* 8b.
[8]See Babylonian Talmud, *Kiddushin* 31a and parallels.
[9]See John Rawls, *A Theory of Justice* (Cambridge, MA, 1971), 27ff.

public law. In other words, social duties are justified by individual rights. But, following this logic, society must be seen as an artificial construct, an epiphenomenon.

However, from a traditional Jewish point of view, this logic is faulty for two reasons. First, it ignores the fact that human society itself is experienced as a natural phenomenon, as part of the order of creation itself. Humans have a need for society as the arena of communication, over and above their need for society as a means to the fulfillment of selfish individual ends. As one of the rabbinic sages put it when he found himself in a community where he could no longer engage in discourse, "either fellowship or death" (*o haveruta o mituta*).[10] This is a more picturesque way of saying what Aristotle meant when he designated the human person as both "having speech" (*logon echon*) and "being a political animal" (*politikon zo'on*), which are actually two sides of the same coin.[11] Indeed, as many philosophers after Aristotle have seen, human society, which is an essentially communicative reality, has always been there in human life; it cannot be constructed *de novo*.[12] Furthermore, the very notion of a contract already presupposes the institution of society, inasmuch as a contract is a *publicly* justified and enforced agreement. How could anyone know that a contract is to be kept (*pacta sunt servanda*) unless he or she already experienced the social order that contracts themselves presuppose? That is the philosophical problem. Second, the theological problem with the social contract theory is that it assumes that the human individual is sovereign, rather than God.[13] Thus, the social

---

[10]Babylonian Talmud, *Ta'anit* 23a. See *Zevahim* 117a, re: Leviticus 13:46.

[11]Aristotle, *Politics*, 1:1/1253a 10–15.

[12]See, for example, Max Scheler, *Formalism in Ethics*, M. S. Frings and R. L. Funk, trans. (Evanston, IL, 1973), 528ff.; Ludwig Wittgenstein, *Philosophical Investigations*, 2d ed., G. E. M. Anscombe, trans. (New York, 1958), 1:18, 8e.

[13]Even Kant, who posits the sovereignty of the human individual only as that of a rational being not acting out of sensual self-interest, still eliminates God's sovereignty either as the source or the end of the moral law. Thus, the truly moral society can only be constituted by these rational self-legislating beings. Transcendence for Kant is that of reason over sense, not that of God over creation. See *Critique of Pure Reason*, B847; *Ground-*

contract theory and its attendant notion of natural rights simultaneously involves an underestimation and an overestimation of the human condition. It underestimates the natural necessity of discursive community in human existence, and it overestimates the importance of human authority in the created order of the cosmos.

Nevertheless, the experience of tyranny in human history, especially the totalitarian tyranny that has so stained the twentieth century, correctly makes most of us wary of the other alternative, namely, that duties entail rights. For this notion seems to regard the claims of human persons to be subject to the will of the state, in the person of those who control it, that is. The epitome of this approach can be seen in the doctrine of the Nazi state, enunciated early in its reign, that the right of humans to their very lives depends on whether the state decides that any human life is *Lebenswertesleben*, "life designated worthy of being allowed to live." Hence, only those whom the state regards as duty-bound to remain present in the world for its sake may do so. Conversely, those whom the state regards as duty-bound to become absent from the world for its sake are to be killed (if they have not already committed suicide). They were designated *Lebensunwertesleben*, "life unworthy of life."[14] In this view, only the state has any real rights, and it alone may exercise them arbitrarily. When anything similar to this notion is put forth, I see the barbed wire of Auschwitz or the gulag on the horizon.

The challenge for a presentation of religious human rights in the world today is to avoid the emptiness of individualistic rights talk without falling into the trap of the excesses of collectivism.

To present Judaism as a system founded on a notion of rights, however, is to run the risk of being challenged with the argument that empirically one can represent Judaism more convincingly as a system of duties. After all, whereas there is no real equivalent in

---

work of the Metaphysic of Morals, H. J. Paton, trans. (New York, 1964), 110–111. Cf. Martin Buber, *Kingship of God*, 3d ed., R. Scheimann, trans. (New York and Evanston, IL, 1967), 136ff.

[14]See Germain Grisez and Joseph M. Boyle, Jr., *Life and Death with Liberty and Justice: A Contribution to the Euthanasia Debate* (Notre Dame, 1979), 242ff.

classical Hebrew to our term "rights," there are certainly equivalents to our term "duty." The literary sources of the normative Jewish tradition continually speak of "commandments" (*mitzvot*) and "obligations" (*hovot*).[15] The closest word to our term "rights" is "permission" (*reshut*). But "permission" refers to those acts that the law has not yet ruled on and has thus left to the discretion of individuals. Nevertheless, considering the whole tendency of the normative Jewish tradition to expand rather than contract the range of the law, there are cases in which areas formerly within the range of "permission" were reinterpreted to become areas of low priority obligations.[16] In the realm of the law, the area of "permission" is arbitrarily epiphenomenal. It is hardly the foundation for which we are still searching.

Yet to leave the description of the Jewish normative tradition at the level of duty alone begs the question. For as we have seen earlier, the very concept of duty cannot stand on its own without the correlative concept of rights. After all, a duty is something one *owes to someone else*. That someone else, therefore, has a *right to that duty*. Both "rights" and "duties" are bipolar terms. The contemporary French Jewish philosopher, Emmanuel Levinas, has made this relationship the cornerstone of his ethical philosophy. As he has powerfully described and argued, the very presence of another person (*l'autre*) is itself a claim upon me, minimally obligating me to respect their right to life by not murdering them.[17] And here we see that although right and duty are correlative, the correlation begins from the point of rights and then extends to the point of duty, but not vice versa. We might say that rights constitute the subject of human action and duty the object. Initially, it is the subject that acts upon the object by intending it before the object reacts upon the subject. Ultimately, then, it is a primary right/ claim that creates a duty, inasmuch as the right is related to the

---

[15]Generally, "commandments" are conditional norms, and "obligations" are unconditional norms. See Maimonides, *Mishneh Torah*, *Berakhot* 11:2.

[16]See, for example, Babylonian Talmud, *Betsah* 36b.

[17]See Emmanuel Levinas, *Totality and Infinity*, trans. A. Lingis (Pittsburgh, 1969), esp. 187ff.

duty as a command. I differ with Levinas, however, in affirming with Jewish tradition that God, not man, is the One who makes the primary claim on our action in the world.[18]

COVENANT: GOD, PERSONS, COMMUNITY

If Judaism is for the most part a system of duties, and if duties imply rights, then it can be said with confidence that Judaism is a system of duties correlative with the supreme rights of God, the creator. The system itself can then be understood to include the following relationships: (1) God to persons; (2) persons to God; (3) God to community; (4) community to God; (5) persons to persons; (6) persons to community; and (7) community to persons. Explicating and illustrating these seven relationships will enable us to see the religious human rights that emerge from Judaism. And I hope it will also at least suggest why this system of relationships and the rights it includes offer a plausible alternative to the individualism and collectivism presently available in contemporary political theory.

God to Persons

It has been a major debate among biblical exegetes since the Middle Ages whether the traditional doctrine of *creatio ex nihilo* is actually taught in the text of the Bible, especially in the creation narrative at the very beginning of Genesis. "In the beginning God created the heavens and the earth. And the earth was an abyss [*tohu ve-vohu*] . . . and God said, 'Let there be light,' and there was light" (Genesis 1:1–3). Now it could be inferred from this text that the "abyss" is some sort of primordial matter out of which God then created a world; or to use Platonic language, God engendered cosmos out of chaos.[19] If so, why did Judaism (and then Christian-

---

[18]See David Novak, *Law and Theology in Judaism* (New York, 1976), 2:15ff.

[19]See Plato, *Timaeus*, 29Eff.; also Jon D. Levenson, *Creation and the Persistence of Evil* (San Francisco, 1988), 3ff.

ity and Islam) more and more insist that creation has no antecedents other than God? The answer, I think, is that only the doctrine of *creatio ex nihilo* affirms the absolute authority of God. If there was anything else that shared God's transcendence of the world as we experience it here and now, then that would imply that God's authority is also shared with something that is not God.[20] *Creatio ex nihilo* is a corollary of the monotheism that Judaism saw as the alternative to the polytheism in which each god's power, and hence each god's authority, are limited by the power and authority of some other god with whom he or she has to co-exist. In the primordial sense, God must be posited in the words of the kabbalistic mystical theology as *Ayn Sof*, "without limit" or "Infinite."[21]

At the most primary level, humans experience the power of God as unlimited. "See now that I, I am He and there is no other power [*elohim*] along with Me. I kill and I give life, human; there is no one who can escape My hand" (Deuteronomy 32:39). "I am the first and I am the last, besides Me there is no power [*ayn elohim*]" (Isaiah 44:6). The response to God at this level is fear of God's absolute power. At this level, even human creatures have no rights at all, inasmuch as they have no power to make any claims on God. As Marx correctly noted, rights without real power are meaningless.[22] Thus, even when Abraham is arguing with God about the question of whether or not God is dealing justly with the people of Sodom and Gomorrah, he is forced to reiterate, "Here I presume [*ho'alti*] to speak to my Lord, even though I am but dust and ashes" (Genesis 18:27). And after God finally appears to Job after all his complaints and all the dialogues with his friends, Job is reduced to utter impotence by God's challenging question, "Where were you when I established earth?" (Job 38:4). Here the very ground under him, that which could be the basis of any claim, is bluntly reclaimed by the God Who created the earth and Job in it—Job, His creature who is now attempting to stand up against God on it.

---

[20]See Maimonides, *Guide of the Perplexed*, S. Pines, trans. (Chicago, 1963), 2:13.

[21]See Gershom G. Scholem, *On the Kabbalah and Its Symbolism*, R. Manheim, trans. (New York, 1969), 73.

[22]See Karl Marx, *The Essential Writings*, F. L. Bender, ed. (New York, 1972), 53ff.

At this point Job is forced to conclude, "Therefore, I abase myself [*em'as*] and repent, being but dust and ashes" (Job 42:5). When faced by God directly, Job has no ontological foundation upon which any moral claim must ultimately rest.

At this most primary level, however, which must be reiterated whenever humans act as if they are equal, let alone superior, to God, God is not yet exercising His right as much as He is exercising His raw power. Such displays of primal power are so overwhelming that their object, man, is in no position to respond with anything but the inactivity of fear.[23] Man, at this level, is in no position to respond with duty, inasmuch as duty is essentially tangible action in the world. But at this level, man has no world in which to stand before God.

Persons to God

Nevertheless, Scripture also teaches that every human person is granted a special status by God in the created world. "And God created man in His image, in the image of God [*be-tselem elohim*] He made him, male and female He created them" (Genesis 1:27). There are various opinions about what is meant by the "image of God." Many have seen it to be some inherent characteristic of human nature, such as reason or free will. In other words, it is seen as the transfer of some Divine power, be it reason or free will, to a special creature, one who is unlike any other creature. But the problem with seeing the image of God as an inherent characteristic of human nature is that such a characteristic can be constituted phenomenologically without reference to God. If God is only the external cause of reason or free will, essential insight into either of these phenomena does not require a causal explanation of how it originally came to be. What does saying "humans receive their reason or free will from God" add to the proposition "humans are rational or possess free will"?[24] In other words, these interpre-

---

[23]See Jerusalem Talmud, *Berakhot* 9:7/14b (Villna, 1907); also, Rabbi Obadiah Bertinoro, Commentary on the *Mishnah: Avot* 1:3.

[24]See David Novak, *Halakhah in a Theological Dimension* (Chico, CA, 1985), 96ff.

tations lose the intimacy *between* God and humans that is suggested by the opening words of God's creation of the human being, "Let Us make the human [*adam*] in Our image" (Genesis 1:26). The only way one can constitute the intimacy of the relationship *with* God that Scripture suggests is a possibility *for* humans from the very beginning and continually thereafter is to see the image of God as that which God and humans share in what they do *together*.[25] The Hebrew verb *asoh* (as in *na'aseh*, "let us make") means both making things and doing acts as, for example, "to do [*la'asot*] the Ten Commandments" (*aseret ha-devarim*) (Deuteronomy 4:13). Similarly, the Hebrew noun *davar* means both a thing and a word as, for example, "the word of our God [*devar eloheinu*] remains forever" (Isaiah 40:8).

Essential human action, which is the practice of the commandments, is unlike all other things that are *made by* the Creator. Rather, it is done *along with* the Creator. In rabbinic teaching, even God himself is imagined to observe the commandments of the Torah in order to share with His people the basic reality of their active life.[26] Thus, the basis of a positive relationship between God and humans is the human capacity, designated as the image of God, to be able to respond to God's commandments with a sense of authentic obligation. Humans not only owe God everything for having made them, but more directly and more positively they owe God everything for descending from beyond to speak to them. Thus, the first of the Ten Commandments, "I am the Lord your God Who brought you out of the land of Egypt, out of the house of bondage" (Exodus 20:2), establishes God's commanding authority both on the basis of the good God has done for Israel by liberating her from slavery, and on the basis of the good God is doing and will do for Israel by giving her commandments that are in her best interest.[27] "And the Lord has commanded us to practice all of these statutes . . . for our own good [*le-tov lanu*] . . . it is beneficial for us [*u-tsedaqah tehiyeh lanu*] that we prepare ourselves to practice all

---

[25]See Franz Rosenzweig, *The Star of Redemption*, W. W. Hallo, trans. (New York, 1970), 154–155.

[26]See Jerusalem Talmud, *Rosh Hashanah* 1:3/57a–b, re: Leviticus 22:9.

[27]See *Mekhilta: Yitro* re: Exodus 20:2, ed. Horovitz-Rabin, 219.

these commandments [*ha-mitsvah ha-z'ot*] before the Lord our God as He has commanded us" (Deuteronomy 6:24–25).

This can be seen in the first explicit address of God to man after creation. "And the Lord God commanded [*va-yitsav*] the human being, saying, 'From all the trees of the garden you may surely eat. But from the tree of the knowledge of good and bad you may not eat, for on the day you eat from it you shall surely die'" (Genesis 2:16–17). In rabbinic exegesis, the human being is both spoken *to* and spoken *about* in this statement. For the Hebrew reads *al ha'adam*, which means both "to the human being" and "about the human being." From this phraseology the Rabbis see an allusion to a prohibition of murder, which is, of course, needed at this point in the biblical narrative if Cain is to be held responsible by God for the murder of Abel.[28] Thus, human dignity is affirmed by the teaching that all humans are capable in one way or another of being commanded by God, responding thereto, and being judged thereon. Accordingly, the ultimate indignity of death is that the dead person is now "free from the commandments," which means to be deprived of essential human nature, to be turned into something else, that is, "to return to the dust" (Genesis 3:19) from which one is made but not what one truly is, at least for "the shadow of our days on earth" (1 Chronicles 29:15).[29] Human persons are regarded as sojourners in the world, who can only find their dwelling in the world when they realize that their authentic identity is neither derived from the world nor from themselves. That identity comes from being related to the One Who Himself transcends the world and directs it, the One to Whom the world is always immanent.[30] "I am a sojourner [*ger*] on earth; do not hide Your commandments from me" (Psalms 119:19).

The idea that God enables humans to be related to Him by means of commandments leads to the idea that humans now have the right to justice both from each other in their societies and, even more so, in the cosmos from God. A relationship consisting of

---

[28]Babylonian Talmud, *Sanhedrin* 56b.

[29]*Niddah* 61b re: Psalms 88:6.

[30]See *Bereshit Rabbah* 39:1.

commandments and not just ad hoc commands involves an order.[31] That order includes God's action as the giver of commandments, the response of humans as keepers of commandments, and then the response of God in the ultimate consequences of either keeping or breaking the commandments. We can see this human right to justice, this claim of man upon the commanding God, throughout Scripture and the literature of the Rabbis.

At the time of the first crime, which was the murder of Abel by his brother Cain, Abel is depicted as claiming justice for himself from God. As God informs Cain, who at that moment is standing in trial before God, "The voice of your brother's blood cries to Me from the soil of the earth [*min ha'adamah*]" (Genesis 4:11). The Rabbis point out that the word for "blood"—*demei*—is in the plural (literally, "blood*s*"), which means that Abel is not only claiming justice for his present that Cain destroyed by the act of murder, but also for his future, namely, the descendents that he could have had but will never hereafter have because of the murder.[32]

After the Flood, which was brought about because of the sin of public violence, God assures the survivors, Noah and his family, who are now the progenitors of restored humankind, that violence against them will not go unrequited. "Indeed, your lifeblood I shall claim [*edrosh*] from the hand of every beast I shall claim it, and from human hands I shall claim it, human life [*nefesh ha'adam*] even a man from his own brother's hand" (Genesis 9:5).[33] This last reference to fraternal violence seems to suggest the crime of Cain against Abel, and that violence is ultimately against our own kin in one way or another and not against total strangers.

------

[31]See David Novak, *Jewish–Christian Dialogue: A Jewish Justification* (New York, 1989), 153–154.

[32]*Mishnah, Sanhedrin* 4:5.

[33]This verse is interpreted in the Talmud (Babylonian Talmud, *Bava Kamma* 91b) as including the prohibition of suicide, viz., God will avenge the blood of any victim, even when the victim and the perpetrator are one and the same person. In other words, there is no individual right to death. As for a communal right to inflict death for certain crimes, Scripture, of course, affirms it (see, e.g., Genesis 9:6). But, for the attempts of some of the Rabbis to so qualify this right as to make it in effect a null class, see *Mishnah, Makkot* 1:10; Babylonian Talmud, *Makkot* 7a; also, David Novak, *Jewish Social Ethics* (New York, 1992), 174ff.

Now, of course, this idea of Divine justice for violence against innocent humans came to be questioned, inasmuch as it is frequently the case that there is good cause to complain "Why does the way of the wicked prosper?!" (Jeremiah 12:1). As a result of such inherently legitimate complaints, the Jewish tradition developed the idea that the full consequences of human justice or injustice are not to be expected in this world but, rather, in a world-yet-to-come (*olam ha-ba*), which will be the Kingdom of God on earth (*malkhut shamayim*).[34] Critics have long seen this type of answer to the question of absent Divine justice to be itself a begging of the question, a way of diverting attention away from a great theological embarrassment. Moreover, to follow the line of the Marxist designation of religion as the "opium of the people," such question-begging is seen as a way of enforcing the status quo, which is assumed to be the unjust exploitation of the masses by those with economic-political power over them.[35] However, in the Jewish tradition, this type of postponement of the question (which is not the same as begging it) has had very different results.

First, it has led to the emphasis of keeping the commandments for their own sake (*li-shmah*) rather than seeing them as instrumental for something else.[36] For, as Aristotle wisely taught, the pursuit of a presently unattainable end cannot be a motivation for purposeful activity here and now.[37] Thus, the final just reward or punishment for either keeping or breaking the commandments in this world is taken to be a future consequence of this action, essentially disjunct from the present, and thus not its actual present *telos*. The purposes of the commandments are seen as being for the sake of the present relationship with God and with fellow human beings. This led to the whole Jewish tendency to discover the "reasons of the commandments" (*ta'amei ha-mitsvot*), that is, those intelligible

---

[34]See *Hullin* 142a re: Deuteronomy 22:7. Cf. *Kiddushin* 39b and *Tosafot*, s.v. "*matnitin.*"

[35]See Karl Marx, *On Society and Social Change*, N. J. Smelser, ed. (Chicago, 1973), 13–14.

[36]See *Mishnah, Avot* 1:3; Babylonian Talmud, *Rosh Hashanah* 28a; Babylonian Talmud, *Nazir* 23b.

[37]Aristotle, *Nicomachean Ethics*, 1:10/1100a–10ff.

ends for which the commandments are seen to function.[38] Indeed, here we see the theological connection with the interest by classical Jewish thinkers in the whole issue of natural law (which they often called by other names, however).[39]

Second, this affirmation of ultimate Divine justice has functioned as an antidote to the despair that often comes when the quest for justice, the response to legitimate human rights, is based on human idealism. For the futility of the finite and mortal human situation, taken in and of itself, belies any idealism in the end. Indeed, total human efforts to bring about justice in the world have inevitably led to more injustice than they purport to cure. One need only think of the colossal fiasco of the utopian promises of Marxism in this century. The pursuit of justice for the sake of human rights can only be maintained in good faith when those who seek it see themselves as participants in a cosmic reality whose final outcome transcends their own fragile efforts.[40] The final victory belongs to God alone. For this reason, human prayer that God will do justice in His world is as important as human efforts to effect justice in our own little domain of activity in that world. It is not, however, a substitute for human efforts that will be judged in the end.[41] As the Rabbis emphasized, prayer to the merciful and gracious God is also to lead to the imitation of these qualities by the humans who affirm them in prayer. "As He is merciful, so you be merciful."[42]

Third, this postponement of ultimate Divine justice to the messianic future (*l'atid la-vo*) led to the emphasis on the practice of justice by humans here and now. For whereas God has all the time He wants to effect justice in the world and can do so alone, mortal humans have only have limited time to attempt to effect justice, always partial justice to be sure, in situations at hand that call for justice to be pursued.[43] Furthermore, they cannot do this alone.

---

[38]See David Novak, *The Theology of Nahmanides Systematically Presented* (Atlanta, 1992), 2ff.

[39]See Novak, *Jewish Social Ethics*, chaps. 1–3.

[40]Ibid., 163–164.

[41]See *Mekhilta: Beshalah* 97, re: Exodus 14:15 (Jerusalem, 1960).

[42]Babylonian Talmud, *Shabbat* 133b, re: Exodus 15:2.

[43]See *Mishnah, Avot* 2:15–16; Babylonian Talmud, *Ta'anit* 21a.

They require the help of others in society. And, in order that human justice not be severed from Divine justice, they require both Divine guidance and Divine example. This now leads us to consider God's relation to human community and the rights and duties that emerge here.

God to Community

In the biblical narrative, the original hope for a united humankind, for one human city on earth, is dashed by the arrogant attempt of the builders of the Tower of Babel to unite humankind against God.[44] According to one ancient tradition, this grandiose attempt to solve the problem of human insecurity in the world also resulted in the neglect of individual human claims for justice to be readily at hand.[45] As a result, humankind is considered to be permanently fragmented; "the Lord has scattered them over all the earth" (Genesis 11:9). This is to be the human situation until the coming of the day "when the Lord will become king over all the earth" (Zechariah 14:9). At that time, God "will turn to the peoples with a clear message [*safah berurah*], summoning all of them in the name of the Lord to serve Him with one accord" (Zephaniah 3:9).[46]

Because of the inherent fragmentation of humankind in this world, the biblical narrative quickly turns to God's relationship with one particular community. In God's choice of Abraham and his descendents, God's direct covenant with at least some humans for the time being is now Scripture's primary concern. The more indirect covenant with the earth and its natural order that came with Noah and the generations who survived the Flood becomes the background for the prime Divine-human reality in the world. The Noahide covenant and its law are the minimal conditions for the emergence and development of this more specific covenant, but they are not rich enough in detail and intensity to suffice for the fuller life with God on earth required by the historicity of the

---

[44]See *Bereshit Rabbah* 38:8, re: Genesis 11:4.

[45]See Louis Ginzberg, *The Legends of the Jews* (Philadelphia, 1909), 1:179.

[46]See Maimonides, *Mishneh Torah: Melakhim*, chap. 11, uncensored ed. (Jerusalem, 1983).

human condition. That historicity consists of singular events and their celebration that can only be the subject of the memory of a singular community among others in the world. The Noahide covenant involves the generality of nature; it does not supply content. It presents negative limits but not the positive claims that can only be made by persons historically situated in a community.[47] Nevertheless, this covenant is considered to be ultimately for all of humankind. Thus, God informs Abraham at the very moment of His initial call to him that "all the families of the earth shall be blessed through you" (Genesis 12:3). The covenant is of universal significance, even if at present it is only a matter of local experience and practice. Minimally, this means that the moral standards of this community are defensible as being in the interest of universally valid human rights.

In the biblical narrative, the covenantal relationship between God and the Abrahamic community (eventually, the people Israel) becomes more exact in terms of its significance for the issue of justice in the world, which takes the form of concern for the human right to justice. God invites Abraham to a dialogue with Him concerning the proposed punishment of the evil cities of Sodom and Gomorrah and all their citizens. The dialogue is initiated by God as follows:

> How can I hide from Abraham what I am about to do? And Abraham is to be a great and important nation through whom all the nations of the earth are to be blessed. For I know him intimately [*yeda'tiv*] and this is to lead [*lema'an*] to his commanding his children and household to follow after him, that they might keep the way of the Lord to practice righteous judgment [*tsedaqah u-mishpat*]. This is to lead [*lema'an*] to the Lord's bringing about all that He has spoken about him (Genesis 18:17–19).

First, there is the question of why God must inform Abraham of what He plans to do with the two cities. The answer to this seems to be that unless Abraham and the community around him (at that time, beginning with his own domestic circle) have actually been assured of God's most elemental justice, they could not possibly

---

[47]See Novak, *Jewish Social Ethics*, 70ff.

model their own practice of justice on it. For justice to be more than a human pursuit, it must be connected to "the way of the Lord." And for the way of the Lord to be a model for human practice, it must be minimally consistent in its application. That is, the innocent and the guilty must not be confused, and the punishment must be appropriate to the crime.[48]

It is not that justice is prior to God. For something to be prior to or even coequal with God, as we have seen when noting the traditional doctrine of *creatio ex nihilo*, would make God inherently limited. But a limited God is not greater than that which necessarily limits it. Instead, the text seems to teach that *if* God wants to maintain a relationship with a community on earth, and *if* that relationship is to be concerned with the human condition itself, which most basically involves the rights of *any* human person to justice, *then* God should act justly. God's autonomous moral authority, which He need not exercise primordially if He does not wish to do so, entails this much responsibility now that He has chosen to exercise it. The "justice" (*mishpat*) that Abraham confronts God about is not a primordial reality in which even God has to participate, as was the case in Plato's constitution of the relation of God and justice.[49] It is, rather, a self-imposed modification of Divine activity; it is to be translated by the adverb "justly" to avoid any notion that it is more than the action that it modifies. "Will the judge of all the earth Himself not do justly?" (Genesis 18:25). Such unjust action admitted by God in His own words with Abraham (as opposed to action whose justice is unknown, as was the case with Job) would make God's claims "obscene" (*halilah*)—that is, it would mark God's authority as the arbitrary exercise of power so familiar from the political experience of all nations.[50] Man, on the other hand, being thrown into the world already before having to make any

------

[48]See *Sifre: Devarim*, L. Finkelstein, ed. (New York, 1969), 303, re: Deuteronomy 25:1; Babylonian Talmud, *Sanhedrin* 90a.

[49]See Euthyphro, 10Aff.; also, David Novak, *Suicide and Morality* (New York, 1975), 31ff.

[50]See Rashi, *Commentary on the Torah*, M. Rosenbaum and A. M. Silvermann, trans. (London, 1946), Genesis 18:25.

existential choices, thus has no such primordial choice. Whereas God does not have to make any choice at all, humans do. Therefore, if humans are to do justly, they must indeed participate in the justice that is not of their own making. Humans are essentially responsive and thus not autonomous in any fundamental sense, contrary to the rights theory that found its most profound enunciation in Kant.[51]

Second, the text from Genesis 18 indicates that the greatness and importance of the Abrahamic nation is not to be a matter of material or military might. The greatness in the eyes of the world is to be moral. "Not by military power [*hayil*] and not by material strength [*koah*], but by My spirit, says the Lord" (Zechariah 4:6).[52] Minimally, that would mean that God's relation to this community results in a system of law in which the concern for human rights would impress anyone having a similar concern. Thus, Moses tells the people of Israel, who are poised to enter the Promised Land, of the universal significance of the law God has given them.

> For it is your wisdom and understanding in the eyes of the nations that will hear all these statutes and will say, "Surely this nation is a wise and discerning people." For what great nation has God so close to them as we do when we call upon the Lord our God? And what great nation has such righteous statutes [*huqqim*] and ordinances [*mishpatim*] as this whole Torah? . . . (Deuteronomy 4:6–8)[53]

Indeed, part of the messianic vision is that the nations of the world will eventually come to Jerusalem for their claims to be adjudicated. They will say, "Let us go up to the mountain of the Lord, to the house of the God of Jacob, and He will direct us from His ways and we will walk in His paths . . . He will judge between the nations and arbitrate [*ve-hokheah*] for many peoples" (Isaiah 2:3–4).[54]

---

[51]See Kant, *Groundwork of the Metaphysic of Morals*, 78–79. Cf. Novak, *Jewish–Christian Dialogue*, 148ff.

[52]Cf. Deuteronomy 8:17–18.

[53]See Maimonides, *Guide of the Perplexed* 3:31 (Chicago, 1972).

[54]See *Tosefta Sotah* 8:6, re: Deuteronomy 27:8 (New York, 1957).

Because of God's claim on His covenanted community to exercise their duty to deal justly, communally as well as individually, the greatest indictment of this community and its institutions by the prophets was the perversion of the rights of the most helpless citizens of the polity by those with the power to do otherwise. Political destruction is promised unless "you seek justice [*that*]; rectify oppression; champion [*shiftu*] the orphan and plead the cause of the widow" (Isaiah 1:17).[55] Because the covenant is with the all-seeing God, no perversion of rights can hide behind the anonymity of faceless institutions. God's concern for the welfare of every human created in God's image gives Him the right to demand proportional concern on behalf of the covenanted community especially. They are to imitate God in His role as "father of orphans and judge for widows" (Psalms 68:6).

That concern for justice is to include just dealings with those outside the community itself; indeed, injustice toward the gentiles, for the Rabbis, entails the sin of "profanation of God's name" (*hillul ha-shem*).[56] Such injustice prevents the gentiles from admiring the inherent justice of the Torah and praising the God Who gave it, as well as desiring to appropriate it. Such injustice would not inspire them to come to Jerusalem, literally or figuratively, for the just response to their rights claims.

God's rights and His championing of the rights of those most in need of justice create numerous duties for the community. But the issue of the just adjudication of rights claims is something that transcends the actual political institutions of the covenanted community. Thus, in rabbinic jurisprudence, when the Jewish authorities are unable to properly adjudicate the rights of persons in their own domain, even Jews are allowed to go to gentile authorities with their rights claims, provided that these authorities practice a law with due process.[57]

---

[55] See Babylonian Talmud, *Sanhedrin* 32b, re: Deuteronomy 16:20.

[56] See Babylonian Talmud, *Bava Kamma* 113a–b.

[57] See Babylonian Talmud, *Bava Batra* 54b, and parallels; Maimonides, *Mishneh Torah: Sanhedrin* 26:7.

Community to God

God's right to command numerous duties of His elect community, prominent among them being the duty to "pursue justice" (Deuteronomy 16:20), does not, however, mean that the covenanted community has no rights itself in its relationship with God. Since God has voluntarily chosen to covenant Himself with Israel (as He voluntarily chose to create the world solely by Himself *ex nihilo*), Israel has the right to demand that God not abandon them by annulling the covenant. The people's claim on God's faithfulness is as indissoluble as God's claim on theirs. Thus, the validity of the covenant is irrevocable even though Israel's disloyalty to it regularly occurs. This comes out in the way the Talmud interprets Moses' dialogue with God after Israel has worshiped the Golden Calf.

> Remember Abraham, Isaac, and Israel, Your servants to whom You Yourself took an oath. . . ." (Exodus 32:13). What does "You Yourself" (*bakh*) mean? Rabbi Eleazar said that it means that Moses really said the following to God: "Master of the universe, if You had taken an oath to them in the name of heaven and earth, I could say that just as heaven and earth are perishable (*betelim*) so is Your oath (*shevu'atekha*) perishable. But now You have taken an oath by Your own great name. Therefore, just as Your great name lives and endures forever, so must Your oath endure forever.[58]

This theological homily is based on the legal fact that in Jewish law only an external authority can annul an oath, thus freeing the person who took it from the obligation to fulfill it. The assumption is that this external authority is higher than the person taking the oath.[59] But God has not recognized any external authority in promising to be covenanted to Israel. Rather, God has based His oath on His own imperishable being, His own unique name. Therefore, there is no way that even God can release Himself from the cove-

---

[58]Babylonian Talmud, *Berakhot* 32a; also, Novak, *Halakhah in a Theological Dimension*, 126ff.

[59]Babylonian Talmud, *Nedarim* 27b.

nant. All He can do in good faith is chastise Israel in the hope that such chastisement will awaken her from her illusions and turn her back to her only authentic covenant partner.

Much of Jewish communal prayer in the form of requests (*baqashah*) is the claim on God to perpetually remember just who His people are. Although Israel is, for the most part, obliged to recognize her own difficulties as stemming from unfaithfulness to the covenant and to praise God for His mercy (*hoda'ah*), there are times when Israel has the right to express her anger with God for what seems to be unjustified harshness. "See, O Lord and look at whom You have done this, women even eat their own children!" (Lamentations 2:20).[60] In fact, the only limit on this expression of anger is the prohibition of blasphemy, the curse that wishes God to be dead.[61]

This right of the covenanted community to be angry with the presently unjustified ways of God assumes special importance for the Jewish people after the Holocaust, particularly regarding their duty to pursue justice and champion human rights. For there is a great temptation to turn away from God because He didn't rescue so many of His people from the murderers. Part of that turning away from God is to conclude that there is no justice at all in the cosmos. But if there is no justice at all in the cosmos, then to maintain human justice as a tiny island in a sea of absurdity seems futile. Jewish abandonment of the universal God because of the experience of gross injustice can quickly lead to the conclusion that justice is not to be done because it has nothing in which to endure. At this point, survival itself becomes the only task. But *in extremis* there are no moral restraints.[62] Everything becomes a matter of self-defense, which is the one area where fear of consequences can justify even killing. Even for those who still want to cling to the ancient tradition of God-talk, without the affirmation of cosmic justice as a reality and an irrevocable (although humanly partial) task, the god they affirm is, for all intents and purposes, a tribal deity,

---

[60]See Babylonian Talmud, *Gittin* 56b, re: Exodus 15:11.

[61]See *Mishnah, Sanhedrin* 7:5.

[62]Babylonian Talmud, *Sanhedrin* 72a. See also Novak, *Jewish Social Ethics*, 167ff.

one who is incapable of judging them but only judges their enemies. Their god becomes a projection of themselves and their power. Such a god is neither the source nor the protector of human rights.

Persons to Persons

The rights that people claim from each other and the duties they owe to each other emerge from the common world that they have to share with each other. Not only is "the earth the Lord's" (Psalms 24:1), but even in the limited sense that "the earth is given to humans" (Psalms 115:16), the earth does not belong to any one of them.[63] The theme that guides discussion in this area is basic human reciprocity. Thus, the Rabbis speculated that the quarrel that led to Cain's murder of Abel was that Cain, as the "tiller of the ground," and Abel, as "shepherd" (Genesis 4:2), fought over who had absolute title to the earth. Cain claimed that the ground belonged to him and thus demanded that Abel forfeit any right to it; Abel claimed that all moveable things belonged to him and thus demanded that Cain forfeit any right to even the clothes he was wearing.[64] Instead of going to God or to his parents to adjudicate this dispute, Cain seized the initiative and thought he eliminated Abel's claim by eliminating him. Conversely, Abraham and the Philistine chieftain Abimelech "take an oath to each other, and conclude a covenant" (Genesis 21:31–32) in order to maintain peace in the land wherein they reside in such close proximity.[65]

The idea of basic human reciprocity, with its rights and correlative duties, is revealed in one of the most famous passages in the Talmud. When a gentile asks Hillel the Elder to "convert me to Judaism on the condition that you teach me the entire Torah while I stand on one foot," the sage answers, "What is hateful to you, do not do to your fellow."[66] Of course, there is much more to the entire Torah than just that, but what this text suggests is that the rights

---

[63]See Jerusalem Talmud, *Berakhot* 6:1, 9d, re: Psalms 24:1.

[64]*Bereshit Rabbah* 22:7.

[65]See Jerusalem Talmud, *Shevi'it* 6:1, 36c.

[66]Babylonian Talmud, *Shabbat* 31a.

and duties that emerge out of basic human reciprocity are the place to begin to appreciate the fuller range of rights and duties with which the Torah is concerned. This is what is meant by the sage's concluding words to the would-be convert, "This is the entire Torah and the rest is commentary. Now go learn." In the Jewish tradition, though, the commentary often surpasses the immediate text at hand.[67] Furthermore, someone without this most basic moral sense is hardly going to be interested in the much more stringent requirements of the entire Torah.[68]

The essential concern with reciprocity found in this text comes out in a comment by the twelfth-century theologian Maimonides on a text in the *Mishnah* that speaks of acts "for which the fruit is consumed in this world even though the principle endures in the world-to-come."[69] Maimonides applies this text to those commandments that pertain to what is "between humans" (*bein adam le-havero*).[70] Unlike those commandments that pertain to what is "between humans and God," whose consequences are transcendent, interhuman commandments have immanent consequences inasmuch as what I do on behalf of someone else is done with the expectation that as much will be done on my behalf.

Human society can only develop when this general openness to mutuality and reciprocity exists. This seems to be what Aristotle meant when he said that "friendship (*philia*) also seems to be the bond that holds communities together" and that it is "considered to be justice in the fullest sense . . . not only a necessity but something desirable per se."[71] Friendship is greater than justice, because it includes justice's negative claims and engenders positive duties as well. In other words, concern with human rights must not remain at the level of a simple demarcation of claims, but it must lead to the emergence of a society in which a common life is de-

---

[67]See *Mishnah, Hagigah* 1:8.

[68]See Babylonian Talmud, *Yevamot* 22a.

[69]*Mishnah, Pe'ah* 1:1.

[70]*Commentary on the Mishnah, Pe'ah* 1:1; Jerusalem Talmud, *Kafih*, ed. (Jerusalem, 1976), 1:55.

[71]*Nicomachean Ethics* 8:1/1155a 20.

veloped, one that is beyond but not at the expense of these human rights exercised by individuals.[72] Persons have duties to the community itself. Indeed, without these communal duties human rights would quickly lose the only context in which they can be exercised with true protection. Concern for the common good enhances human rights by teaching those virtues that include respect for the human dignity of each and every person (*kevod ha-beriyot*).[73]

Persons to Community

In the Jewish tradition, society functions as much more than the mere arbitrator of the conflicting claims of individuals. The good of society is something worthy in and of itself and is not just instrumental for something else. Being a community, this entity has rights that claim the duty of individuals who live and flourish there as the social beings they are by nature.

Jewish law is replete with duties that the community claims from individuals.[74] Most of these duties are formal legal obligations—that is, there are sanctions for the refusal to obey them. Some of these duties involve the community removing certain rights that individuals previously had.[75] Such removal is always justified by considerations of the common good, which are considered to override the private good that the exercise of an individual right intends. An example of this transfer of rights, so to speak, is the following:

> Ulla said that the literal law of Scripture is that a debtor may pay his debt even with the poorest quality produce (*ziburiyot*), as it says: "You [the claimant] are to stand outside [the dwelling of the debtor]

---

[72]Ibid., 8:1/1155a 25–30. See Babylonian Talmud, *Bava Batra* 100a, and David Novak, "Is There a Concept of Individual Rights in Jewish Law?" in *Jewish Law Association Studies* (Atlanta, 1994), 129ff.

[73]See Babylonian Talmud, *Berakhot* 19b, and parallels.

[74]See, for example, Babylonian Talmud, *Shabbat* 23a. For the criteria for making these new duties, see Babylonian Talmud, *Avodah Zarah* 36a–b.

[75]See, for example, *Mishnah, Arakhin* 5:6, and *Mishnah, Gittin* 9:8.

and the man whose debt you are claiming shall bring the pledge out to you" (Deuteronomy 24:11). Now, what does one usually bring out, is it not the least valuable stuff among his things (*pahot she-ba-kelim*)? Therefore, what is the reason the sages rule that a debtor is to be paid with at least medium quality produce (*beinonit*), is it not so that (*kedei*) the door will not be closed in the face of borrowers?[76]

This is one of several rabbinic rulings that in effect removed a scripturally granted right to an individual for the sake of the economic good of the entire community.[77] The assumption is that the full exercise of the right of debtors basically to unload merchandise that is difficult to sell as repayment of their debts will in the end stifle the ready lending of money.[78] Those who have money to lend will regard lending as entailing just too much trouble to want to bother with it at all. Such a breakdown of communal responsibility on the part of borrowers will have bad consequences for the entire community.

What we have just seen is how the transfer of a right was formally legislated. However, there are some cases in which the transfer of a right is not legislated but only encouraged. The following is an example of this voluntary transfer of an individual right for the sake of the common good:

Rabbi Eliezer, the son of Rabbi Yose the Galilean, says that it is forbidden to submit one's case to arbitration (*asur li-vetsoa*) and whoever does so is a sinner . . . but let the legal ruling (*ha-din*) pierce the mountain. . . . Rabbi Joshua ben Korhah says that it is meritorious (*mitzvah*) to submit one's case to arbitration, as Scripture says: "True and peaceful judgment [*that shalom*] you shall adjudicate in your gates" (Zechariah 8:16). But is it not so that when there is judgment there is no peace and when there is peace there is no judgment? So what kind of judgment contains peace? That is arbitration.[79]

---

[76]Babylonian Talmud, *Bava Kamma* 8a.
[77]See, for example, Babylonian Talmud, *Yevamot* 89b.
[78]Cf. Babylonian Talmud, *Gittin* 36a.
[79]Babylonian Talmud, *Sanhedrin* 6b.

The phrase used by the first opinion, "let the legal ruling pierce the mountain," means that whereas it is easier to go around a mountain, the most direct way to get beyond it is to go through it. In other words, the law is to be upheld without regard for social consequences. In this case, the law is for the sake of the rights of the litigant judged by the authorities to be the innocent party in a case. He benefits; the litigant judged to be the guilty party suffers.

However, in the second opinion there is the political issue of the peace of the community over and above the legal issue of whose individual rights are to be enforced and whose are not to be enforced. In this opinion, the authorities must combine concern for individual claims (*mishpat*) with concern for the common weal (*shalom*). There is only one way to do this with legal integrity: before any decision is made in a private monetary dispute, both parties must themselves agree to waive their respective right to the possibility of total legal victory and thus agree that neither one will win and neither one will lose. Both are willing to compromise (*pesharah*) for the sake of the common weal, from which they and the entire community ultimately benefit.[80] Now, even though no one is literally obligated by the law to agree to arbitration in lieu of a formal trial, the later Jewish authorities often urged that litigants at least be subjected to social pressure to do so.[81] That social pressure is to be persuasion based on an appeal to the essential reasonableness of naturally social beings, who should rise above the level of even legitimate private interest for the sake of what is more important in the end.[82]

Nevertheless, in our century especially, when we have seen how the rights of individuals have been crushed under the weight of collectivist regimes, many people have good reason to be suspicious of a system that seems to always place *bonum commune* over *bonum sibi*—that is, the notion that man is made for the state rather than the other way around.

---

[80]For the right to not exercise, that is, to waive, one's right, see Babylonian Talmud, *Kiddushin* 32a; Babylonian Talmud, *Sotah* 25a.

[81]See Maimonides, *Mishneh Torah: Sanhedrin*, 22:4–6, Isodore Twersky, trans. (New Haven, 1976); *Tur: Hoshen Mishpat* 12 (Jerusalem, 1992).

[82]See Babylonian Talmud, *Bava Metziah* 48b.

Community to Persons

The debate over how much weight should be placed on individual rights as opposed to communal duties, and vice versa, is currently being waged by those who call themselves "liberals," on the one side, and those who call themselves "communitarians," on the other side.[83] The preponderance of data from the Jewish tradition, certainly from the Jewish legal tradition, would seem to place this tradition within the communitarian camp. The question is, how can one have a generally communitarian perspective and still reserve an important role for individual rights, even though at times they are at odds with the claims of the community?

One can, of course, simply argue for some sort of balance between the two claims. However, the problem with such a stipulation is that in particular instances one never knows for sure just which side to emphasize. Thus, without a middle term to mediate between these two disjuncts, we do not seem to see how they can function in essential harmony. Is not leaving the matter at this level like agreeing to agree?

It seems to me that if one looks more carefully at the idea of the covenant (*ha-berit*), the essential harmony needed between individual rights and communal duties can be found in Judaism. For in the covenant both individuals and the community as a whole are directly related to God.[84] The community does not mediate that relationship between God and individual persons any more than individuals create the community as an instrument for the fulfillment of their own private needs. Thus, the Torah, as the constitution of the covenant, addresses its commandments both to the community and to the various individuals within it. Everyone has the duty of enhancing the rights/privileges (*zekhut*) of other people

---

[83]For a good discussion of this debate as it relates to Judaism, see Alan Mittleman, "From Private Rights to Public Good: The Communitarian Critique of Liberalism in Judaic Perspective," *Jewish Political Studies Review* 5 (1993): 79ff.

[84]Even that quintessential modern apostate from Judaism, Baruch Spinoza, was favorably impressed by this aspect of the covenant. See *Tractatus Theologico-Politicus*, chaps. 16–17.

in order to enable them to practice more of the Torah's command-ments. Each is therefore responsible for the other.[85] As the *Mishnah* puts it: "God wanted to privilege (*le-zakot*) Israel, therefore He increased the number of commandments for them."[86] In this re-ciprocal fashion, one of the community's main duties is enhancing the right of its members to practice the Torah's commandments. Thus, individuals also have a covenantal claim on the community, beyond the usual personal and property rights they expect soci-ety to protect. And it is for the common good that the community acts on behalf of these individual rights. Here is a vivid example of this covenantal process at work:

> An instance about Rabbi Eliezer: Once when he entered the syna-gogue and did not find ten [the quorum required for public wor-ship]. So he freed his slave on the spot so that he could be the tenth. . . . But how could he do this? Didn't Rav Judah say that whoever frees his slave violates the positive commandment "you shall enslave them forever" (Leviticus 25:46)? But this was a matter of fulfilling a commandment (*le-dvar mitzvah*). Yet doesn't this consist of a com-mandment whose condition is a sin [and hence not the valid prac-tice of the commandment]? No, a public commandment (*mitzvah de-rabbim*) is different.[87]

To appreciate the dialectic in this talmudic discussion, one must be aware of how the institution of slavery developed, from the time of the proof text from Leviticus to the time of Rabbi Eliezer (first century C.E.). In biblical times, it seems that gentile slaves of Jews were only considered to be part of the covenanted community in the sense that certain legal restrictions, such as working on the Sabbath, also applied to them.[88] They were primarily chattel, although their basic human right to bodily integrity was legally enforced.[89] But by rabbinic times they were considered to be

---

[85]See Babylonian Talmud, *Shevu'ot* 39a, re: Leviticus 26:37.

[86]*Mishnah, Makkot* 3:16.

[87]Babylonian Talmud, *Berakhot* 47b. Cf. Babylonian Talmud, *Sukkah* 30a, and parallels.

[88]See Exodus 20:10.

[89]See ibid., 21:20, 26–27. See also Jerusalem Talmud, *Ketubot* 5:5/30a, re: Job 31:15.

quasi-members of the covenanted community. Thus, both male and female slaves had to undergo the same rites of initiation required of a convert.[90] The only difference between a slave and a convert was that a convert had all the rights of a native-born member of the community (with a few minor exceptions), whereas a slave had virtually none of them.[91] Certainly, one of the greatest of these rights is the right to be counted as part of the quorum for public worship. Nevertheless, considered only on the level of individual rights, the scripturally-based law that applies to the community regarding holding slaves might still take precedence. However, when the community itself needs the participation of a slave for purposes of the common good, then its interest and that of the slave actually coincide. A task for the community's religious authorities might well be to look for ways to legally expand the range of such social needs in order to include more persons in the authentic life of the community.[92]

The institution of slavery is, of course, something that has happily disappeared from our world today. I cannot think of anyone who could put forth a morally persuasive argument to look upon it with favor, let alone advocate its return. But what we see from this talmudic text is typical of the way in which the Jewish tradition increasingly made slavery a thing of the past. The way this was done was to see the slave's right to freedom as his or her claim to be a full participant in the life of the community, someone given the opportunity to contribute to the common good. In the case of public worship, we have the best example of the harmony between the private and the public, the individual and the communal. For public worship includes personal prayer, just as personal prayer finds

---

[90]See Babylonian Talmud, *Shabbat* 135b; also, Novak, *Law and Theology in Judaism*, 2:87ff.

[91]The question of whether slaves themselves regarded their status as beneficial or detrimental depended on whether a slave valued physicial security (of slavery) over communal rights (of freedom) or vice versa. See Babylonian Talmud, *Gittin* 12b.

[92]See, for example, *Mishnah, Bikkurim* 1:4; Jerusalem Talmud, *Bikkurim* 1:4/64a, re: Genesis 17:5; Maimonides, *Mishneh Torah: Bikkurim* 4:3.

a deeper context when it is part of public worship.[93] Being communal is different from being collectivist. Indeed, when worship becomes collectivist, it loses the personal devotion (*kavvanah*) that is considered to be its very essence.[94]

CONCLUSION

At the beginning of this chapter, I emphasized how the mandate of this volume actually deals with two different questions: first, the question of religious liberty; and second, the question of the religious foundation of human rights. Therein I indicated my preference for the second question. Nevertheless, the two are closely related. For without the emphasis of religious liberty in a society that is secular by definition, those who see a religious foundation for the human rights that are affirmed by a secular society such as ours have no entry into the moral discourse of the public square. The task of religious believers who wish to enter this moral discourse (although there are quite a few who regard such entry as more dangerous than beneficial to their religious integrity and thus opt for sectarian seclusion) is to persuade others that a religious foundation for human rights can respect the realm of the secular where these rights are exercised much easier than "secularism" can respect the realm of the religious. In other words, the task of the religious believer—Jewish, Christian, or Muslim—is to provide a better foundation for the moral claims of a secular realm in which the vast majority of its citizens profess religious belief and, indeed, see their very allegiance to that secular realm as itself being religious.[95]

---

[93]See Babylonian Talmud, *Rosh Hashanah* 34b.

[94]See Babylonian Talmud, *Ta'anit* 2a, re: Deuteronomy 11:13.

[95]See Richard John Neuhaus, *The Naked Public Square* (Grand Rapids, 1984), esp. chap. 1.

2

FORMING RELIGIOUS COMMUNITIES AND RESPECTING DISSENTERS' RIGHTS: A JEWISH TRADITION FOR A MODERN SOCIETY

Michael J. Broyde
Emory University

The observance of law is one of the ways in which groups of people cohere and form a society.[1] The observance of religion is another.[2] The complex intersection of these two methods of social formation in the Judaic tradition is a critical part of the Jewish understanding of "religious human rights."

---

[1] For a review of the recent literature on this issue, see Lawrence M. Friedman, "The Law and Society Movement," *Stanford Law Review* 38 (1986): 763.

[2] For a detailed discussion of the impact religion has had on the formation of society, see Jerold S. Auerbach, *Justice Without Law* (Oxford, 1983). The thesis of Auerbach's book—that many religious systems can create justice without any formal system of law—is quite debatable and beyond the scope of this paper. It is clear that Jewish law is not such a system, although, as Auerbach notes, it is a system of justice without lawyers, which is not the same as a system of justice without law. Justice without law and justice without lawyers are by no means identical, although to those involved in the common law model of justice it might appear that they are the same. The Jewish legal system certainly had all of the apparent indicia of a legal system (unlike the Amish, who, Auerbach maintains, lack a legal system), although the Jewish tradition had no lawyers as part of its legal system. For more on this issue, see Michael J. Broyde, *The Jewish Perspective on Practicing Law* (Yeshiva University Press, 1995). The

This chapter first focuses on the legal process that Jewish law[3] uses to form communities and to exclude people from them.[4] It addresses the sources within Jewish law for the power to shun

---

confusion that results from comparing a system of law without lawyers (such as Jewish law) with a system of justice without law (such as Amish society) can sometimes be found in Auerbach's book.

[3]Jewish law (called *halachah*, in Hebrew) is the term used to denote the entire subject matter of the Jewish legal system, including public, private, and ritual law. A brief historical review will familiarize the new reader of Jewish law with its history and development. The Pentateuch (the five books of Moses, the *Torah*) is the historical touchstone document of Jewish law and was revealed to Moses at Mount Sinai. The Prophets and Writings, the other two parts of the Hebrew Bible, were written over the next seven hundred years, and the Jewish canon was closed around the year 300 B.C.E. From the close of the canon until 250 C.E. is referred to as the era of the *tanaimim*, the redactors of Jewish law, whose period closed with the editing of the *Mishnah* by Rabbi Judah the Patriarch. The next five centuries was the epoch in which the two Talmuds (Babylonian and Palestinian) were written and edited by scholars called *amoraim* ("those who recount" Jewish law) and *savoraim* ("those who ponder" Jewish law). The Babylonian Talmud is of greater legal significance than the Palestinian Talmud and is a more complete work.

The post-talmudic era is conventionally divided into three periods: the era of the *gaonim*, scholars who lived in Babylonia until the mid-eleventh century; the era of the *rishonim* (the early authorities), who lived in North Africa, Spain, Franco-Germany, and Egypt until the end of the fourteenth century; and the *achronim* (the latter authorities), who encompass all scholars of Jewish law from the fifteen century up to this era.

From the period of the mid-fourteenth century until the early seventeenth century, Jewish law underwent a period of codification, which led to the acceptance of the law code format of Rabbi Joseph Caro, called the *Shulchan Aruch*, as the basis for modern Jewish law. Many significant scholars—themselves as important as Rabbi Caro in status and authority—wrote annotations to his code, which made the work and its surrounding comments the modern touchstone of Jewish law. The most recent complete edition of the *Shulchan Aruch* (Vilna, 1896) contains no fewer than 113 separate commentaries on the text of Rabbi Caro. In addition, hundreds of other volumes of commentary have been published as self-standing works, a process that continues to this very day.

or excommunicate[5] people and the goals of such practice. It then discusses the Jewish legal problems raised when excommunication and shunning are used in a modern secular community, whose primary means of self-classification is not normally through religion.

This chapter then analyzes illustrative American, British, and Canadian cases that have reviewed the use of such excommunication and shunning. None of these legal systems ultimately provides satisfactory protection for the right and rite of excommunication. The chapter thus proposes a number of changes in prevailing secular laws in order to protect the community's right to form itself and to define its membership and the individual's right to leave such communities. Current secular law doctrine in these three countries does neither well.

For a more literary history of Jewish law, see Menachem Elon, *Jewish Law: History, Principles and Sources* (Philadelphia, 1994); and for a shorter review of the literary history of Jewish law, see Suzanne Last Stone, "In Pursuit of the Counter-text: The Turn to the Jewish Legal Model in Contemporary American Legal Theory," *Harvard Law Review* 106 (1992): 813, 816 n.13.

[4]Classically, this is known as shunning and excommunication. The term "excommunication" has its origins in the exclusion of a person from the Christian right to communion, and thus the term is not itself of Jewish origins. See James H. Provost, "Excommunication," in Mircea Eliade, ed., *Encyclopedia of Religion* (New York, 1987), 5:218. Notwithstanding its origins, it has become the accepted term to use to refer to this status. The adoption of legal phrases with origins antithetical to a particular religious practice of rabbinic Judaism, and then their subsequent incorporation into the literature of rabbinic Judaism has precedent; see, for example, Aaron Kirschenbaum, "The Good Samaritan: Monetary Aspects," *Journal of Halacha & Contemporary Society* 17:83 (1989): 84–87.

[5]In Hebrew, the word *cherem* means "to destroy"; see Exodus 22:19 and Deuteronomy 13:16. However, in modern and rabbinic Hebrew it means "to excommunicate"; see Rabbi Joseph Caro, *Shulchan Aruch, Yoreh Deah* 334:1. This isolation is sometimes also expressed through the term *nidui* or *shamta*. The precise linguistic differences between these various terms is beyond the scope of this paper. For more on this, see "Cherem," *Encyclopedia Talmudit* (Jerusalem, 1976), 16:326.

The conclusion notes that exclusions from religious sub-communities are not only fundamental to the ways in which a religious community forms itself, but are profoundly compatible with general moral and legal notions of minority rights and represent the most equitable way a religious community can form itself in a modern society.

JEWISH LAW ON EXCLUDING

Classical Jewish law offers a broad variety of penalties for those who violate the law. The Bible has four different types of death penalties[6] for a variety of offenses, some of which could hardly be described as "criminal."[7] Generally, those offenses for which death is not the prescribed punishment were punished by whipping, according to Jewish law.[8] A small number of offenses were punished by *karet*, a Divinely mandated punishment that humans had no hand in. Some violations were not punished at all.[9] Beyond those penalties found explicitly in the Bible, a Jewish court had available *makot mardut*, literally, the "whipping of a rebel"—a process that allowed the court to punish a person who defied the law—through judicially mandated beatings.[10] So, too, a Jewish court had available the *kipah*, a Jewish version of "three strikes and you're out,"

---

[6]Stoning, burning, slaying, and strangling; see Deuteronomy 17:17, Leviticus 10:2, and Deuteronomy 13:16.

[7]See Maimonides, *Sanhedren* 14:1 and 15:3, Isidore Twersky, trans. (Jerusalem, 1976), who lists the 36 different offenses for which there is a death penalty.

[8]See, for example, ibid., 16:1, and 18:1–2, listing 207 different violations for which lashes are mandated. The codifiers after Maimonides declined to cite these punishments in their codes precisely because they felt them to be inapplicable in modern times. Thus, no listing of death penalty or lashing cases is even found in the classical code of Jewish law, the *Shulchan Aruch*.

[9]Ibid., 18:1–3.

[10]See Rabbi Chezkeya Demedina, *Sedai Chemed* (New York, 1960), 4:287–288, for more on this issue. As a matter of legal theory, Jewish courts might still be entitled to use this punishment; see Menachem Elon, *Prin-*

where a repeat offender could be (informally) killed if he violated the law with impunity.[11]

Despite these classical formulations, Jewish law has not had the judicial authority to inflict any of these punishments for nearly two thousand years.[12] Indeed, Jewish law has functioned for the past two millennia with only two real jurisdictional bases to punish violations—the "pursuer" grant of jurisdiction, and excommunication or shunning.[13] The pursuer rationale (*rodef*) is the jurisdictional source of power for a Jewish court or community to intervene to prevent a murder—by force if need be, and even if that use of force violates the rules of the host country.[14] This area of Jewish law is widely known and much written about.[15] It is irrelevant to the formation of a sub-

---

ciples of Jewish Law (Jerusalem, 1974), 534–35. However, it is clear that Jewish courts do not *ever* order this punishment in modern times, and it is thus considered a punishment no longer applicable.

[11]Babylonian Talmud, *Sanhedren* 81b. This penalty is also inapplicable in modern times.

[12]Formal jurisdiction ended forty years prior to the destruction of the Second Temple (ibid., 41a). While perhaps some sort of criminal jurisdiction might have been granted to the Jewish community in Spain in the 1300s and in various other times in Jewish history by the civil government, even that jurisdiction was not directly based on Jewish law and involved punishments unheard of in Jewish law. For a further discussion of this issue, see Elon, *Principles of Jewish Law*, 529.

[13]Perhaps there is also some emergency jurisdiction, although this author is inclined to view this form of jurisdiction in post-talmudic times as a broad manifestation of the pursuer rationale. See further, H. Ben-Menahem, *Judicial Deviation in Talmudic Law* (Boston, 1991). Essentially complete civil jurisdiction is still part of Jewish law and is beyond the scope of this paper.

[14]Thus, for example, if one saw "A" going to murder "B" in Atlanta, Jewish law would allow one to kill "A" if that is the only way to prevent the crime. In fact, the scope of the pursuer rationale is quite a bit broader than that case, and it perhaps provides the governing jurisdictional grant (and perhaps the substantive laws) for such areas as abortion, spousal abuse, armed robbery, and other violent crimes; for more on this, see *Shulchan Aruch, Choshen Mishpat* (Jerusalem, 1992), 425:1–3.

[15]See further, Marilyn Finkelman, "Self-Defense and Defense of Others in Jewish Law: The Rodef Defense," *Wayne State Law Review* 33 (1987): 1257.

society in modern times, since the cases it governs are crimes that are also nearly always violations of basic moral principles and thus subject, on a practical level, to the concurrent jurisdiction of the secular government. Thus, the normal response—even in a very insular, fastidiously observant, Jewish society—to a murder would be to call the police.[16]

The remaining powers that Jewish courts have, with which to address routine problems involved in forming a sub-society, are those of excommunication and shunning.[17] The power to form a sub-community and to exclude people from that sub-community is a power that can frequently encourage conduct in ways that formal law itself either cannot or will not accomplish. The creators of Jewish law and culture were quite aware of that fact and designed within their legal and ethical system rules that relate to the use of social pressure.

A recent case arising in the rabbinical courts of Israel demonstrates this well and presents itself as a modern—but classical— example of the power of a Jewish court to order social shunning of a person whose conduct is not in full compliance with the ethical dictates of Jewish society. The Supreme Rabbinical Court in Israel

---

[16]See, for example, *People v. Drelich*, 506 N.Y.S.2d 746 124, A.D.2d 441 (2d App. Div. 1986).

[17]One other significant power is present, which is the religious authority to exclude people from the privileges Jewish law mandates that one adherent extend to another. For example, in a society where the secular law does not mandate that one return lost property to its rightful owner, Jewish law directs that one nevertheless return such property to a fellow Jew who observes Jewish law. This type of privilege can also be used to create communities and exclude individuals. This author has argued elsewhere that these privileges are, in fact, quite similar in purpose to excommunication—creating a community committed to a similar level of observance—but are used on a much higher level. See Michael J. Broyde and Michael Hecht, "The Gentile and Returning Lost Property According to Jewish Law: A Theory of Reciprocity," *Jewish Law Annual* (forthcoming). Thus, as will be shown later in this chapter, excommunication and shunning were used only to prevent public defiance of community norms, whereas these remaining reciprocal privileges were used to distinguish personal observance. This is quite a difficult topic, and the conclusion found in that paper could be contested.

is discussing what to do in a situation in which a divorce seems proper and is desired by the wife, yet the husband will not cooperate in the processing of the divorce.[18] The court states:

> In the appeal,[19] which was presented before us on January 7, 1985, the court did not find sufficient cause to compel[20] the husband to divorce his wife. The Court did, however, try to persuade the man, who is religiously observant, that he follow the proper path and to obey the decision of the court [that it is proper for him to issue the divorce], for it is a good deed to heed the words of the Sages who religiously obliged him to divorce his wife and that he has chained his wife needlessly.[21]

The court gave the husband an extension of three months within which to grant a divorce to his wife. However, when the Court saw that three months passed without a response, they declared:

> [W]e instituted the separations of Rabbenu Tam as found in the *Sefer HaYashar* (*Chelek HaTeshuvot* 24), which states: Decree by force of

---

[18]For more on this topic, see Irwin H. Haut, *Divorce in Jewish Law and Life* (Targum, 1983), 18, and Irving Breitowitz, "The Plight of the Agunah: A Study in Halacha, Contract, and the First Amendment," *Maryland Law Review* 51 (1992): 312.

[19]For a discussion of the appellate process in Jewish law, see Eliav Shochetman, *Civil Procedure in Jewish Law* (Jerusalem, 1994), 443–71.

[20]In Jewish divorce law, a court has three choices. It can compel the issuing of a divorce (and in such a situation, Jewish law would allow court-ordered compulsion to force a bill of divorce to be written). However, there are few grounds for such an order—essentially adultery or serious marital misconduct. Alternatively, a court can rule that one is "religiously obliged" to participate in a divorce. In such a situation, judicial force cannot be used. The grounds for such an order are numerous, and that was the order in this case. Finally, it can rule that a divorce is not mandated by Jewish law and should only be given with the full and complete consent of both parties. See, generally, *Shulchan Aruch, Even Haezer* 154.

[21]Jewish courts, unlike common law courts, not only decide cases but give moral advice based on the teachings of Jewish law and ethics. See Menachem Elon, *Jewish Law: History Sources, Principles 4* (Philadelphia, 1994), 1863–71.

oath on every Jewish man and woman under your jurisdiction that they not be allowed to speak to him, to host him in their homes, to feed him or give him to drink, to accompany him or to visit him when he is ill. . . .

We added to these strictures that no sexton of any synagogue in the area where the husband resides be allowed to seat him in the synagogue, or call him to the Torah, or ask after his welfare, or grant him any honor. All people are to distance themselves from him as much as possible until his heart submits and he heeds to voices of those instructing him that he grant his wife a divorce. And so it was done, at which time the husband submitted and granted his wife a divorce.[22]

This case involved the use of the communal sanction of mild shunning to encourage a person who wished to be part of the religious community in Israel[23] to obey the mandates of Jewish law and ethics. A person who felt no desire to belong to the community, and thus was not threatened by the possibility of exclusion from it, would not have reacted in the manner this person did. The sanction would have had no effect.

One should not think that such methods of persuasion occur only in Israel. For example, in the case of *Grunwald v. Bornfreund*[24] the plaintiff sought an injunction from a United States District Court prohibiting the "Central Rabbinical Congress of the United States and Canada, its Rabbinical Court and its members (the 'Rabbinical Congress'), and defendants from making any efforts to have plaintiff withdraw his action from this Court and submit it to a rabbinical or ecclesiastical court and from temporarily or permanently

---

[22]Like many opinions of the Supreme Rabbinical Court, this case was initially published as part of the Responsa literature of its judges; see Rabbi Obadiah Yosef, *Yabia Omer*, 7:23 (Jerusalem, 1993) (Even HaEzer) and Rabbi Eliezer Waldenberg, *Tzitz Eliezer*, 7:53 (Jerusalem, 1989).

[23]Note how the court states: "We did, however, try to persuade the man, *who is religiously observant*, that he follow the proper path and to obey the decision of the court, for it is a *mitzvah* to heed the words of the Sages who obliged him to divorce his wife . . ." *Yabia Omer* 7:23 (emphasis added).

[24]696 F. Supp. 838 (E.D.N.Y. 1988).

excommunicating plaintiff, his counsel, and staff."[25] Modern rabbinical courts can and do excommunicate. Indeed, excommunication and its lesser cousin, shunning, remain valid expressions of religious will within the Jewish community to this very day, and they are used to express communal disdain for a person's actions.

The Power and Purpose of Exclusion

The Talmud discusses the legal rules related to shunning in some detail,[26] and over time the legal rules have grown in detail and purpose.[27] One overarching theme emerges from the legal discussion: Unlike the many forms of punishment found in classical Jewish law, the purpose of the exclusion process is to deter future violations of Jewish law—primarily by other members of society, but also by the excluded person. Punishment and retribution as aims were not thought to be part of the process, as they were in classical Jewish criminal law.[28]

---

[25]The affidavit submitted described the consequences of this excommunication as follows: "Plaintiff may be totally excluded from the community, he will not be able to shop at the stores of members of the community, his *tzitzit*, a fringed garment worn by observant Jews, may be cut off, the *mezuzah*, religious verses in a container, may be removed from his door, and there will be no religious prohibition on injury to his property or, indeed, his murder" (ibid., 839). The movant's affidavit is clearly incorrect as a matter of Jewish law. As noted by the Court, it mixes the legal sanctions for excommunication with that of informing, a far more serious violation of Jewish law and ethics. The Jewish tradition simply excluded people when excommunication was ordered. No other penalty should be imposed.

[26]Babylonian Talmud, *Mo'ed Katan* 14b–17b.

[27]Perhaps one could suggest that as other remedies were abolished in response to societal concerns, the uses of exclusion to form a community increased. Thus, it is quite reasonable that Rabbi Asher ben Yecheil (Spain, 1300s) can essentially abandon the use of exclusion as a punishment (see *Responsa of Asher* 43:9), as the Jewish community in Spain at that time had criminal jurisdiction over the Jewish community, including the statutory authority to execute. See *Responsa of Asher* (Jerusalem, 1991), 17:1; *Responsa of Yehuda ben Asher* (New York, 1957), 75.

[28]See, generally, Elon, *Principles of Jewish Law*, 469–475.

Any analysis of the rules relating to excluding people raises two questions. First, may one shun or excommunicate a person when the shunning process might (or will) drive this person completely away from the religious community or religious observance?[29] Second, may one shun or exclude the relatives of a person in order to encourage the person to cease his or her activities? These two questions are central to the seminal issue of this chapter: *What is the purpose of excluding people from the community?*

The problem of excluding people from the community when they will abandon religious observance in response is part of a very important discussion as to whom Jewish law is seeking to deter through the process of excommunication. Is it the person who is flaunting community standards, or is it the community at large that will witness the person's exile from the community, and thus be deterred? If it is the former, then one does not shun a person who will abandon the faith when shunned. If it is the latter, then that factor is not relevant. Indeed, this discussion reflects the ultimate reality concerning all shunning cases: in modern times and in democratic countries, the penalty of exclusion works on the one being shunned only if the person desires the approbation of the faith that is excluding him or her.

This fact itself reflects a profound historical change in the purpose of excluding people from the community. Classical Jewish law held "that a person on whom an excommunication ban lies can be regarded as dead."[30] Indeed, flogging was perceived as a

---

[29]At first glance this might seem like a peculiar question. After all, is not the goal of excommunication to remove the person from the community? It is clear that in talmudic times, that was not the goal. For example, the great sage, Rabbi Eliezer was excommunicated by the talmudic Sages for defiance of the majority on a particular issue. Notwithstanding his excommunication, he remained one of the premier talmudic scholars of his time, to whom other scholars went to hear lecture—all the while making sure that they stayed more than four cubits away from him, as required by Jewish law. He was excommunicated to indicate that his view on a particular topic was wrong, and his defiance was unacceptable. However, he clearly remained in the faith-group of rabbinic Judaism. For more on this, see *Bava Metziah* 59a–b.

[30]Elon, *Principles of Jewish Law*, 543.

more merciful punishment than excommunication in classical Jewish law.[31] In a closed and tightly knit community, surrounded by a generally hostile society, exclusion from the Jewish community was a very severe penalty. Many classical Jewish law authorities would thus not shun or excommunicate under any circumstances.[32] This has changed in post-emancipation times. As noted by a secular critic:

> Shunning and excommunication became so common in the later centuries that they no longer made any impression and lost their force [to the uncommitted]. They became the standard rabbinic reaction to all forms of deviation or nonconformity considered incompatible with or dangerous to Orthodoxy. As such, they are sometimes imposed by extreme Orthodox authorities at the present day, but as neither the person afflicted nor the public at large regard them as bound by them, they have ceased to be a terror or have much effect."[33]

Particularly today, a person who is shunned can simply leave the community and join a different community that adheres to different religious principles.

Rabbi Moses Isserless, one of the codifiers of Jewish law, writing in his glosses on *Shulchan Aruch*, resolves the issue of the purpose of exclusion by stating: "We excommunicate or shun a person who is supposed to be excommunicated or shunned, even if we fear

---

[31]Jacob ben Asher, *Tur, Yoreh Deah* (Jerusalem, 1992), 334.

[32]See Rabbi Jacob Moellin, *Minhagai Maharil* (Jerusalem, 1991), 34.

[33]Haim Cohen, quoted by Elon, *Principles of Jewish Law*, 544. It is worth noting that (notwithstanding their ineffectiveness) the British Mandate law governing Palestine appeared to outlaw these pronouncements as a form of criminal conspiracy; see *Criminal Ordinances of Palestine*, sect. 36. I am inclined to disagree with Cohen's thesis as to the cause of the ineffectiveness of the current penalties. While Cohen appears to maintain that the penalty became ineffective because of overuse by the "extreme Orthodox," I am inclined to maintain that the penalty became ineffective due to the emancipation and the general change in social status of the Jewish community. Once one can legally move out of the Jewish district/ghetto and avoid the community's sanction, excommunication becomes a much weaker penalty.

that because of this, he will bring himself to other evils [such as leaving the faith]."[34] The rationale for this is explained clearly by later authorities. The purpose of the shunning or excommunication is to serve notice to the members of the community that this conduct is unacceptable, and also, secondarily, to encourage the violator to return to the community. In a situation where these two goals cannot both be accomplished, the first takes priority over the second.[35] This is true even in situations where there is a reasonable possibility that the person will leave the Jewish faith completely and simply abandon any connection with the community to avoid the pressures imposed on him. The shunning and excommunication can be said to have accomplished its goals in such a situation—even if the shunned person continues in the path of defiance and leaves the faith community.[36] Not unexpectedly, the vast majority of civil suits related to excommunication in-

---

[34]*Yoreh Deah* 334:1.

[35]See comments of Rabbi Shabtai ben Meir Hacohen, *Nekudat Hakesef* 334:1; Rabbi Yair Bachrach, *Responsa Chavat Yair* (Jerusalem, 1968), 141; Rabbi Yakov Emden, *Responsa Yavetz* (Lemberg, 1887), 1:79; Rabbi Avraham Yitzchak Kook, *Da'at Cohen, Yoreh Deah* (Jerusalem, 1983), 194; Rabbi Moses Feinstein, *Iggrot Moshe Yoreh Deah* (New York, 1959), 1:53, OC 2:33; Rabbi Yitzchak Isaac Herzog, *Hechal Yitzchak* (Jerusalem, 1961), OC, 30(3); and *Pitchai Teshuva* commenting on *Yoreh Deah* 334:1.

[36]These dual goals of shunning and excommunication are found in religions other than Judaism. For example, a recent court case discussed the process of withdrawal of fellowship from the Church of Christ. It noted: "Withdrawal of fellowship is a disciplinary procedure that is carried out by the entire membership in a Church of Christ congregation. When one member has violated the church's code of ethics and refuses to repent, the elders read aloud to the congregation those scriptures which were violated. The congregation then withdraws its fellowship from the wayward member by refusing to acknowledge that person's presence. *According to the Elders, this process serves a dual purpose: it causes the transgressor to feel lonely and thus to desire repentance and a return to fellowship with the other members; and secondly, it ensures that the church and its remaining members continue to be pure and free from sin*" (*Guinn v. The Church of Christ of Collinsville*, 775 P.2d 766, 768, n. 2 [Okl. 1989]) (emphasis added).

volved people who have left the faith community in response to their exclusion.

It is worth noting that there is a minority opinion to the contrary, which rules that one should not shun or excommunicate a person who will leave rather than be excommunicated. Rabbi David Halevi, writing in his commentary *Turai Zahav*, states that he disagrees with the approach of Rabbi Isserless, and in his opinion it is prohibited to shun a person when one suspects that the person shunned will withdraw from the Jewish community in response.[37] However, many commentators, while noting his remarks, make a crucial distinction as to why people might be excluded. They note that while as a matter of theory one could be shunned or excommunicated merely for violating any law, or even for avoiding a financial obligation,[38] in fact, that is not how and why exclusion is used. Exclusion, these authorities state, is used as a deterrent, to prevent other people from violating the law, and is no longer used as a method of punishment. Thus, these authorities note that Rabbi Halevi's point is true, but inapplicable. In a case where a person is violating the law, and the punishment imposed will drive him further away—but there is no other community value at stake—it might be that Rabbi Halevi's point is correct, that it is prohibited to punish by exclusion. However, such is no longer the purpose of shunning and excommunication; inevitably, more is at stake than this single person's violation.[39]

The process of shunning or excommunicating individuals relates not solely to their violation of religious law, but also to their apparent status as members of the community in good standing. For example, Jewish law reserves the right, as a matter of jurisdiction, to assert that any Jew who willfully deviates from Jewish law may

---

[37]Commenting on *Yoreh Deah* 334:1.

[38]Indeed, this is quite clearly stated in *Shulchan Aruch, Yoreh Deah* 334:1.

[39]Indeed, this remark is part of a broader posture of modern Jewish law that the punishment of criminals for any reason other than deterrence of future crime is no longer within the jurisdiction of Jewish law. Just as the pursuer rationale permits only the use of force to prevent crime, and not to punish it, so, too, the essential goal of the shunning process is to deter future violations (either by this person or others). It is not to punish.

be excluded. However, the law is established that such shunning or excommunication does not, in fact, occur unless it is actually pronounced by a Jewish court, and such pronouncements are not forthcoming unless the person started as a member of the faith community and now is publicly deviating from it in a way designed to hinder communal organization.[40] Thus, in modern times vast numbers of Jews are distant from any version of traditional Judaism, happy with that status, and yet are not under any decree of excommunication;[41] the few who are excluded appear to be people who are insiders, deeply within the faith, but yet are actively dissenting.[42]

The legal status of a "non-member" of the Jewish community is considerably better than that of one who joins and is expelled or wishes to leave.[43] This is consistent with the essential purpose of shunning and excommunication in the Jewish tradition—to establish a religious community. Nonmembers do not disrupt such a community: dissenters do.[44]

---

[40]See *Shulchan Aruch* 334:12 and commentaries ad locum; see also comments *of Nekudat HaKessef* on *Taz Yoreh Deah* 334:1.

[41]For a discussion of levels of observance in the Jewish community, see Harold DellaPergola and Uziel Schmelz, "Demography and Jewish Education in the Diaspora," in H. Himmelfarb and S. DellaPergola, eds., *Jewish Education Worldwide: Cross Cultural Perspectives* (Lanham, MD, 1989), 43, 55.

[42]Thus, for example, the three court cases discussed in this paper that address legal aspects of excommunication within the Jewish tradition all are clearly concerned with insiders who are flouting the will of the community and yet wish to remain part of that community.

[43]Within the Jewish tradition, one who was never part of the community almost inevitably has the status of a "child who was kidnapped" from the faith and is thus excused from any penalty for his violation, based on his complete lack of familiarity with the faith. The Jewish tradition directs that one must befriend such persons to bring them closer to the faith; certainly such people cannot be shunned. See further, Maimonides, *Mamrim* 3:3 and Rabbi Abraham Isaiah Karletz, *Chazon Ish, Yoreh Deah* (Bena Brak, 1962), 1:6, 2:160, and 2:28.

[44]This is hinted at in Robert Bear's recounting of his exclusion from the Reformed Mennonite Church. He states "Because I have been excommunicated I am considered to be more sinful than if I had never known 'the truth'" (Robert Bear, *Delivered Unto Satan* [Philadelphia, 1974], 10).

The second issue that needs to be addressed within the Jewish tradition is whether one may shun the relatives of a person in order to encourage the person to cease his disruptive activities. This situation also crystallizes the purpose of this treatment. As a general principle, classical Jewish law prohibits punishing an innocent person as a way of punishing another person for a violation of the law.[45] Thus, the question is whether shunning is really a form of punishment, or is it some other type of activity not bound by the jurisprudential rules of punishment?

Once again, Rabbi Isserless adopts the legal rule that posits that punishment is not the goal. He states: "It is within the power of a Jewish court to order [as part of a shunning] that a violator's children not be circumcised, that his dead not be buried, that his children be expelled from the school, and that his wife be removed from the synagogue until he accepts the ruling of the court."[46] Thus, Rabbi Isserless endorses exclusion not only of those who defy the community, but he also recognizes that people can be excluded from the community when their inclusion, through no fault of their own, will prevent the formation of the community.[47] Letting the close family of an excluded person participate in the religious sub-community—using its synagogue, cemetery, or schools—still allows the "excluded" person to be part of the community even though he is "excluded."

This is, by no means, the only ruling possible. Commenting on this phrase, Rabbi David Halevi, writing in his classical commentary *Turai Zahav*, states: "Heaven forbid this. The world is only in existence because of the studies of children in school. It makes sense to prohibit circumcising children, as that obligation is solely the father's;[48] the same is true for burying his dead. . . . However, studying by children has no restitution. . . . So, too, to exclude his

---

[45]Deuteronomy 24:16.

[46]*Yoreh Deah* 334:6, quoting from a responsa of Rav Palti Gaon (ninth century).

[47]It is important to realize that Rabbi Isserless is not discussing the exclusion of the relative who assists in the disruption. Rather, he permits the exclusion from the community of people who, if allowed to remain, will cause disruption through their mere presence.

[48]Until children reach adulthood, the primary obligation to circumcise is limited to the father; see *Shulchan Aruch, Yoreh Deah* 360:1.

wife from the synagogue is improper; if he sinned, what was her sin?"[49] Clearly, this approach assumes that excommunication and shunning are a form of judicial punishment, subject to the general rules regulating the fairness and propriety of any punishment. This ruling is consistent with Rabbi Halevi's analysis, discussed above, which prohibited exclusion when the person will leave the community in retaliation. It is predicated on a judicial model of exclusion bound by the rules of punishment.

Rabbi Isserless, and those authorities who follow his view, simply assume that the normal rules regulating judicial punishment do not apply in the case of shunning and excommunication—not because on a practical level the innocent person is unhurt, but because on a philosophical level, exclusion is not punishment. Rabbi Hershel Schachter, agreeing with Rabbi Isserless's ruling, states that the one being shunned "would agree to obey the law, in the particular area which he is remiss, in order to afford his wife and children a proper religious environment. *Using the children as leverage is not to be confused with punishing them unjustly.*"[50]

The question is, why is leverage not to be confused with punishment? Certainly the children or spouse would feel that they are—for all apparent purposes—being punished. Rabbi Schachter's point goes to the purpose of the shunning or excommunication, rather than to its apparent impact—to compel communal cohesiveness and to exclude people who prevent it. In a situation where shunning relatives would have no impact on the conduct of the principal and would not admit the person to the community, such conduct is prohibited.[51]

In summary, Jewish law has an institution called shunning and excommunication, the goal of which is to exclude from the community people who seek to dissent from central tenets of the com-

---

[49]Actually, he is quoting from the works of the Rabbi Shlomo Luria, *Yam Shel Shlomo*, a major scholar of Jewish law who lived two generations prior to Rabbi Halevi.

[50]Rabbi Hershel Schachter, "Synagogue Membership and School Admission," *Journal of Halacha and Contemporary Society* 12:50 (1986): 64 (emphasis added).

[51]Ibid.

munity. However, it is not used as a form of punishment and does not have its origins in any judicial institutions. It is designed to encourage people to conform to communal norms or else cease to be part of the religious sub-community.[52]

Shunning: For Which Offenses

Having established the legal basis for shunning and excommunication, it is now necessary to determine the offenses that merit such exclusion. As noted earlier, the theoretical talmudic law is clear:

---

[52]This raises the issue of recognized diversity within a particular religious faith. Within Judaism there are certain well-established differences of practice, custom, and law that are based on the historical separation and isolation of certain geographical groups. Thus, for example, there are Eastern European Jews, commonly called *Ashkenazim*, and Oriental Jews, commonly called *Sefardim*; these two groups have their own customs, and frequently also their own laws, that govern many matters. There is a considerable body of literature discussing the establishment of practices within the community when the "community" is made up of members with different customs, traditions, and laws.

In a nutshell, Jewish law recognizes not only the right of a community to exclude people from the sub-society who are in deviation from the basic tenets of the community in violation of Jewish law, but also to compel members of a different recognized Jewish community to adhere to the norms of the majoritarian Jewish practice in the community where they reside. Thus, for example, a Jew of Eastern European descent who would normally follow the rites and laws of the Ashkenazic Jewish community must publicly follow the strictures of the Oriental (Sefardic) community were he to reside in such a community. Of course, Jewish law would recognize the right of this person to form his own community following the Ashkenazic rite when a mass of such people were present. However, the Jewish tradition clearly grants to the majority community the right to insist that all of the participants in its community adhere to the same public rites on significant issues—or leave the community to form its own religiously separate community (which is perfectly proper). It matters not at all whether the deviation from communal norm is one that is "historically legitimate" or not. For a recent Hebrew work on the issue of interactions between various communities in Israel, see Tal Doar, *Tal Amarti* (Jerusalem, 1992), 1–26.

"[O]ne who violates any prohibition may be shunned."[53] That is, however, only the beginning of the rule. One of the commentators immediately notes that this is limited to a situation where the person has already been formally warned that his public conduct violated Jewish law.[54] So, too, one may not excommunicate or shun a person who unintentionally violated Jewish law; indeed, one may not—Jewish law rules—shun a person who is aware of what the rule of law is, tries to observe it, and occasionally slips.[55]

The classical code lists specific offenses for which shunning is proper. All involve breaches of community discipline. For example, the classical code lists as one who ought to be shunned a person who denigrates a community scholar or an agent of the Jewish court while he is doing his job, or a person who mocks—not who violates—one of the rules of Jewish law. Other offenses include desecration of God's name[56] or refusing to accept the jurisdiction of the Jewish court system.[57] Such offenses hinder the creation or maintenance of a community and can destroy the community if not stopped.

The Jewish tradition thus differs significantly from various Christian practices of using shunning to enforce observance of the details of the law and to supervise the private conduct of its

---

[53]*Shulchan Aruch, Yoreh Deah* 234:1.

[54]See comments of Rabbi Shabtai ben Meir Hacohen, *Seftai Cohen, Yoreh Deah* 334:2.

[55]*Shulchan Aruch, Yoreh Deah* 334:38, and see comments of Rabbi David Halevi (*Taz*), n.18. The classical example of that is the case of a person who is aware that it is wrong to use God's name in vain, generally abstains from so doing, but occasionally in moments of frustration does so. Such a person cannot be excluded.

[56]*Yoreh Deah* 334:43.

[57]A Jewish court would not order exclusion as an economic remedy for such a violation—indeed, it cannot. See *Shulchan Aruch, Chosen Mishpat* 13. It would only order exclusion if the one who lost the case defied the court and declined to implement the economic remedy ordered by the Jewish court. In that case, exclusion might be ordered; it, however, is not an economic remedy, but rather a form of contempt of court, whose punishment bears no relationship to the underlying issues in the case.

members. That was never its use in the Jewish tradition. Adultery, polytheism, Sabbath violations, ritual violations, and other central tenets of the faith, which were grounds for excommunication from the Christian community, were never subject to shunning by the Jewish tradition unless the person engaged in this conduct in a public manner intended to indicate defiance of the Jewish tradition.

The differences between Jewish and Christian views of shunning can be seen in cases brought before American courts by disgruntled excommunicants. While there are a wealth of American tort cases involving shunning and excommunication by various Christian denominations, these cases are categorically different from excommunication cases involving Jewish law. A brief summary of the allegations contained in these cases is itself worthwhile, as it highlights uses of exclusion and excommunication by different faiths. Of the reported American cases[58] that deal directly with a suit related to an excommunication or a shunning by a Christian denomination, four allege that a religious denomination publicized the sexual practices of one of its congregants or former congregants in the process of excommunication.[59] Four cases allege alienation of affection from spouses based on religiously motivated abandonment because of one partner's lack of observance, which resulted in excommunication.[60] Three cases allege that the church engaged in financial slander against a member

---

[58]As of September 1, 1994, on Westlaw.

[59]*Guinn*, 775 P.2d 775 (excommunication based on fornication); *Ventimiglia v. Sycamore View Church of Christ*, 1988 WL 119288 (Tenn. Ct. App. 1988) (excommunication resulting from adultery); *Hadnot v. Shaw*, 826 P.2d 978 (Okla., 1992) (excommunication based on fornication); *Synder v. Evangelical Orthodox Church*, 264 Cal. Rptr. 640, 216 Cal. App. 3d 297 (Cal. Ct. App. 1989) (excommunication based on adultery).

[60]*Hester v. Barnett*, 723 S.W.2d 544 (Miss. Ct. App. 1987) (alienation of affections suit resulting from excommunication ordered by pastor); *O'Neil v. Schuckardt*, 733 P.2d 693 (Idaho 1986) (alienation of affections suit resulting from excommunication ordered by denomination); *Radecki v. Schuckardt*, 361 N.E. 543 (Oh. Ct. App. 1976) (same); *Carrieri v. Bush*, 419 P.2d 132 (Wash. 1966) (alienation of affections suit resulting from excommunication ordered by church).

when it publicized an alleged fiscal impropriety of the member in
the process of excommunication.[61] Four cases allege financial
claims relating to misappropriating church funds by church officials, resulting in excommunication by the one alleging the impropriety (or otherwise protesting a fiscal practice of the church).[62]
Two cases deal with excommunications as a result of attempts to
fire the pastor.[63] Only in one case does the plaintiff pose a general
challenge to the practice of shunning without a specific allegation
of impropriety.[64] The cases reflect both the routineness of the excommunication process in these denominations and its general use
as a method of governance in the community.

The only two American cases that discuss the Jewish excommu-
nication process reflect the different interest associated with the
Jewish use of excommunication. In one case, a member of a chasidic
Jewish community was suing the educational institution of his com-

------

[61]*Molko v. Holy Spirit Association for the Unification of World Christianity*, 252 Cal. Rptr. 122, 46 Cal. 3d 1092, 762 P.2d 46 (1988) (allegation of
financial fraud as the cause of an excommunication); *Bear v. Reformed
Mennonite Church*, 462 Pa. 330, 341 A.2d 105 (1975) (financial ruin resulting from allegation of fraud leading to excommunication); *Lide v.
Whittington*, 573 S.W.2d 614 (Tex. Ct. App. 1978) (excommunication resulting from an allegation of business misconduct and slander).

[62]*Lozanoski v. Sarafin*, 485 N.E.2d 669 (Ind. App. 1985) (excommunication resulting from church financial dispute); *Macedonia Baptist Foundation v. Singleton*, 379 So.2d 269 (La. App. 1979) (excommunication resulting from inter-church dispute about fundraising matters); *Davis v.
Church of Jesus Christ of Latter Day Saints*, 258 Mont. 286, 852 P.2d 640
(Mont. 1993) (allegation of fraud and breach of fiduciary duty leading to
excommunication resulting from medical injury in a church building); *St.
John's Greek Catholic Hungarian Russian Orthodox Church of Rahway v.
Fedak*, 96 N.J. Super. 556, 233 A.2d 663 (N.J. Super. A.D. 1967) (excom-
munication resulting from property dispute in church).

[63]*Bowen v. Green*, 275 S.C. 431, 272 S.E.2d 433 (S.C. 1980) (excommunication resulting from attempt to fire pastor); *Bentley v. Shanks*, 48
Tenn. App. 512, 348 S.W.2d 900 (Tenn. App. 1960) (excommunication
resulting from firing of pastor).

[64]*Paul v. Watchtower Bible and Tract Society of New York, Inc.*, 819 F.2d
875 (9th Cir. 1987) (excommunication resulting from disfellowship of
parents).

munity, alleging systemic corruption on the part of the institution against the government and various students.[65] He was excommunicated for bringing forth that violation.[66] The second case involved a witness in a grand jury proceeding who was set to testify against a Jewish institution, alleging systemic fraud by the institution. He wished to avoid testifying, based on the fact that he would be excommunicated if he did so.[67] Both of these cases raise the specter of "community issues" that go far beyond the question of the propriety of an individual person's conduct. These cases are typical of the issues that result in removal from the community. *Exclusion is not for the "garden variety" sin in the Jewish tradition.*

Indeed, the differing approaches to exclusion reflect a deeper difference concerning the more general issue of noncompliance with religious obligations by members of one's faith. How does a faith go about forming its own sub-community? Does it, as the Church of Christ does, seek only to have the already committed join the faith, and then use the process of shunning and excommunication to enforce discipline among the already committed?[68] Or does it adopt the policy of the modern Catholic Church, which automatically excommunicates for serious violations, and in addition, reserves the right to excommunicate for political or public defiance of the church.[69] Classical Judaism adopted neither of these policies. It excommunicated *only* for public violations of the law and only when these violations were designed to undermine the community or the ability to form a community. Thus, as a general matter, Jewish communities are made up of people of various levels of observance. Shunning and excommunication are not used

---

[65]*Grunwald*, 696 F. Supp. 838.

[66]Ibid., 839.

[67]*In re Fuhrer*, 419 N.Y.S. 426 (1979).

[68]*Guinn*, 775 P.2d 768–69.

[69]Thomas J. Green, "Future of Penal Law in the Church," *The Jurist* 35 (1975): 212–275. See, generally, The National Conference of Catholic Bishops, *Resolution of National Conference of Catholic Bishops* (Washington, 1989), and Ari L. Goldman, "O'Connor Warns Politicians Risk Excommunication Over Abortion," *New York Times* (June 15, 1990): A1, B2 ("Catholics in public office must also have this commitment to serve the state; but service to God must always come first.").

as methods encourage observance, but to exclude people from
the community who did not accept and vocally disagreed with the
communitarian tenets of the group.

EXCLUSION AND SECULAR LAW

The choices a religion makes concerning the exclusion policy it
enforces affect the nature of the community that is formed. So, too,
does the secular law of the society it lives in. The next section of
this article will address the impact of American, British, and Canadian law on Jewish (and, by comparison, other religious) doctrines
concerning exclusion.

Exclusion and American Tort Law

Religious doctrines do not live in a vacuum. The way American tort
law rewards or punishes certain behavior—including religious
behavior—affects the frequency and form of the behavior. As the
United States Court of Appeals for the Ninth Circuit ruled: "Permitting prosecution of a cause of action in tort, while not criminalizing
the conduct at issue, would make shunning an 'unlawful act.' Imposing tort liability for shunning on the Church or its members
would in the long run have the same effect as prohibiting the practice and would compel the Church to abandon part of its religious
teachings."[70] Jewish communities frequently confronted this issue

---

[70]*Paul*, 819 F.2d 877. There are a few examples of excommunications having unquestioned secular law consequences. One such case is
Borntrager v. Commissioner, 58 T.C.M. (CCH) 1242 (1990), which involved
the rights of an excommunicated member of the Old Order Amish to keep
his religious exemption from Social Security benefits, taxes, or even having a Social Security number. The court ruled that the statutory exemption of the Amish was at least in part based on the Amish community's
self-sufficiency in caring for its members; since Borntrager was no longer
a member in good standing in the Amish community and would not be
assisted by the Amish communal welfare system should he need it, he is
not entitled to Social Security exemption.

in Eastern Europe, whose governments generally outlawed the use of excommunication and shunning. Not surprisingly, when confronted with significant governmentally imposed sanctions against this practice, the Jewish authorities ceased using exclusion as a method of community formation or maintenance.[71]

American cases on excommunication and shunning have raised two related issues: (1) May courts impose damages against religious communities for torts such as the intentional infliction of emotional distress that impose liability for a plaintiff's nonphysical damages, such as alienation of affection or interference with a contractual relationship? or (2) Do the First Amendment religion clauses immunize religious groups from such tort suits? These two doctrines are the counterbalances that form American tort law in this area.

The reader is entitled to one caveat. The religious parameters relating to excommunication and shunning differ from religion to religion. It is vitally important to grasp that these same terms mean drastically different forms of treatment toward shunned and excommunicated individuals depending on the faith group. For example, the Church of Scientology of California at one point—and perhaps still[72]—adopted a policy of "fair game" toward individuals who are excommunicated. One court described the doctrine as follows: "Under Scientology's 'fair game' policy, someone who

---

[71]For a Jewish law discussion of the issues raised by a governmental ban on excommunication, see Rabbi Yecheil Michael Epstein, *Aruch HaShulchan, Yoreh Deah* 334 (preface and section 42) (Hobokin, 1992). In my opinion, the material in the preface is not an authentic representation of the position of Jewish law, but was placed there for the purpose of permitting the publication of the work in response to censorship by the Czarist government. An examination of the *Aruch HaShulchan, Choshen Mishpat*, indicates that this was his method of speaking exclusively to the censor. His actual explanation for the legal basis for not using the power to exclude when prohibited by the secular government from using it is found in *Yoreh Deah* 334:42, buried among other issues in a way that the censor, most likely not completely familiar with Hebrew, would not find.

[72]See *Hart v. Cult Awareness Network*, 13 Cal. App. 4th 777, 16 Cal. Rptr. 2d 705 (Cal. Ct. App. 1993), which discusses the doctrine of "fair game" in some detail.

threatened Scientology by leaving the church may be deprived of property or injured by any means by a Scientologist. . . . [The targeted defector] may be tricked, sued, or lied to, or destroyed."[73] The state interest in protecting an excluded member from such practices clearly is greater than the interest in protecting a person from the more common version of religious shunning, which the Ninth Circuit described as follows:

> Members of the Jehovah's Witness community are prohibited—under threat of their own disfellowship [shunning]—from having any contact with disfellowshiped persons and may not even greet them. Family members who do not live in the same house may conduct necessary family business with disfellowshiped relatives but may not communicate with them on any other subject.[74]

Indeed, this is similar to the manner a person would be treated if excluded from the Jewish community, which sought to punish only through the removal from the community.[75]

The numerous cases that address the problems of religious exclusion, shunning, and excommunication apply one of three categories of legal rules. First, some courts hold as a matter of law

---

[73] *Wollershein v. Church of Scientology*, 212 Cal. App. 3rd, 260 Cal. Rptr. 331 (1989) (brackets are in the original opinion).

[74] *Paul*, 819 F.2d 877. The court went on to describe how such a person would be treated: "[A shunned person] visited her parents, who at that time lived in Soap Lake, Washington. There, she approached a Witness who had been a close childhood friend and was told by this person: 'I can't speak to you. You are disfellowshiped.' Similarly, in August 1984, [defendant] returned to the area of her former congregation. She tried to call on some of her friends. These people told Paul that she was to be treated as if she had been disfellowshiped and that they could not speak with her. At one point, she attempted to attend a Tupperware party at the home of a Witness. [Defendant] was informed by the Church members present that the Elders had instructed them not to speak with her."

[75] *Shulchan Aruch, Yoreh Deah* 334:2–11. Exclusion in the Catholic canon law tradition contains within it a number of different levels of varying severity, none of which permit violence against the person. See Green, "Future of Penal Law in the Church."

that religious discipline can never be actionable when the disciplined member remains a member of the religious organization that is disciplining him or her.[76] In this theory, consent proves to be the underlying defense to allegations of tortious misconduct by a religious organization. Absent membership in the faith, or after withdrawal from membership, the activities of the church are no different from any other organization in terms of tort law treatment.[77]

The essential failure of this theory, in my opinion, is that it focuses on the status of the person being injured and misses one of the fundamental purposes of church discipline: to inform the faithful that a person's conduct violated the religion's tenets, and thus they have been excluded.[78] To allow lawsuits, particularly for the intentional infliction of emotional distress or similar torts for the use of this information (even after resignation), deprives the religious organization of its ability to standardize the conduct of its members by publicizing cases of exclusion. The community is formed by publicly establishing norms of conduct. Such cannot be done under this legal rule, since the moment a person resigns from the church, the church loses any ability to announce their exclusion.

Second, some courts have held that the "religiously motivated disciple is entitled to First Amendment protection and cannot form

---

[76]See *Guinn*, 775 P.2d 767–69.

[77]See Comment, "Religious Torts: Applying the Consent Doctrine as Definitional Balancing," *University of California at Davis Law Review* 19 (1986): 949, 975–83, for a list of such cases. The earliest of the American cases defends this theory by stating: "[t]hey joined the church, with a knowledge of its defined powers, and as the civil power cannot interfere in matters of conscience, faith, or discipline, they must submit to rebuke or excommunication, however unjust, by their adopted spiritual rulers" (*Gartin v. Penick*, 68 Ky. [5 Bush] 110, 120 [Ct. App. 1869] [Robertson, J.], quoted in *Chase v. Cheney*, 58 Ill. 509, 539 [1871]).

[78]Thus, in *Guinn*, the court held actionable the fact that: "Parishioner was publicly branded a fornicator when the scriptures she had violated were recited to the Collinsville Church of Christ congregation on October 4. As part of the disciplinary process the same information about Parishioner's transgressions was sent to four other area Church of Christ congregations to be read aloud during services" (*Guinn*, 775 P. 2d 768).

the basis"[79] for a suit in tort.[80] These courts, including the United States Court of Appeals for the Ninth Circuit, rule that: "Because the practice of shunning is a part of the faith of [a religion], we find that the 'free exercise' provision of the United States Constitution . . . precludes the plaintiff from prevailing. The defendants have a constitutionally protected privilege to engage in the practice of shunning."[81]

The most significant failure of this approach is that it places outside the scope of governmental regulation potentially egregious conduct. Indeed, a very strong case can be made that the current interpretation of the First Amendment does not require that government immunize religion from tort laws that are generally applicable. Whatever the merits of *Employment Division v. Smith*[82] in the context of criminal law, one could see very significant problems developing were religions granted general tort law immunity for all conduct that is religiously directed or compelled.[83] Even limiting such an immunity to "intangible or emotional harm"[84] pro-

---

[79]Hayden, "Religiously Motivated Outrageous Conduct: 'Intential Infliction of Emotional Distress' as a Weapon against Other People's Faiths'," *William & Mary Law Review*, 34 (1993): 579, 642–43.

[80]*Paul*, 819 F.2d 875, and *Burgess v. Rock Creek Baptist Church*, 734 F. Supp. 30 (D.D.C. 1990).

[81]*Paul*, 819 F.2d 876. I have deleted the court's discussion of the constitutional law of the State of Washington.

[82]494 U.S. 872 (1990).

[83]Indeed, the United States Supreme Court's ruling in *Employment Division v. Smith*, 494 U.S. 872, 879 (1990), which states that "the right of free exercise does not relieve an individual of the obligation to comply with a 'valid and neutral law of general applicability,'" undercuts the whole validity of *Paul*, which compels a religiously motivated exception to a tort law doctrine. See Douglas Laycock, "The Remnants of Free Exercise," *Supreme Court Review* (1990): 45–46. However, the application of these principles to cases that call for the application of general tort law rules is quite unclear. Indeed, a claim could be made that *Smith* has overruled any dicta to the contrary that implies a heightened governmental deference to religious claims in the face of a neutral state law, such as its tort law. Of course, if tort law doctrines were specifically modified to prohibit a particular religious activity, that would lead to a much stronger First Amendment challenge; see *Church of Lukumi Babalu Aye, Inc. v. City of Hialeah*, 508 US 520 (1993).

[84]*Paul*, 819 F.2d 883.

vides a level of immunity to a religious practice that would leave many uncomfortable and a license to injure enjoyed by no one else. Notwithstanding one commentator's endorsement of this "First Amendment" approach of complete immunity for religious organizations,[85] the fact remains that the granting of immunity in the face of religiously motivated tortious conduct can produce profoundly negative consequences.

Third, some courts rule that shunning or excommunication can be—by itself—tortious conduct subject to liability. This theory assumes that the state interest in preventing shunning and excommunication is strong enough to allow state interference in all of these decisions. The first American case to adopt this posture, *Bear v. Reformed Mennonite Church*, advanced this argument in its simplest form, arguing that the church's shunning practice[86] "may be an excessive interference within areas of 'paramount state concern,' that is, the maintenance of marriage and family relationship, alienation of affection, and the tortious interference with a business relationship, which the courts of this Commonwealth may have authority to regulate, even in light of the 'Establishment' and 'Free Exercise' clauses of the First Amendment."[87] Other courts have also agreed with this basic approach and ruled that shunning and excommunication are actionable conduct even when it is unaccompanied by any other activity.[88]

---

[85]Hayden, "Religiously Motivated Outrageous Conduct," 653.

[86]The court earlier had described the practice as: "[T]he church and bishops, as part of the excommunication, ordered that all members of the church must 'shun' appellant in all business and social matters. ('Shunning,' as practiced by the church, involves total boycotting of appellant by other members of the church, including his wife and children, under pain that they themselves be excommunicated and shunned.)" (ibid.).

[87]*Bear*, 341 A.2d 105.

[88]*Van Schaick v. Church of Scientology*, 535 F. Supp. 1125 (D. Mass. 1982). This can also be implied from *Christofferson v. Church of Scientology*, 644 P.2d 577 (Or. Ct. App.), petition denied, 650 P.2d 928 (Or. 1982), which held that there was no liability, but implied that liability was possible, as a matter of law. This lack of protection can also be derived from a long line of cases that deny any First Amendment immunity to recruitment practices of faiths; see *Murphy v. I.S.K.Con. of New England,*

This approach has the potential to vastly limit the scope of religion's right to self-associate and exclude others. If, in fact, as *Bear* rules, the Constitution provides no protection from tort law liability for interfering with a spousal relationship when a minister announces that associating with a particular person—even by that person's spouse—violated the rules of the faith, tort law has accomplished what no other set of legal rules can do under the Constitution. It has prevented a faith from announcing its opinion on the ethical conduct of a portion of society, even when the faith makes no attempts to coerce compliance with its doctrines or punish adherents of other faiths.

Exclusion and the Financial Ramifications: The British and Canadian Approaches

A much more problematic case of exclusion, and the judicial response to it, occurs when the faith that is doing the excluding bundles religious rights with financial claims. A classical case of that is the division of property by a religious commune when it orders the excommunication of members, and the forfeiture of those members' property rights. There are no United States cases addressing this issue, for the Supreme Court has ruled that ecclesiastical disputes command secular court abstention if called upon to resolve matters of religious belief or governance. As stated in *Serbian Eastern Orthodox Diocese v. Milivojevich*: when "hierarchical religious organizations . . . establish their own rules and regulations for internal discipline and government, and . . . create tribunals for adjudicating disputes over these matters, [then the] . . . Constitution requires that civil courts accept their decisions as binding *upon them*."[89]

Inc., 571 N.E.2d 340 (Mass. 1991); *McNair v. Worldwide Church of God*, 242 Cal. Rptr. 823 (Ct. App. 1987); and *Molko v. Holy Spirit Ass'n*, 762 P.2d 46 (Cal. 1988).

[89]*Serbian Eastern Orthodox Diocese v. Milivojevich*, 426 U.S. 696, 724–25 (1976) (emphasis added). While American courts will hear the fiscal aspect of these cases, they will not (and cannot) review, in any form, the ecclesiastical determinations. See also *Jones v. Wolf*, 443 U.S. 595 (1979).

Such is not the case in many other common law countries, which will freely review such determinations. Indeed, an example of the problems faced by a court in such a case can be found in *Lakeside Colony of Hutterian Brethren v. Hofer*, issued by the Canadian Supreme Court.[90] In this case, the Court confronted the excommunication (and expulsion) of the Hofer family from a colony of the Hutterian Church of Canada for pressing a patent claim against another colony of the Church. Under relevant Church doctrine, which was codified in the articles of incorporation of the commune, expelled members lost their financial claim to the assets of the commune.[91] After reviewing the actions of the Church for conformity to Canadian corporate law and adherence to its own associational bylaws, the Supreme Court announced that expulsions from these types of religious associations are also governed by "natural justice." The Court stated: "The content of the principles of natural justice is flexible and depends on the circumstances in which the question arises. However, the most basic requirements are that of (1) notice; (2) opportunity to make representations; and (3) an unbiased tribunal."[92] The Court then determined that the notice provided to the excommunicated members by the Church was insufficient and that the expulsion and excommunication were thus void. The Court ordered the excommunicated individuals returned to the colony as members.[93]

This Canadian approach to the problems of exclusion is no better, in my opinion, than its American counterpart. Under the guise of reviewing a property settlement, the court imposed sub-

---

[90]97 D.L.R. (4th) 17; 36 A.C.W.S. (3d) 512 (1992). This case is an appeal from the judgment of the Manitoba Court of Appeal, 77 D.L.R. (4th) 202, 70 Man. R. (2d) 191, 25 A.C.W.S. (3d) 2, dismissing an appeal from a judgment of Ferg J., 63 D.L.R. (4th) 473, 62 Man. R. (2d) 194, 18 A.C.W.S. (3d) 117, declaring that the defendants were no longer members of a Hutterian community and that their excommunication was valid.

[91]The legality of that contractual arrangement had been affirmed in *Hofer v. Hofer*, 13 D.L.R. (3d) 1 (1970). The dissent in this case indicates that this precedent is ripe to "revisit." Ibid., 64.

[92]Ibid., 36.

[93]Ibid., 58.

stantive requirements of "natural justice" that might be completely foreign to any particular religious tradition's system of laws. Based on these laws of "natural justice," the Court will reverse a determination that a particular form of conduct merited excommunication from a particular religious denomination.[94] These types of judicial determinations should, simply put, be beyond the scope of any secular court. To allow procedural review of an ecclesiastical court's determinations in the context of the property rights of the excommunicated has a certain amount of validity, as that property ownership issue is at its core secular. However, the question of membership in the colony of the church should be beyond review of a secular court. The rights of the faithful to excommunicate for violations of religious doctrine—without conforming to Canadian notions of due process—would seem to be protected. Any restrictions on that religious right should be incompatible with freedom of religion and association guaranteed in the Canadian Bill of Rights.[95] One cannot help but recall the words of the learned Zechariah Chafee, who observed: "In very many instances the courts have interfered in these [ecclesiastical disputes] and con-

---

[94]Indeed, the failures of this three-part test of natural justice is recognized in the Canadian Supreme Court's own discussion of the third prong of the test, the requirement of an unbiased tribunal. The Court stated: "There is no doubt that an unbiased tribunal is one of the central requirements of natural justice. However, given the close relationship amongst members of voluntary associations, it seems rather likely that members of the relevant tribunal will have had some previous contact with the issue in question and, given the structure of a voluntary association, it is almost inevitable that the decision-makers will have at least an indirect interest in the question. Furthermore, the procedures set out in the rules of the association may often require that certain persons make certain kinds of decisions without allowing for an alternate procedure in the case of bias" (ibid., 37). These issues are even further compounded when the issues are theological in nature. Is it really possible to produce an "unbiased tribunal" to discuss an issue of theology?

[95]The dissent correctly noted that the proper way to resolve the property claims of the excommunicated would be for that group to make a claim "for a division of the assets and judgment for their share" (ibid., 63–64).

sequently have been obliged to write very long opinions on questions that they could not well understand. The result has often been that the judicial review of the highest tribunal of the church is really an appeal from a learned body to an unlearned body."[96] Such is certainly the case when a court reviews ecclesiastical determinations for conformity with the ethereal requirements of "natural justice."

A better example of how a court should address this type of challenge to exclusion can be found in the case of *Regent v. Chief Rabbi of the United Hebrew Congregations of Great Britain and the Commonwealth (Ex parte Wachmann)*,[97] concerning the authority of the Chief Rabbi of Great Britain to defrock a clergyman for sexual misconduct. The clergyman appealed the decision to the Queen's courts, which ruled that the ecclesiastical functions of the Chief Rabbi, in determining who was religiously fit and who was not, were religious in nature and thus not subject to any secular review. This is true, the Court ruled, even though the declaration on the unsuitability of the applicant to occupy a position as a rabbi resulted in the applicant being "unemployable as a rabbi and . . . stripped of all religious status."[98] The Court spurned the plaintiff's arguments from "natural justice": "[Plaintiff] would be prepared to rely solely upon the common law concept of natural justice [to overturn the decision of the Chief Rabbi]. But it would not always be easy to separate out procedural complaints from consideration of substantive principles of Jewish law which may underlie them."

Jewish law does not recognize the elaborate requirements of natural justice in these types of cases,[99] and the British Court rightly recognized that the exclusion of a person from a particular ecclesiastical function, or an exclusion of a person from a particular faith group, is itself not subject to any judicial review external to the faith

---

[96]Zechariah Chafee, "The Internal Affairs of Associations Not for Profit," *Harvard Law Review* 43 (1930): 993, 1024.

[97][1993] 2 All ER 249 (Q.B.).

[98]Ibid., 253. This religious status granted him certain rights under British law, including the right to perform marriages.

[99]As there is no "right" to be a congregational rabbi.

that makes that determination.[100] Of course, as noted by the British Court, this determination of ecclesiastical exclusion by the Chief Rabbi would have no relevance to a determination of a breach of contract, or other financial rights and duties owed by one party to another.[101] Those determinations would be made by the secular courts, independent of the ecclesiastical rules of the Chief Rabbi.

The Value of Excluding

This author is inclined to look at the fundamental values encapsulated by the practices of religious discipline, and to determine which of these central values are worthy of governmental protection, and to limit the privilege to cases in which those values are furthered. As noted, the Jewish tradition recognizes two possible theoretical models for religious discipline: punishment of the offender and formation of a community through exclusion.[102] The Jewish tradition opted for the second model as the jurisprudential basis for its practice of exclusion.

---

[100]Indeed, the essence of plaintiff's claim was that the Chief Rabbi did not conform to the substantive requirements of Jewish law, which, in plaintiff's opinion, require that this type of determination be made by three *dayanim*, sitting Jewish law judges, in the context of a formal *beit din*, a Jewish court, and not as an administrative determination by the Chief Rabbi (ibid., 255). I am inclined to agree with the posture of the Chief Rabbi that such determinations need not be made by a formal *beit din*. The rationale for such an informal procedure is that a determination of actual sexual impropriety and the legal consequences of such conduct can only be made by a Jewish court. However, a rabbi can be defrocked by the much lower standard of mere appearance of impropriety (see Rabbi Moshe Isserless (*Rama*), *Choshen Mishpat*, 25:2), which is an administrative determination. One thing is clear: the British Court correctly realized that the proper standard to use is beyond the determination of the Queen's Bench.

[101]*Chief Rabbi*, 2 All ER, 255. In this case the Court seems to find that there was no employment contract, and thus no breach of secular law (ibid., 255–256).

[102]Subsumed within this second justification is the possibility that the person will repent and wish to return to the community.

Of these two models, only the second is worthy of tort law immunity and First Amendment protection. Punishment of individuals for violations of the law (religious or otherwise) is to be left to the governmental authorities (and to God). Attempts by religious groups to use their many members or their economic might to punish people for violations should not be protected as a religious value. These are fundamental governmental prerogatives that should not, and may not, be delegated.[103] That is not, of course, to say that such conduct is always tortious; rather, as conduct by a religious group it should have no First Amendment protection. The assertion that a person who is punished by his former co-religionists for a violation of religious law is entitled to any less protection of his rights than others is difficult to support. In one case the court stated:

> [Plaintiff] did not suffer his economic harm as an unintended by-product of his former religionists' practice of refusing to socialize with him any more. Instead, he was bankrupted by a campaign his former religionists carefully designed with the specific intent to bankrupt him. Nor was this campaign limited to means which are arguably legal, such as refusing to continue working at Wollersheim's business or to purchase his services or products. *Instead the campaign featured a concerted practice of refusing to honor legal obligations . . . owed [plaintiff] for services and products they already had purchased.*[104]

Religious conduct with the intent to punish—if protected by tort or criminal immunity—delegates to the sectarian community a core governmental authority. As noted by the Supreme Court: "At the time of the Revolution, Americans feared not only a denial of religious freedom, but also the danger of political oppression through a union of civil and ecclesiastical control."[105] Laurence Tribe, in his treatise on American constitutional law, elaborates on this problem:

---

[103]See, generally, *Larkin v. Grendel's Den, Inc.*, 459 U.S. 116 (1982).

[104]*Wollersheim v. Church of Scientology*, 212 Cal. App. 3d 872, 890, 260 Cal. Rptr. 331, 343 (Cal. Ct. App. 1989).

[105]*Larkin*, 459 U.S. 126, n.10.

Even if a state ceded power to a church in a way that avoided any ongoing administrative entanglement, the action would be unconstitutional. . . . [Under] the vesting entanglement[106] test, breadth is irrelevant so long as the power remains a traditionally governmental one. . . . Thus, *any* degree of vesting entanglement—not merely excessive entanglement—is prohibited."[107]

More generally, government has an interest in preventing religion from punishing people who leave it; absent such protection, the freedoms of the First Amendment appear vacuous. *The right of religious dissent is no less precious than the right of religious conformity.*[108]

In my opinion, a solid middle ground is implied in many of these cases. This middle ground provides a doctrinal basis for discussing secular legal responses to shunning and excommunication that neither protects religious rights to oppress those who scorn or violate the faith, and yet grants legal protection to a faith community's right to form its own insular sub-group and exclude people who violate the rules of the community.

The First Amendment should only protect the right of a faith community to exclude members; thus shunning, excommunication, and other methods of isolation are all protected only when they are used to exclude. However, claims based not on the need of the faith community to exclude, but on its need to convince the "unfaithful" to return, or to punish them for their violation, should

------

[106]"Vesting entanglement" is the term used for the problem that results when the government delegates its authority to an ecclesiastical group.

[107]Laurence Tribe, *American Constitutional Law*, 2d ed. (St. Paul, MN, 1988), 1229 (notes omitted, emphasis in original).

[108]This is consistent with Supreme Court precedent, which has repeatedly declined to recognize "religious group rights" as a value higher than the aggregate of individual group rights. See *Ohio Civil Rights Commission v. Dayton Christian Schools, Inc.*, 477 U.S. 619 (1986) and *Corporation of the Presiding Bishop v. Amos*, 483 U.S. 327 (1987). For an article arguing that "religious rights should be recognized as of a higher value," see Fredrick Gedicks, "Toward a Constitutional Jurisprudence of Religious Group Rights," *Wisconsin Law Review* (1989): 99.

be subject to scrutiny of tort and criminal law and enjoy no protection. This approach can be found implicitly in a number of cases, although this distinction is not found as the controlling rule in any single case. For example, in *Guinn*, the Supreme Court of Oklahoma, after ruling that the crucial feature in determining protected status is membership, goes on to note:

> For purposes of First Amendment protection, religiously motivated disciplinary measures that merely exclude a person from communion are vastly different from those which are designed to control and involve. A church clearly is constitutionally free to exclude people without first obtaining their consent. But the First Amendment will not shield a church from civil liability for imposing its will, as manifested through a disciplinary scheme, upon an individual who has not consented to undergo ecclesiastical discipline.[109]

A similar result was reached in *Gruenwald v. Bornfreund*.[110] After discussing the protected status of a mere act of exclusion by any religious organization, the Court indicates that were the defendant to have proven that he would suffer "battery, trespass, or theft," or any other tortious act as a result of the excommunication or other conduct by a religious group, it would enjoin this conduct.[111]

The virtues of this "middle ground" approach are clear. First, religious adherents must have the right to form their own subsociety. While the melting pot may be some people's image of an ideal American society, the rights of those who do not wish to melt but wish to keep their own unique identity must be protected. These people have not only the right to avoid governmentally compelled blending, but also to avoid the internal confusion of allowing multiple voices to speak in the name of its faith-group.

---

[109]*Guinn*, 775 P.2d 780.

[110]696 F. Supp. 839.

[111]Judge Sifton states: "To the extent that the Weg affirmation alleges that plaintiff will suffer battery, trespass, or theft in the absence of a religious prohibition against those acts, plaintiff has failed to show that such injury is imminent or likely. The harm which will give rise to an injunction must be not remote and speculative but actual and imminent."

However, granting religious groups unfettered rights to stifle internal dissent creates the possibility that religions will use that right to compel religious orthodoxy or adherence to its religious norms. Such action also is contrary to (at the least) the spirit of the First Amendment. Focusing on the purpose of the exclusionary act forces the courts—and thus eventually the faiths themselves—to ask why a particular person is being excluded.[112] Once a clear understanding of why people are excluded is articulated by each faith, tort law can grant or deny protection to those exclusions whose purpose is consistent with the protected First Amendment values of forming a religious sub-community.[113]

Second, this "middle ground" approach is superior in application to any of the three tests found in the various court opinions. It is simply more nuanced than either the blanket First Amendment protection granted by the *Paul* case or the generic nonprotection

---

[112]This also fits in well with the purpose of the Restatement. Once the purpose of the excommunication is not to hurt or punish the person but simply to exclude him, the tort of intentional infliction of emotional distress is inapplicable. *Restatement (Second) of Torts* (1965): 46(1) now states: "One who by extreme and outrageous conduct intentionally or recklessly causes severe emotional distress to another is subject to liability for such emotional distress, and if bodily harm to the other results from it, for such bodily harm.

"There are three basic elements that must be shown in order to allow a recovery under this tort: (1) Defendant must have intended to inflict severe emotional distress; (2) The conduct must be 'extreme and outrageous'; (3) severe emotional distress must result."

A religion that announces a violation of its norms of conduct, without any intent to punish the violator, or otherwise cause that person harm—but whose motives are merely to tell the faithful what conduct conforms to the norms of the faith—will never "intend to inflict severe emotional distress" and thus will never be liable under this tort. The purer the religious motives are, the less likely a recovery will be allowed.

[113]Of course, religions with unprotected motives will not likely announce their motives as such. However, once a legal test of purpose is announced, religious exclusion practices—whatever their "true" motives—will have to craft themselves around the fact that excommunication and shunning practices that appear designed to punish will probably not be granted tort law immunity. Eventually, such practices will cease.

advocated by the *Bear* case. Both of these cases appear to adopt standards that are too easily prone to abuse. *Bear* creates civil liability for core religious functions and contains the capabilities of destroying any faith's exclusionary policies. Once one allows a civil action for alienation of affection when a minister advises a spouse to leave a marriage on religious grounds (as *Bear* does), there is little sacred religious advice that is not actionable in tort.[114] The potential to destroy religious communities is clear. *Paul* allows religious communities to persecute those who leave a faith. This simply cannot be tolerated in a free society. *Paul* also appears to allow, or at least could be read to allow, such practices as "fair game" or "freeloader debt" that can be used to prevent people from exercising their right to leave a religion and not be part of the community.[115]

More significantly, this test is superior to the more nuanced "consent test" advocated by *Guinn*. There are crucial problems with this test. Most significantly, *Guinn* allows people to be disciplined based on their apparent consent, when they join the Church. While this theory might have a certain amount of validity in a highly organized and well-disciplined church, as was the case in *Guinn*, this test has little validity for the many faiths where synagogue or church membership is by no means a commitment to observance of the normative rules of the faith. To assert, for example, that mere membership in the Catholic Church would give the local parish the right to publicize who is using a prohibited method of birth control, or membership in a synagogue would give the rabbi the right to announce who does not keep kosher, misses the fact that these religions do not use membership as a litmus test of full observance. The *Guinn* court has taken a very specific rule of the

---

[114]Thus, for example, there are situations where Jewish law encourages divorce; indeed, Jewish law categorically prohibits reconciliation in certain circumstances. Accepting the test used in *Bear*, one could easily conclude that a rabbi who informs a congregant of the position of Jewish law, and tells him that the Creator desires him to obey, is liable.

[115]Tribe correctly classifies these rights as "rights of religious autonomy." See Tribe, *American Constitutional Law*, 1154. The crucial insight is autonomy and not coercion of others.

Church of Christ and turned it into a general rule of law when it should not have.[116]

Moreover, the consent test allows the church to punish violators, even if they clearly do not wish to have that done against them. The whole notion of consent, even in a situation where the church uses membership as a litmus test of observance, is suspect. Thus, even in *Guinn*, it is clear from the facts of that case that the woman did not wish to have information concerning her sexual life publicized to church members.[117] Whether she was or was not a member at the time of the publication, *it is clear that she did not consent* to be disciplined.

So, too, Professor Hayden's assertion, in defense of the consent rule, is debatable. Professor Hayden writes:

> A second related strength of the consent theory in this context derives from the nature of free exercise itself: individuals should be free to practice one religion or another, or none at all. When a person has chosen one organized belief structure, he should be held to it until he chooses to withdraw, and therefore he should not be able to sue his fellow members for disciplining him in accordance with church doctrine and policy. As soon as that person chooses to leave one religion, however, either to join another or to join none at all, the government has an interest in the individual's free exercise of that choice to leave.[118]

Why should the government allow religions that have organized belief structures to punish people who wish to belong to the faith

---

[116]A modified version of the *Guinn* test can be found in Comment, "Religious Torts," 975–83, which argues that membership in a religious faith creates a rebuttable presumption that one consents to the faith's rules. The problem is that this consent is simply untrue when it comes to religious discipline. People rarely if ever consent to public humiliation. Particularly in situations where the one being punished by the faith employs a lawyer to deter the faith's activity, the "consent through membership" doctrine is simply inapplicable.

[117]For example, see *Wollersheim v. Church of Scientology*, 260 Cal. Rptr. 331 (Ct. App. 1989), which rules that all discipline is, in fact, nonconsensual.

[118]Hayden, "Religiously Motivated Outrageous Conduct," 651.

and yet violate its rules? It makes more sense to limit the faith's rights to actions that exclude these people and not actions designed to punish them. Carried to its logical conclusion, Professor Hayden's analysis would permit even physical disciplining of members and not limit immunity to the tort of "intentional inflection of emotional distress" but to such crimes as assault. It is clear that the consent obtained is not genuine.

In short, the consent doctrine is at best a narrow doctrine suitable for only select faiths and at worst a fiction that allows religions to publicize private details of people's lives against their will. This problem clearly comes to the fore when one examines the difficulties later cases have had in applying the test developed in *Guinn*.[119]

The same values that would seem to preclude most damage awards for excommunication and shunning in tort law would prevent judicial review of the merits of excommunication through the guise of resolving a property law dispute. The approach of the Canadian Supreme Court in *Lakeside Colony of Hutterian Brethren*, which allows for judicial review of orders of expulsion and exclusion to ensure their conformity with natural justice would seem to be unwise, for it evaluates the "correctness" of what are core theological determinations when these same factors can be avoided and the property law dispute be resolved independent of a merit determination of the correctness of the faith's exclusion. A better rule would be either to adopt the American approach enunciated in *Milivojevich*, which mandates complete abstention, or the British approach in *Chief Rabbi*, which allows formally for review, but with a completely deferential standard of review.

This chapter started with a Jewish perspective on shunning and excommunication, and it argues that Jewish law in this area is re-

---

[119]For example, in *Hadnot v. Shaw*, 826 P.2d 978 (Okla. 1992), the Oklahoma Supreme Court had to address the issue of constructive withdrawal and implied consent. Indeed, it appears that the court allowed post-withdrawal action needed to re-enforce discipline under some form of a consent theory, even when it was clear that the disciplined individuals considered themselves free from the religious dictates of the church and did everything except actually send in a letter of withdrawal.

spectful of both minority and majority rights and gives each the ability to form its own exclusive community. The common law of torts and constitutional law should aim to do the same. The goals of such doctrines and practices should be to allow the formation of self-selected sub-communities sharing common religious values, which are protected in their right to exclude but prevented from harassing in the name of religion. The law must reflect both of these goals, and it currently does not.

CONCLUSIONS

Painting with a broad brush, certain conclusions can be drawn as to the nature of shunning, excommunication, and other exclusionary practices devised by Jewish and other religious communities to allow them to form a sub-community within modern secular society.

Many religious communities cannot be fully open to any and all conduct by its members. Jewish communities established a mechanism and procedure for the exclusion of members of the faith who reject basic tenets of the community or faith. Such mechanisms include partial shunning, complete shunning, and, in rare situations, excommunication. Other faiths use comparable processes in different ways to shape their communities. These mechanisms of exclusion should be allowed to affect only people who wish to remain part of the religious sect that issued the shunning. People should be free to leave the faith group and avoid the penalty.

Government has a regulatory interest in governing these religious—and all other—collective groups that engage in activity designed to exclude people from a particular benefit. Government is (or should be) precluded on various freedom of religion grounds, however, from regulating purely ecclesiastical or faith matters.[120] These grounds should also be understood as precluding the government from preventing faith groups from forming

---

[120]*Milivojevich*, 426 U.S. 724–25.

their own special sub-communities, which exclude based on religious criteria. In that way, religious groups are entitled to more protection than mere commercial enterprises.[121]

The right to religious exclusion cannot, however, rise to the level of implicit (or explicit) coercion to religious conformity. This issue was clearly noted in a discussion within Jewish law concerning coercion and minority rights. Writing in the early 1600s, Rabbi Shabtai ben Meir Ha Cohen protested against a particular form of shunning and asserted that in the social framework of Eastern Europe in the seventeenth century, it was tantamount to coercion and should not be allowed.[122] Essentially, he stated that in an insular and thoroughly intertwined Jewish community, which was the norm in the pre-emancipation communities of Eastern Europe, shunning was a form of compulsion and was thus only permitted when actual physical force was legally permitted according to Jewish law. Absent continuous interaction with the community, a single person who wished to rebel would perish. Shunning was coercion in that social setting. In such a society, religious minority rights disappear if even low level exclusion is allowed, and government must intervene to protect people's freedom of religion.

Such an intertwined society does not exist in America and other democratic polities. Shunning and excommunication as practiced by many faiths, including Judaism, are no longer designed to compel or force observance by the shunned one. The pressures imposed will no longer prevent a person from functioning or cause him or her to starve. Rather, the process of shunning and excom-

---

[121]Thus, for example, government clearly can prevent a nondenominational social club from limiting, based on religious faith, its membership. A religious social club should have that right. See *New York State Club Association, Inc., v. City of New York*, 487 U.S. 1 (1988).

[122]Rabbi Shabtai ben Meir Hacohen, *Gevurat Anashim* 72, cited in *Pitchei Teshuva Even Haezar* 154:30. Many commentaries on the *Shulchan Aruch* other than *Pitchei Teshuva* express dissent to *Gevurat Anashim*'s rule. See *Aruch Hashulchan, Even Haezer* 154:63; *Maharam M'Lublin* 1 and 39 (Jerusalem, 1960), *Eliyahu Rabbah* 1–3; *Rav Betzalel Ashkenazi* 6 and 10; Chief Rabbi Yitzchak Isaac Halevi Herzog, *Techuka Liyisrael Al Pi Hatorah* 3:202 and 209.

munication creates a choice. It forces people to decide in which society they wish to reside. Only coercion to choose is involved. It does not, in its modern form, actually compel any particular activity. Just as a person has the right to remove himself or herself from a particular religious society, that society has a right to remove itself from him or her. Minority rights in the context of religious freedom has to include the right to leave a sect. It does not, however, include the right to remain part of a group, while defying that group's wishes.

Ultimately, religious freedom has to include the right to choose and to form one's own co-religionists and religious community members. This is the best protection government can give to religious minorities and still maintain a freedom of religion.

3

WOMEN IN JUDAISM FROM THE PERSPECTIVE OF HUMAN RIGHTS

Michael S. Berger and Deborah E. Lipstadt
Emory University

"He dreamt that he saw a ladder, which rested on the ground with its top reaching to heaven, and angels of God were going up and down upon it." Genesis 28:12

The task of examining the norms of a particular religious tradition from a human rights perspective presents us with both an anomaly and a challenge. On the one hand, the term "religious," at least in the Western experience, inclines one to look to the heavens for the source of correct action.[1] Obligations stem from a law-giving deity whose will has become known to us through various forms of revelation. On the other hand, the word "human" is not simply an adjective describing the kind of rights being discussed, as opposed to, say, animal rights. Emerging in the early Enlightenment, the notion grounds our obligations to one another in the individual's humanity, an aspect of the person independent of his or her race, religion, or ethnic identity. The universalism inherent

---

[1]The Eastern religious traditions, both in their polytheistic and non-theistic forms, provide very different models for understanding human rights in a religious context. See the essays on Hinduism, Buddhism, and especially Confucianism in Leroy S. Rouner, ed., *Human Rights and the World's Religions* (Notre Dame, 1988). Rouner's introductory essay (ibid., 1–14) is very helpful in comparing and contrasting the Western and Eastern approaches to human rights.

in this idea is one of the hallmarks of modernity, serving as the benchmark for treatment of minorities, prisoners of war, and criminals.[2] Therefore, the term "religious human rights" strikes us as a virtual oxymoron, for while religions focus on the top of Jacob's ladder, Enlightenment philosophers and ethicists are exclusively concerned with Jacob at its base.

Nevertheless, many of us, whether secular scholars of religion or religiously committed scholars and laypersons, are involved in this project precisely because we do not see such an abyss separating the two realms. In our perception, there is a close, intimate connection between human rights and religion. Violations of human rights, whether locally or across the world, offend many of us as morally and religiously repugnant. On the positive side, advocates of human rights frequently link arms with priests, ministers, and rabbis, joining in common cause, such as in the American civil rights crusade of the 1960s. The dreams and goals of those who pursue and defend human rights are clear echoes of ancient prophetic voices who also hoped for an ideal society based on justice and truth. In short, the challenge of this volume is that we want to be those angels, ascending and descending the ladder, some more easily than others, in an effort to better understand the connections and relationships between the two spheres.

This chapter concerns women's rights within Jewish communities. One way of approaching this subject is simply to list a woman's rights and obligations according to *halachah* (Jewish law): what she is obligated to do for others, such as her spouse, children, and parents, and how, in turn, others are obligated to act with respect to her. As in any legal system, there will be privileges as well as restrictions that developed over time and that need to be seen from precisely that historical perspective. This, in itself, would be an ambitious project, and indeed is the necessary backdrop for any informed discussion of the topic. But if we are to be true to the challenge we believe this project sets before us, then we must

---

[2]See Jacob Katz, "Post-Emancipation Development of Human Rights: Liberalism and Universalism," in David Sidorsky, ed., *Essays on Human Rights: Contemporary Issues and Jewish Perspectives* (Philadelphia, 1979), 282–96.

sketch out, however theoretically, the potential contribution of viewing the issue from the perspective of human rights.

We should state, from the outset, that we are not merely engaged in the critical review of Jewish law by using contemporary canons of human rights. This project was not established to expose aspects of religious traditions that affront and even violate accepted standards of recent human rights commissions and conventions. Not only would that undermine the spirit of cooperation that distinguishes this project, it would necessarily put the various religions on the defensive, forcing an apologetic posture that would preclude the openness and candor crucial to our enterprise.

Nor is our aim to show, in the classical tradition of apologia, that a particular religious tradition anticipated or even served as the source of modern human rights, essentially claiming that contemporary views are simply redundant. Rather, our aim is to lay bare some of the assumptions and premises of each system, and then examine if any fruitful intersection is possible. We begin with a brief analysis of the different notions of rights in each tradition, followed by an overview of laws relating to women in *halachah*. We then take a particular case, considerably pressing on the contemporary Jewish scene, and explore some ways that our discussion might illuminate that issue.

JEWISH LAW AND HUMAN RIGHTS

The overlap of Jewish law and human rights in practical terms is an important starting point for our analysis of the respective assumptions of each system.[3] *Prima facie*, the Jewish Bible's persis-

---

[3]The attention this subject has received over the last twenty years is impressive, producing a staggering number of articles, books, and symposia on the relationship of Jewish law and human rights. S. Daniel Breslauer has recently collected the extensive literature in *Judaism and Human Rights in Contemporary Thought: A Bibliographical Survey* (Westport, 1993). The comprehensive introduction reviews the theoretical axes along which the various approaches to the subject can be organized.

tent concern for "the stranger, the orphan, and the widow,"[4] as well as for the poor person, is an expression of the basic moral posture of Jewish law, insuring the care and equal treatment due every member of society regardless of economic condition or social status.[5] The Rabbis continued in this vein, instituting laws and practices that would prevent abuses of these disadvantaged classes.[6] Medieval Jewish communities were almost universally characterized by locally supported institutions and funds established and maintained to help widows, orphans, and the poor—features that still distinguish modern Jewish communities across the spectrum. For those interested in human rights, Jewish history appears to stand proudly by its record of concern for the disadvantaged and unfortunate.

However, this practical intersection belies a fundamental theoretical difference between Jewish law and modern notions of human

------

[4]The three-part formulaic expression appears no less than ten times in the Book of Deuteronomy alone: 14:29; 16:11, 14; 24:17, 19, 20, 21; 26:12, 13; and 27:19.

[5]There are many scholars who see in the Bible and rabbinic literature a clear and unequivocal emphasis on ethics. See, for example, Louis Jacobs, "The Relationship between Religion and Ethics in Jewish Thought," in Gene Outka and John P. Reeder, eds., *Religion and Morality* (New York, 1973), reprinted in Menachem Marc Kellner, ed., *Contemporary Jewish Ethics* (New York, 1978).

[6]For instance, measures were taken to insure *she-lo tin'ol delet bifnei lovin*, literally, "that the door should not be locked in the face of the borrowers," who were generally poor. In other words, when legal procedure or even biblical law could serve as an excuse not to lend money to the poor, the Rabbis eased the requirements or found a way to circumvent the law. Thus, Jewish law requires, according to one opinion, three ordained judges to adjudicate a dispute in civil suits. The Rabbis allowed three knowledgeable laymen to comprise the court to make it easier for the lender to sue for his money, thus removing a technical obstacle from the initial act of lending (Babylonian Talmud, *Sanhedrin* 2b–3a. Hillel's prosbul, which allowed lenders to collect their loans even after the sabbatical year that biblically cancelled all debts, was intended to benefit the poor, who found it increasingly difficult to borrow money as the seventh year approached (Babylonian Talmud, *Gittin* 36a–b; cf. Jerusalem Talmud, *Gittin* 4:3 [Villna, 1907]).

rights.[7] Borrowing Robert M. Cover's phrase,[8] the "narrative" behind the "nomos" of *halachah* is two-fold. First, it is the idea that all humans are created in the image of God, an idea that itself has two corollaries. One is that everyone is endowed with a measure of absolute worth, even sanctity, which obligates people to act with a basic degree of respect toward each other. The Genesis story refers to the first human as created with a Divine image (1:26–27), and that this creation was "very good" (1:31). The Torah's imperative to "love your neighbor" (Leviticus 19:18) is predicated on the equal worth of every human being. For the Rabbis, this principle served as an indication of the infinite value of human life; thus, witnesses in capital crimes were warned by the judges: "Anyone who destroys the life of a single person, it is as if he destroyed an entire world."[9] When testimony is to have such potentially grave consequences, it is crucial to underscore the infinite worth of each individual. In rabbinic literature, the commandment not to leave an executed criminal hanging until dusk (Deuteronomy 21:22–23) is presented as a basic expression of the Divine image of the person, even one who violated the law.[10]

The notion that mankind is created in God's image has a further, perhaps more significant, corollary for human action: the imperative to imitate God. As beings with a Divine aspect,[11] persons are enjoined to live up to their potential and act in Divine ways toward one another. The Pentateuchal injunction "You shall be holy, for I, the Lord your God, am holy" (Leviticus 19:2) is an echo of this notion, as is the rabbinic interpretation of Exodus 15:2: "Just as He is merciful and compassionate, so you shall be merciful and com-

---

[7]Much of this analysis is based on Lenn Evan Goodman's penetrating yet brief "Equality and Human Rights: The Lockean and the Judaic Views," *Judaism* 25 (1976): 357–62. See also Ze'ev W. Falk, *Law and Religion* (Jerusalem, 1981), 75–89, esp. 79–86.

[8]Robert M. Cover, "Nomos and Narrative," *Harvard Law Review* 97 (1983): 4.

[9]*Mishnah, Sanhedrin* 4:6.

[10]Babylonian Talmud, *Sanhedrin* 46b.

[11]This notion is expressed in Psalms 8:5: "What is man that You should remember him, but You made him little less than a god [or angels]."

passionate."[12] These are the clearest expressions of the idea that human beings are under the obligation to actualize their own Divine image by acting ethically.[13]

Secondly, the biblical account of the Exodus from Egypt functions, already in the Torah itself, as the ultimate equalizer. As an epilogue to a lengthy chapter on how one is to treat the poor, especially those who are forced to sell either their inherited land or even themselves, the Torah states: "For it is to Me that the Israelites are slaves, they are My slaves, whom I brought out of Egypt; I am the Lord your God" (Leviticus 25:55). Economic lordship is the most common form of "subjugation" in a society; the law insists on protecting the dignity of those who are forced to depend on others. For a nation that owes its collective existence to a benevolent and undeserved act of Divine redemption, all members stand in equal relation to God. With God at the vertex, all Jews are equal.

These two *religious* conceptions of equality are in marked contrast to the philosophical basis of modern human rights. For while the opening sentence of the American Declaration of Independence, in a deistic mimicry of the biblical stance, states "All men are created equal," in fact, the eighteenth-century notion of mankind's equality was simply the latest incarnation of an idea that traces its origins to the Greek Sophists, and whose heirs were Machiavelli, Hobbes, and Locke. Broadly speaking, all these thinkers express the idea that the basic equality of people is their capacity—and willingness—to destroy everyone else in the un-

---

[12]Babylonian Talmud, *Shabbat* 133b. Cf. Babylonian Talmud, *Sotah* 14a, which actually enumerates specific activities that God performed and persons should emulate: clothing the naked, visiting the sick, comforting mourners, and burying the dead.

[13]Maimonides, when discussing the treatment of slaves, also refers to the dual notion of every person's worth and the commandment to imitate God (*Mishneh Torah*, Laws of Slaves, Isadore Twersky, trans. [New Haven, 1976], 8:9). However, S. D. Goitein, who also saw in Maimonides a dual ground for the treatment of slaves, understood the first notion to be the *unity* of mankind, not the infinite worth of the individual. See S. D. Goitein, "Human Rights in Jewish Thought and Life in the Middle Ages," in Sidorsky, ed., *Essays on Human Rights: Contemporary Issues and Jewish Perspectives*, 254.

checked pursuit of each person's own self-interests. Hobbes' famous description of humanity's pre-civilized state as "the war of all against all" is the necessary consequence of seeing people as individuals engaged in the ceaseless and relentless pursuit of power.[14] Echoing the Sophists, Locke as well asserts that the sole significance of a person as regards others is his or her being a source of potential danger. The critical corollary for Locke is that the primary function of government (and law) is to protect citizens from one another, restraining the innate but subdued aggression that is constantly threatening to surface. This pessimistic, naturalistic view of humankind is in stark contrast to the predominant view in Judaism, which both sees the person as a being with Divine qualities and portrays the role of law and government to be the nurturing of a person's moral character within a society actively cooperating to attain a higher ideal.[15]

---

[14]Thomas Hobbes, *Leviathan*, part 1, chap. 11.

[15]We say "predominant view" because rabbinic literature does contain expressions of the Sophist position: "R. Hanina, the priestly understudy, says: 'One should pray for the welfare of the government [*malkhut*, literally, 'monarchy'], for were it not for the fear of [government], people would swallow one another alive" (*Mishnah Avot* 3:2, Herbert Darby, trans. [London, 1944]). Babylonian Talmud, *Avodah Zarah* (4a), sharpens the image further, depicting people as fish of various sizes, with the larger ones swallowing the smaller ones, were it not for the presence of government. This is certainly an echo of the pessimistic view of human beings found later in Hobbes and Locke. Nevertheless, one must be careful to note that in his comment, R. Hanina is referring to a foreign government, in this case, the Roman governorship of Judea. While there were many in the land of Israel at the time who prayed for the government's downfall for a variety of political reasons, R. Hanina reminded them that the very presence of the government insured some measure of law and order in an otherwise anarchic society and should thus be supported. (Josephus attests to the priestly allegiance to the Roman authorities; see *Antiquities of the Jews*, Book 10, chap. 10.) Moreover, R. Hanina is not referring to law, but to the system of government that administers justice and metes out punishment, a function that the Jewish court system did not significantly perform during the later years of the Second Temple period. R. Hanina's comment cannot be seen as a general view of the purpose of *halakhah*, or Jewish law as a legal system.

In this light, the modern notion of human rights is not just a reconceptualization of an ancient moral impulse, formulated in immanent rather than transcendent terms. The descent down Jacob's ladder from religious obligations to human rights suggests a fundamental transformation of the social significance of persons. For the biblical worldview, humans are created in the Divine image and as such deserve dignity and respect as equals to every other person. People are obligated to help one another, both to improve collective conditions and to assist in the other's material and spiritual development.[16] In contrast, for the modern *Weltanschauung*, "human rights" refers to one's claims against society—a menacing group of self-interested individuals who literally endanger one's well-being. For obvious reasons, minorities, women, children, and the handicapped require the protection of human rights, for they are most vulnerable in a society formed solely to prevent the natural aggression of which all humans are capable and which they are willing to use.[17]

We now turn to the issue of the rights of women in Jewish law. We will briefly sketch the general contours of women's rights and

---

[16]While there seems to be ample evidence of the moral character of Jewish law, a thorough analysis would require examining the *vitality* of ethics within Jewish law. In other words, even as many laws achieve what we would identify as moral ends, the legal exegesis and discussion within the sources of Jewish Law themselves rarely, if ever, invoke ethical principles. See Sid Z. Leiman's "Critique of Louis Jacobs" in Menachem Marc Kellner, ed., *Contemporary Jewish Ethics* (New York, 1978), 58–60; Gerald J. Blidstein, "Moral Generalizations and Halakhic Discourse," *S'vara* 2:1 (1991): 8–12.

[17]Strict capitalism is, of course, the economic equivalent of this conception of human value. A person's worth is his labor, self-interest propels the system, and those who are not successful are deemed either incompetent or simply not actualizing the aggressive potential with which each person is naturally endowed. Governmental interference is therefore shunned and even feared as introducing an unfair factor into the "natural state" of men: those most aggressive will "naturally" succeed. The contemporary debate about "rights" to health insurance, retirement benefits, and other forms of welfare is an effort to superimpose the Lockean model of government on the economic state of society.

obligations, highlighting the rules and procedures that were instituted over time, both to insure a woman's dignity and to protect her from potential abuses implicit in the unequal relationships in which most women found themselves: father–daughter and husband–wife.

WOMEN IN JEWISH LAW: AN OVERVIEW

"I find women more bitter than death" (Ecclesiastes 7:26). "He who finds a wife has found happiness" (Proverbs 18:22). These two biblical passages from the *Ketuvim* (the Writings) alert us to the multiplicity of voices contained in the Jewish tradition. Rarely does one find only one opinion on a subject within the sources of Judaism, even on such fundamental issues as idolatry or martyrdom. From a methodological standpoint, then, it is difficult to draw general conclusions about any subject from traditional Jewish law. Its authoritative texts span millennia, from the Bible to contemporary codes and rabbinic responsa.[18] The tradition is self-consciously exegetical and interpretive, using careful analysis of prior texts and codes to yield solutions to any problem. Historically, the majority of *halachah*'s earliest and most authoritative sources date from the rabbinic period, roughly spanning from about the second century B.C.E. to the sixth or seventh century C.E. During this time, an immense body of legal material evolved in the oral culture of the academies, initially summarized in the *Mishnah* in the late second to early third century C.E. by the patriarch Rabbi Judah, and later redacted with greater detail and commentary in the Palestinian and Babylonian Talmuds. We shall focus on these sources in reviewing the legal status of women in Jewish law.[19]

---

[18]For an overview of the history of Jewish law, see David Feldman, *Marital Relations, Birth Control and Abortion in Jewish Law* (New York, 1974), 3–18, reprinted in Menachem Marc Kellner, ed., *Contemporary Jewish Ethics*, 21–40.

[19]Two main works that summarize this particular realm of law are Judith Hauptman, "Images of Women in the Talmud," in Rosemary Radford

In matters of civil or criminal law, men and women are essentially equal, whether they be victim or criminal. Thus, *halachah* forbids harming a man or a woman, and both are held liable for assault.[20] The consequences of harming a slave were identical whether the slave was male or female.[21] According to biblical law, both parents were due equal respect, and striking either parent was punishable by death.[22] Both partners to an illicit sexual union were executed,[23] and in contrast to other ancient Near Eastern codes, such as that of Hammurabi, neither the class nor the sex of the victim affected compensation.

While women enjoy access to all legal forms of redress, they are restricted from its process. They can serve neither as witnesses in criminal proceedings nor as judges in any court of law.[24] This exclusion from public life extends to all areas of communal service in its official forms.[25] Historically, however, women were not absent entirely from the public sphere. Both Talmuds are replete with legal cases involving women engaged in serious, even large-

---

Ruether, ed., *Religion and Sexism* (New York, 1974) and Judith Romney Wegner, *Chattel or Person? The Status of Women in the Mishnah* (New York, 1988). As the respective titles imply, each book focuses on a different rabbinic legal text as its source.

[20]See, for example, Exodus 21, *passim*. In general, the *midrishei halakhah* go to great exegetical lengths to ensure that all torts laws apply equally to men and women. See, for example, *Mekhilta de-rabbi Yishmael* to Exodus 21:18ff., Horovitz-Rabin, trans. (Jerusalem, 1960).

[21]Exodus 21:26–7.

[22]Exodus 20:10; 21:15.

[23]*Sifre* to Leviticus 19:29.

[24]The source of their disqualification as witnesses is an exegesis found in *Sifre* to Deuteronomy 19:17 (New York, 1969); cf. *Mishnah, Shevuot* 4:1, and Babylonian Talmud, *Shevuot* 30a. This exclusion, as noted, was limited to criminal cases; in ritual matters, women's testimony was accepted to establish the status of certain objects, whether they were permissible or not. Regarding women's inability to serve as judges, this exclusion is derived from a mishnaic identity between eligibility to testify and eligibility to serve as a judge. See *Mishnah, Niddah* 4:4. Women were, however, permitted to render halakhic decisions in an extra-judicial capacity; see *Pitchei Teshuvah* to *Shulhan Arukh, Hoshen Mishpat* 7:4 (Jerusalem, 1992).

[25]Babylonian Talmud, *Yevamot* 45a. Cf. *Sifre* to Deuteronomy 17:15.

scale business transactions, and are often represented as possessing their own land.

It is with respect to ritual law where the clearest distinction between men and women is evident. According to the *Mishnah*, women are exempt from all positive laws that are of a time-bound nature.[26] This encompasses most festival laws unless a specific exegesis re-obligates women in the observance, such as eating unleavened bread at the Passover seder. This exemption had wide-ranging consequences for, according to Jewish law, in "verbal" laws such as prayers and blessings, one can discharge one's responsibility by listening to another recite the required formula as long as the two persons were of equal obligation. While women were permitted to recite the prayers, the time-bound nature of praying (morning, afternoon, and evening) meant that women were essentially exempt and thus could not discharge a male's obligation. Women were not counted in the quorum for prayer, thus excluding them from synagogue services except as spectators. According to the Talmud, women were allowed to be called up to the Torah when it was publicly read, but subsequent rabbinic legislation excluded them from this sphere as well, due to "the congregation's honor," a vague notion.[27]

This exemption from time-bound commandments is generally taken to be based on the social need to have the woman available at all times to meet the needs of her husband and children. Imposing an additional set of demands would simply be unfair. However, even this theory, reasonable from a socio-historical standpoint, is

---

[26]*Mishnah, Kiddushin* 1:7.

[27]Babylonian Talmud, *Megillah* 23a. The exact quote is as follows: "Our rabbis taught: All are qualified to be among the seven [who read the Torah], even a minor and a woman, but the Sages said that a woman should not read because of the congregation's honor." Some interpret this to mean that someone might enter the service and, seeing a woman reading, would conclude that no male present is capable of reading from the Torah scroll, a genuine skill given the absence of vowels or punctuation in the Torah text. The term "the congregation's honor" is used on several occasions in the Babylonian Talmud, each with a different connotation. See, for example, Babylonian Talmud, *Megillah* 24b. It is therefore difficult to retrieve the precise meaning of this source.

not universally accepted. Given a woman's obligation in several time-bound commandments, such as hearing the Scroll of Esther on Purim, lighting Hanukkah candles, and others, this explanation is not adequate. Moreover, this account should lead to the conclusion that single women, or elderly women with no children or husbands any longer, should still be obligated. Due to these objections, Saul Berman has argued that what truly underlies this exemption is the perceived needs of Jewish society, which the rabbis believed were best served by keeping women in the family context.[28] The critical distinction between the commandments, according to Berman, is those that can be performed at home and those that must be performed in the communal sphere. The primary goal of this exemption was family stability, a goal best achieved if the woman was not given the chance to choose between familial duties and communal performances.[29]

Berman's theory may also account for the other significant exemption of women in Jewish law: they are not obligated to study Torah. For traditional Jews, the Torah is not merely a set of rules and laws, but the embodiment of the Divine word, the record of God's revelation to the Jewish people. The oral traditions that developed around it are the essence of rabbinic Judaism, and being left out of the enterprise could, arguably, deprive a Jew of connecting with her people's spiritual heritage. Nevertheless, Torah study, particularly in the rabbinic period, left the familial realm of parent to child (Deuteronomy 6:7, 11:19) and entered the academy, where one first heard *tannaim* recite the oral traditions of previous generations, and then personally debated its meaning with contemporary scholars. Torah was no longer a family affair but a communal one, and, once again, women were excluded from that sphere.

Even this explanation, however, does not explain why the exemption was extended to all women, even those who presently are not, or are no longer, in the context of the traditional family. Moreover, given the temperament of many men today, these fathers'

---

[28]Saul Berman, ''The Status of Women in Halakhic Judaism,'' in Elizabeth Koltun, ed., *The Jewish Woman: New Perspectives* (New York, 1976), 114–128.

[29]Ibid., 123.

involvement in family duties should exempt them as well from some time-bound commandments.[30] Rather, what we have here is, as Berman suggests, a fundamental split between the private and the public spheres. However, when this functional distinction is mediated through laws and is expressed in legal language (the only one available to the rabbis), many consequences that flow from the original distinction are sacrificed in order to create a clear and easily implemented system. These legislative concerns led the rabbis to exclude all women from the public realm in order to facilitate the situation of most of them—a concern that law school professors often appreciate but the man (sic) in the street does not.[31]

Thus, in certain respects, women enjoyed the same rights as men, while in others, particularly in ritual and academic settings, women were excluded and consigned to the home. This mixed image, where women and men are sometimes treated equally by the law and sometimes not, is even more noticeable in the next realm we will examine: marriage and divorce.

MARRIAGE AND DIVORCE

"A bad wife is as hard [to bear] as a stormy day."[32] "If your wife is short, bend down to listen to her."[33] As these two passages indicate, an analysis of Jewish attitudes and practices in the realm of marriage and divorce demonstrates there has been significant development over the centuries, virtually all of it designed to enhance the status of the woman and to make her less vulnerable. These changes reflect both the dynamic quality of Jewish law and a basic attitude toward the woman as a person. As will be demon-

---

[30]The single father with custody of his children, or even when he has visitation rights, are situations that immediately come to mind.

[31]See Saul Berman's response to Pnina Lahav in *S'vara* 3:1 (1993): 51–54, esp. 52.

[32]Babylonian Talmud, *Yevamot* 63b.

[33]Babylonian Talmud, *Bava Metziah* 59a.

strated, this almost inherent dynamic quality has not been mar-
shalled to address a situation in which many Jewish women
today suffer abuse and extortion to simply bring an end to their
marriages.

The first chapter of *Mishnah Kiddushin*, which deals with issues
of betrothal and property, opens with the statement that a woman
is "acquired by three different means: money, document, or sexual
intercourse."[34] Some contemporary scholars, focusing on the word
"acquired" (*niknait*) and the first two transactional means mentioned in this *mishnah*, have argued that this rendered the woman
a form of property.[35] There was, they contend, virtually no difference between acquiring a woman and acquiring other kinds of
property. Their argument is strengthened by the fact that the subsequent paragraphs in this chapter of the *Mishnah* deal with the
acquisition of other forms of property, such as slaves, animals, real
estate, and portable objects.

One can only speculate about the nature of marriage in pre-
rabbinic times; there are simply too few sources of only dubious
reliability. In any event, by the time of the *Mishnah*'s redaction, the
Rabbis had already significantly moved away from the concept of
women as chattel, if it ever obtained at all. They did so in a number of ways. First, the amount that was used to effect the marriage
was so minimal that it is hard to consider this transfer of funds a
purchase.[36] It was in essence a symbolic payment to recognize the
man's "acquisition." What the husband was acquiring in this transaction was the sole right to have sex with this woman. In contrast
to the purchase of property, before a marriage could be arranged,

---

[34]*Mishnah, Kiddushin* 1:1. By the early amoraic period, the Rabbis opposed using sexual intercourse as a means of effecting a marriage. See
Babylonian Talmud, *Kiddushin* 12b.

[35]Wegner, *Chattel or Person,* 43, 227, n. 84.

[36]The School of Shammai argued that a *dinar* was a sufficient amount.
The School of Hillel, whose view was accepted, argued that it was only a
prutah, the eighth part of an Italian *issar*. Although we are not sure of the
exact equivalent, we do know that these were exceptionally minimal
amounts. A *prutah* might well be the contemporary equivalent of a penny.
Even a *dinar* was not more than the contemporary equivalent of five dollars (*Mishnah, Kiddushin* 1:1).

the consent of the woman had to be obtained.[37] Moreover, the man could not sell a woman he acquired for a wife, nor could he compel her against her will to do certain things, as was the case of English law until the end of the nineteenth century. Nor could he treat her as an animal: Though wife-beating was recognized as a form of chastisement, it was considered by many rabbis as grounds for compelling a man to divorce his wife.[38]

Furthermore, on two occasions, the Bible records the payment of a bride-price (*mohar*) to the father for his daughter.[39] This seems to reflect the prevalent custom in the ancient Near East of actually buying a bride.[40] In the Second Temple period, however, economic conditions prevented young men from amassing sufficient sums to pay the *mohar* in advance. This led to the conversion of the *mohar* into a marriage settlement for the *bride* (*not* her father), providing for her in the event of divorce or widowhood. R. Simeon ben Shetah, the leader of the Pharisees in the Hasmonean period (mid-second century B.C.E.) reportedly strengthened the settlement by introducing the husband's pledge of all his possessions as security. The substance of the settlement is embodied in the marriage contract (*ketubah*) that witnesses sign before a wedding, attesting to the husband's acceptance of his obligation. In general, the sum of the settlement is roughly the equivalent of living expenses for one or two years. Subsequent rabbinic legislation insured the protective capacity of this settlement by prohibiting any couple from marrying without a *ketubah*; if it were later lost, rabbinic law forbade their living together until a new one was written and signed by witnesses. Furthermore, if the *ketubah* had to be

---

[37]Babylonian Talmud, *Kiddushin* 41a.

[38]An eleventh-century rabbi ruled that a man who beat his wife was to be treated more severely than a man who beat another man, because he was not obligated to honor his fellow man but he was obligated to honor his wife more than himself. For additional discussion of this point, see Rachel Biale, *Women and Jewish Law: An Exploration of Women's Issues in Halakhic Sources* (New York, 1984), 93–96.

[39]According to the Bible, her father received the bride-price from a man who violated or seduced his daughter (Exodus 22:15–16; Deuteronomy 22:28–29).

[40]Hauptman, "Images of Women in the Talmud," 185.

collected, she was to receive the money before any other distributions were made from his estate. If the inheritance was insufficient,
the rabbis ruled that the sons were to go begging, allowing the
mother and the daughters to be maintained by whatever funds were
available in the estate.[41] These enactments collectively had the impact of rendering marriage easier and divorce more difficult.[42]

Finally, the paragraph in *Kiddushin* that speaks of the "acquisition" of the wife is, in fact, the last time the *Mishnah* uses the term
niknait, "acquired," in reference to a marriage. All subsequent
references use the term *kiddushin*, "exclusively designated," but
also connoting an aura of holiness. In Judaism something that is holy
is set aside for special use. In terms of marriage, *kiddushin* denotes
exclusivity. According to the Rabbis, the man was sanctifying the
woman to himself, that is, for his sole access to her sexual functions.[43] While this was the husband's privilege, it was not his prerogative to allow others to "use" his wife, even by the seemingly
legitimate means of divorce and subsequent re-marriage.[44]

While the rabbinic portrayal of *betrothal* was clearly dissimilar
to the acquisition of chattel, it was particularly the rabbinic understanding of *marriage* and the mutual obligations it entailed that
reveal true sensitivity and concern for protecting the woman. The
Mishnah enumerates and the *Gemara* expands upon an entire series of rights and protections accorded the wife. Recognizing that
from a social and economic perspective, the wife was the dependent partner in the relationship, the tradition provided her with a
host of protections. When a wife fell sick, the husband had to provide for her.[45] Should he die, she could not be evicted from the

------

[41]*Mishnah, Bava Batra* 9:1.

[42]Babylonian Talmud, *Ketubot* 82b; Jerusalem Talmud, *Ketubot* 8:11;
Elliot N. Dorff and Arthur Rosett, *A Living Tree: The Roots and Growth of
Jewish Law* (New York, 1988), 443.

[43]Biale, *Women and Jewish Law*, 48.

[44]Deuteronomy 24:1–4. See the *Commentary of Nachmanides*, Charles
Chavel, trans. (New York, 1971) and *Commentary of Sforno* (Jersualem,
1981), *ad loc*, and the explanation in the *Sefer ha-Hinukh*, commandment
580 (Jerusalem, 1991).

[45]*Mishnah, Ketubot* 4:9.

marital residence.[46] Most significantly, the *Mishnah* recognized that she has certain emotional and social needs. Her husband could not arbitrarily prevent her from visiting her parents or attending community gatherings such as weddings or funerals. If he did attempt to do so, he was obligated to grant her freedom by divorcing her and granting her the funds promised her in the *ketubah*.[47] One thousand years later, Maimonides, who insisted on a wife's right to visit her parents' home, as well as her friends and neighbors, observed that "she is not in a prison from which she cannot come and go."[48] Most importantly, her husband was liable for her support, burial, and ransom should she be kidnapped.[49] All these practices are manifestations of her dependency on him and his responsibilities toward her.

A wife had certain reciprocal obligations toward her husband. According to the *Mishnah*, she was obligated to wash his face, hands, feet, make his bed, and prepare his wine.[50] The Talmud expanded and contracted these to reflect those acts that, according to local custom, are performed by a wife for her husband. Thus, today washing feet would *not* be included. In certain places, she was obligated not only to raise the children and perform household duties, but also to spin, weave, and sew the family's clothing. If she had the means, either from her husband's wealth or her own

---

[46]*Mishnah*, *Ketubot* 4:12.

[47]*Mishnah*, *Ketubot* 7:4, 5.

[48]To this, Maimonides appended the following comment: "On the other hand, it is unseemly for a woman to be constantly going out abroad and into the streets, and the husband should prevent his wife from doing this and should not let her go out, except once or twice a month, as the need may arise" (*Mishneh Torah*, Laws of Marriage 13:11). This comment by Maimonides must be seen in light of contemporary Islamic law; see Goitein, "Human Rights in Jewish Thought and Life in the Middle Ages," 256.

[49]*Mishnah*, *Ketubot* 4:4. While she could relieve him of certain obligations toward her, such as the responsibility to feed and clothe her, she could not waive his obligation to ransom her. See Samuel Morrell, "An Equal or a Ward: How Independent Is a Married Woman According to Rabbinic Law?" *Jewish Social Studies* (Summer/Fall, 1982): 190.

[50]Babylonian Talmud, *Ketubot* 61a.

assets, she was allowed to hire others to do these chores for her,[51] though Rabbi Eliezer cautioned that she should not remain idle but should be compelled, if necessary, to undertake certain tasks because "idleness leads to promiscuity."[52]

Furthermore, the husband's financial responsibilities to his wife granted him rights to her earnings while they were married, and to the usufruct from the fields she brought into the marriage.[53] But even in this regard, the husband's rights were limited. In contrast to Anglo-American law, any assets she brought to the marriage remained her property and were returned to her in the case of a divorce. While he controlled what was done with these during the marriage, he could not sell them without her consent.[54]

Perhaps the true test of a woman's rights within society, according to Jewish law, is the status of the *unmarried* woman. In contrast to the traditional patriarchal system, there are entire classes of Jewish women who have total control over all aspects of their lives. While the dependent women—the minor daughter, wife, and levirate widow[55]—have a nexus of rights, some of which have been enumerated here, their person is greatly controlled by the men upon whom they depend. In contrast, the divorcée, the widow, and the adult unmarried daughter (after age twelve) are totally independent. There is extensive anecdotal evidence of these women arranging their own marriages, conducting business affairs, and functioning in all but the realm of ritual as autonomous and independent persons. Though a wife was forbidden from selling her own property without her husband's permission, a divorcée could have

---

[51]*Mishnah, Ketubot* 5:5.

[52]*Mishnah, Ketubot* 5:5. The talmudic discussion of this view does not indicate whether Rabbi Eliezer's opinion is normative, although Maimonides does codify it. See ibid., 21:2. This sort of rabbinic suspicion of female sexuality is not uncommon in rabbinic literature.

[53]*Mishnah, Ketubot* 4:4, 6:1.

[54]*Mishnah, Gittin,* 5:6.

[55]The levirate widow was a woman whose husband died without having had male children. She was to marry her brother-in-law so that he could perpetuate his brother's line. If he does not wish to marry her, he must perform a ceremony releasing her. If he does neither, she remains an *agunah*, unable to marry anyone else, until his death.

the court compel her former husband to sell his property in order to gain what is due her as enumerated in the *ketubah*. The widow had even greater latitude. Not only did she control her own property, but she did not need court approval to sell portions of her late husband's estate. Moreover, a widow who was not a levirate could marry whomever she wished.[56] The adult single daughter could engage in all sorts of business transactions without obstacle, for she had sole claim to her property. This belies claims made by those such as Simone de Beauvoir that Judaism is a pure patriarchal system.[57] Only in the realm of ritual and Torah study were these otherwise independent women curtailed in their activities.

Perusal of both the laws and the general statements about marriage in the Talmud offers valid grounds to argue that the tradition considered marriage to be a complex set of entitlements and obligations that each partner had toward the other. As Judith Hauptman concludes, the Talmud considered marriage to constitute a relationship between two human beings, each with his or her own set of needs and responsibilities. The man was clearly the dominant partner in this relationship, owing to a variety of social, economic, and religious reasons. But the wife's personal rights were protected in a sophisticated arrangement of reciprocal duties and privileges.[58]

Reciprocity, however, does not imply equality, and this is the crux of the matter. In the biblical and rabbinic conception, marriage is not the union of two adults mutually consenting to spend their lives together—although the Rabbis did insist that both partners agree to the marriage.[59] Rather, marriage is the man's acqui-

---

[56]Wegner, *Chattel or Person*, 170.

[57]Simone de Beauvoir, *The Second Sex* (New York, 1974). See, generally, Wegner, *Chattel or Person*?

[58]Hauptman, "Images of Women in the Talmud," 186.

[59]Babylonian Talmud, *Kiddushin* 41a, warns that a man should not marry off his minor daughter, but should wait until she matures and can express her own opinion about whom she wants to marry. Nor should a man betroth a woman without seeing her first, lest he subsequently find her repulsive. It is interesting that the talmudic justification for this is that he may subsequently come to hate her, thus violating the biblical command "Love your neighbor as yourself" (Leviticus 19:19). Samuel Morrell points out

sition of exclusive legal claim to his wife's sexual function. The only
Pentateuchal reference to either marriage or divorce is significant
in this regard:

> When a man takes a wife and has intercourse with her, and if she
> fails to please him because he finds something obnoxious about her,
> he should write her a bill of divorce, hand it to her, and send her
> away from his house. She will leave his household and [may] be-
> come the wife of another man. [If] this latter man rejects her, writes
> a bill of divorcement, hands it to her, and sends her away from his
> house, or [if] the man who married her last dies. Her first husband,
> who divorced her, shall not take her to be his wife again. . . .[60]

The expression in the first verse "and has intercourse with her" is
the essence of the marital relationship. In Hebrew, the word for
husband derives from the same root as "to have intercourse"—
b.'a.l. To be sure, even these rights were limited by *halachah*: rabbinic tradition recognized rape within marriage, and forbade it.[61]
Even more far-reaching was the notion that intercourse was a wife's
right and a husband's duty,[62] and a man could not withhold conju-
gal rights as part of a stipulation of marriage[63]—in sharp contrast
to other ancient Near Eastern traditions.

What these verses make clear is that the model of marriage was
unilateral acquisition of sexual rights, perhaps requiring (as the
Rabbis later did) the woman's consent. And if this is how marriages
are forged, then there exists only one way to dissolve them: the
man must surrender the rights he possesses and return them to
the woman. This explains why the verse concentrates on the
husband's dissatisfaction with his wife (for whatever reason), and

---

that this talmudic teaching is significant because it treats the woman purely
as a person and not as a wife. See Morrell, "An Equal or a Ward," 189.

[60]Deuteronomy 24:1–4.

[61]Maimonides writes: "[a husband] must not rape her by having intercourse against her will, but rather [let him perform the act] with her consent
and in mutual arousal and joy" (*Mishneh Torah*, Laws of Marriage, 15:17).

[62]*Ketubot* 47b, 56a.

[63]Babylonian Talmud, *Kiddushin* 19b.

not the reverse; only he can initiate marriage, so only he can initiate a divorce.

Once again, it is rabbinic tradition that went very far in protecting the woman from the abuses inherent in a system in which only
one party has control. Even a brief survey of Jewish divorce law
will reveal that the Rabbis acted to enhance her clearly vulnerable
position by making it harder for him to divorce his wife. The rabbis conceived of a variety of avenues to safeguard a wife from a
capricious and vengeful husband who, because of jealousy or in-
stability, would try to wreak havoc with her life. The harder it was
to divorce her, presumably, the more protected she would be.

The vast majority of the tractate of the *Mishnah* on divorce is
concerned with the technical matter of standardizing the *get*, the
writ of divorce. The bill had to be written with certain kinds of ink,
on particular forms of paper, and by a scribe. These various requirements were apparently intended to prevent the husband from
sitting down in anger and simply scribbling a few lines that would
radically affect his wife. It is striking that in rabbinic law, marriage
entails far fewer technical details than divorce, reflecting both the
preference for marriage (and the desire to facilitate it), as well as
the bias against divorce and the belief that the woman needed
protection.

According to Jewish law, a married woman who committed
adultery was executed, and if there were children from the act, they
had the status of a *mamzer*, which prohibited them from marrying
anyone but another *mamzer*. Given these serious consequences,
the rabbis went to pains to make sure that the divorce was genuine and that the woman was clear about her own status. Rabban
Gamliel, patriarch of the second century c.e., therefore enacted
that if a man sends a *get* through an agent to his wife (a common
practice if he happened to be far away from her), he is not allowed
to cancel that agency in a court.[64] The *Mishnah* declares that
Rabban Gamliel did this "for the betterment of the world" (*tikkum
'olam*), and the Talmud offers two reasons for this enactment. One
opinion maintains that if the nullification of the agency were allowed
to be valid, then the wife might receive the divorce, mistakenly

---

[64]*Mishnah, Gittin* 4:1.

assume it was valid (even though it had been canceled), and proceed to marry someone else. The children of this second marriage would then be *mamzerim*, a consequence to be avoided at all costs. The other possible situation, maintained by a different scholar, was that women, fearful that their husbands have canceled the writ, might be paralyzed into inaction after receiving writ of divorce through an agent. These women might never re-marry, fearful that they were still legally married to their first husbands.[65] It is not at all clear whether this was a prevalent practice, or whether Rabban Gamliel was merely preventing an anticipated abuse. In any event, according to both views, it was the woman's future that was the patriarch's primary concern.

Nor could the husband's control extend beyond the termination of the marital relationship. Thus, once a woman had her *get*, she was free to marry whomever she wished. Her first husband could not stipulate either during the marriage or in the *get* that he divorced her on the condition that she would not marry a specific person.[66] Divorce meant total liberation from the first husband.

The Rabbis of the Babylonian Talmud, concerned about producing greater equity in the entire procedure, established a means for the woman to sue for divorce. In a variety of situations, she could turn to a Jewish court and ask it to force her husband to grant her a divorce: if her husband was afflicted by a physical condition that made him repulsive to her, if he did not uphold his obligation to maintain or support her as he stated he would in the *ketubah*, or if she found him sexually repulsive and could not have relations with him.[67] Maimonides' formulation vividly portrays the *halachah*'s sympathy for the woman caught in an unbearable marital bond:

---

[65]Babylonian Talmud, *Gittin* 33a.

[66]The Talmud's exegesis (Babylonian Talmud, *Gittin* 82b) is clear that this would not constitute a genuine divorce: "'And he shall give her a writ of *keritut* (severence)'—we require total severence, and there is none [in this case]." In other words, if even after divorce, the former husband controlled her choice of a second spouse, then the woman was not entirely her own person.

[67]Babylonian Talmud, *Ketubot* 63b, 70a–77b; Hauptman, "Images of Women in the Talmud," 189.

> [She] should be questioned as to the reason for her rebelliousness
> [that is, her refusal to have relations with her husband]. If she says,
> "I have come to loathe him and I cannot willingly submit to his in-
> tercourse," he must be compelled to divorce her immediately, for
> she is not like a captive woman who must submit to a man who is
> hateful to her.[68]

Medieval rabbinic authorities added other grounds on which to sue for divorce, such as wife-beating or the husband's frequenting prostitutes.[69] Divorce initiated by the man, however, was strictly a matter of individual judgment and discretion.[70]

But even this rabbinic effort to redress the inequity of divorce proceedings could not change the biblical character of divorce: a unilateral action by the husband. At best, the court could compel him to give her the *get* if it found her suit legitimate. The man's consent was the *sine qua non* of the entire process.

Two other steps were taken in the early Middle Ages to balance the powers in divorce, and both are credited to Rabbi Gershom of Mainz (960–1028): One banned polygamy on penalty of social excommunication (*herem*), the other forbade divorcing a woman against her will.[71] These two rulings marked the end of the man's absolute right of divorce, for not only was her consent now necessary, but the man no longer had the option of ignoring his first wife and marrying another woman. Divorce had to be effected before he could move on with his life. Prior to this ruling, the only leverage available to the woman was the financial consequences of divorce for the husband, the amount having been pre-set in the

---

[68]*Mishneh Torah*, Laws of Marriage 14:8.

[69]Rabbi Moses Isserless to *Shulchan Aruch, Even ha-Ezer,* Laws of Divorce 154:3.

[70]For a summary of this discussion, see Biale, *Women and Jewish Law,* 73–79. The Rabbis believed that if marital infidelity was the sole reason for a divorce the husband might be tempted to simply be unfaithful as a means of causing the divorce to proceed.

[71]There is evidence that these rulings were in effect even before Rabbi Gershom. See Ze'ev W. Falk, *Jewish Matrimonial Law in the Middle Ages* (Oxford, 1966), 13–18; Blu Greenberg, *On Women and Judaism: A View from Tradition* (Philadelphia, 1981), 130.

ketubah. In general, only the wealthy could afford a divorce, since the *ketubah* granted her the legal right to claim her dowry even if it meant "taking the shirt off his back."[72]

However, the method by which Rabbi Gershom instituted these rulings inherently contained a loophole: a rabbinic ban can be overridden if the dispensation of one hundred rabbis (*heter me'ah rabbanim*) is obtained. Thus, if a man's wife became mentally unbalanced, preventing her from accepting a *get,*[73] the husband could secure the agreement of one hundred rabbis and marry a second wife, provided his first wife's needs were met. This strategy is, in fact, available to any man whose wife refuses to accept the bill of divorce for what are deemed illegitimate reasons, a decision rendered by the rabbinical court involved. In this scenario, the husband actually writes a *get* and deposits it in the court, appointing the members of the court as his proxies to deliver the *get* to his wife whenever she chooses to come to the court and accept it. Thus, the *heter me'ah rabbanim* does not leave her chained, but allows him to go on with his life even if she is recalcitrant and refuses to accept the *get.* No such recourse, however, is open to her; if her husband was beset by a mental illness, or refused to write the bill of divorce, she became an *agunah,* a chained woman, unable to remarry.

The unfortunate situation of the *agunah* is well-known in Jewish law and was already addressed by the rabbis of the *Mishnah.* The typical case was a husband who never returned from traveling abroad, and while the precarious nature of travel justified a presumption of death, hard evidence was lacking that would clearly establish this fact and free her to remarry. To prevent this, some rabbis suggested writing a conditional form of divorce, whereby the writ would become valid if the husband did not return by a specified time.[74] In the event that the husband did not have this

---

[72]Babylonian Talmud, *Yevamot* 63b; Babylonian Talmud, *Gittin* 58a; *Mishnah, Nedarim* 9:5; Falk, ibid., 115.

[73]In Jewish Law, the receipt of a *get* is taken to be a type of transaction, and thus requires the mental competence of both parties, as in any transaction.

[74]*Mishnah, Gittin* 6:5.

foresight, the rabbis were prepared to relax the rules of evidence, which normally require two witnesses to establish fact,[75] and accept the testimony of only one witness.[76] The Rabbis were even willing to accept the testimony of those who would, under normal circumstances, be disqualified, such as a woman, a minor, or even the wife herself despite her vested interests.

The more insidious type of *agunah* is the woman whose husband refuses to grant her a divorce. Whether out of anger, revenge, or spite, he will not give her the document that will allow her to terminate the marriage and remarry. Traditionally, rabbis treated this situation, known as "the recalcitrant husband," with familiar and tested methods to force him to divorce his wife. Various social pressures, ranging from public declarations and humiliation in the synagogue to outright social excommunication, were at a rabbi's disposal to compel the husband to release his chained wife. These options, however, were effective when Jewish communities were fairly independent entities with virtually complete control over their internal affairs. If a man did not grant his wife her freedom, the court could socially excommunicate him and make it impossible for him to live in that community. Because people were much less mobile, the community could also more easily monitor his movements and warn other communities not to have any dealings with this married man who refused to accede to the court's ruling and issue his wife a divorce. Today, however, when the rabbinic courts do not possess such power, and men are free to travel far to communities unaware of their recalcitrance, the plight of the *agunah* has become quite severe. Even in the State of Israel, where rabbinic courts enjoy exclusive jurisdiction over marital matters, including the right to jail recalcitrant husbands,[77] there are still men who

---

[75]See Deuteronomy 17:6, 19:15.

[76]*Mishnah, Yevamot* 10:1.

[77]Part of the problem is the unwillingness of the rabbinical courts to use the power they have on the men, preferring to advise the couple to work things out rather than separate. While in some cases this is justified and reflects a healthy effort to see divorce as a quick and easy solution to any marital strife, the rabbinical courts at times refuse to recognize cases of abuse from which the woman needs immediate recourse. Between 1948 and 1986, the rabbinical courts in Israel only used compulsory *get*

prefer to suffer this punishment rather than issue their wives a *get*.[78] To be sure, for many cases it might be a simple matter of legislation, enacting a law that makes the consequences of recalcitrance much more severe, such as freezing assets, garnishing wages, and the like. Nevertheless, the procedural rules of divorce themselves prevent rescuing the woman whose husband ignores all these punitive measures and remains recalcitrant. He alone can grant her freedom to remarry, and his refusal to grant the *get* necessarily chains her to him for life.

More significantly, many women are able to secure a divorce only by meeting the extortionate demands of their husbands. Thus, women regularly find themselves subject to severe financial, custodial, and other sorts of stipulations in order to have their husbands agree to grant them a divorce. To avoid becoming permanent *agunot*, some women agree to pay their spouses exorbitant sums of money or to forgo child support. Inequitable divorce settlements are reluctantly agreed to, at times involving serious and delicate custody issues, in order to secure the *get*. Most regrettably, some rabbis have even come to see this kind of conduct by the husband as acceptable, providing the demands are not extraordinary. This kind of abuse is endemic to a divorce procedure that places the full responsibility of divorce on one party alone, and given today's world, social pressure will solve only a handful of the most severe *agunah* cases. The overwhelming majority of women will either capitulate to their husbands' demands or suffer in silence and solitude.

There are, in essence, two sets of problems here: attitudinal and halakhic. For a long time, the traditional community denied that

---

measures on recalcitrant husbands fourteen times; between 1980 and 1985, ninety-five men whose wives refused to accept a divorce were given permission to take second wives. The tendency of the court, however, to use its power to compel the husband to give his wife a divorce is increasing. In 1992 alone it used that power five times. See Naomi Grossman, "Women Unbound: Breaking the Chains of Jewish Divorce Law," *Lilith* (Summer, 1993): 8–10.

[78]Recently, the newspapers reported that a man in Israel who had been incarcerated since *the early 1960s* for not giving his wife a *get*, died in jail. All this time, his wife could not remarry.

there was a problem. As recently as the late 1970s, many modern Orthodox rabbis and much of the Orthodox community dismissed the problem as one of little significance.[79] Today, however, increasing numbers of rabbis are willing to acknowledge that this is a serious problem.[80] In part, their recognition of the problem is rooted in the fact that their daughters and granddaughters have faced this difficult situation.[81] The situation involving a recalcitrant spouse has increasingly been recognized by Orthodox rabbis as a problem that must be resolved. There are still those who believe that, while it is a tragedy, nothing essentially can really be done to change the situation. Men must simply be pressured to agree to the Rabbinic Court's ruling. Some of the rabbis who take this position argue that the woman who finds herself in this situation somehow deserves it.[82] In contrast, one rabbi publicly conceded that this situation was a tremendous *Hillul Hashem*, a desecration of God's name.[83]

Rabbis of the Conservative movement have adopted their own solution. They have relied on the conditional divorce, inserting a clause in the marriage agreement that makes the marriage null and

---

[79]Conversation with Rabbi Saul Berman, September 3, 1994.

[80]Blu Greenberg, "Woman Today—An Orthodox View," in Steven Katz, ed., *Frontiers of Jewish Thought* (New York, 1992), 76–81.

[81]The publisher of a major Jewish newspaper in New York that caters to the Orthodox community refused the request of a number of organizations to publish the names of men who had refused to accede to the court's directive to issue their wives *gets*. However, when his daughter was subjected to the blackmail of a recalcitrant husband who demanded an interest in the paper in exchange for issuing the *get*, the publisher's attitude changed. He now publishes the list and has become a major supporter of legislation by the State assembly to strengthen the position of Jewish women facing a divorce.

[82]One of the apologists referred to at the outset of this paper wrote in 1986 that "in the case where a wife is oppressed or remains an *agunah*, one may say that it is the divine will, for whatever reasons He deemed fit" (H. E. Yedidiah Ghatan, *More Precious than Rubies: The Unique Status of Women in Judaism* [New York, 1986], 135).

[83]Basil Herring, "Putting an End to the Agunah Problem," *Amit* (September, 1994): 18–19.

void if a civil divorce is not followed by a Jewish divorce within six months. The other Conservative strategy has been to have the rabbinic court annul the marriage if they deem it necessary to do so in the interests of justice. They justify this action on the passage in the Talmud "everyone who betroths does so at the discretion of the Rabbis."[84] This is understood to mean that there is an implicit condition in every Jewish marriage that it is subject to annulment by Jewish legal authorities.[85] The Reform movement has simply done away with the need for a religious divorce altogether.

The Orthodox community does not accept the validity of the Conservative movement's solutions, finding technical halakhic difficulties both in the concept of a conditional marriage, and in the applicability of the talmudic prerogative of annulment, which, admittedly, was only rarely used historically.[86] Many within the Orthodox rabbinate diagnose the problem in a much different way. The fault lies not in the halakhic system per se; the fact that a large number of *agunot* have appeared only recently is evidence that the existing system is sufficiently viable. What these Orthodox leaders bemoan is the changing conditions that have rendered traditional methods of coping with this problem essentially useless. The reliance on social pressure assumes both a tight-knit community and the individual's need for a community to supply his identity. Neither of these conditions obtain for the average Jew, excepting those who have chosen to live in the ultra-Orthodox community, particularly the hasidic sects. Given the mobility of people and their willingness either to join a different community or simply not to identify with an Orthodox community altogether, the old strategies

---

[84]Babylonian Talmud, *Gittin* 33a and parallels. According to the medieval Franco-German Tosafists, this idea came to be expressed in the betrothal formula "Behold, you are betrothed to me with this ring *according to the laws of Moses and Israel*." Thus, rabbinic approbation is a condition of every marriage. See ibid., s.v. *kol*.

[85]Dorff and Rosett, *The Living Tree*, 526.

[86]See David Novak, *Law and Theology in Judaism* (New York, 1974), 31–54; J. David Bleich, "The Device of the 'Sages of Spain'" as a Solution to the Problems of the Modern Day Agunah," in id., *Contemporary Halakhic Problems* (New York, 1989), 3:329–343.

will no longer work. New methods must therefore be proposed to meet the challenges posed by the *agunah* problem.

Since secular governments have assumed many of the legal and social functions previously held by the autonomous community, the Orthodox rabbinate naturally first turned to these authorities to address the problem of *agunot*. This approach was tried in the State of New York, which, given the large population of Orthodox Jews, heard many cases of *agunah*. The New York legislature passed a law that would withhold a civil divorce from a couple until "all barriers to the other party's remarriage" are resolved. Barriers to remarriage specifically include "any religious or conscientious restraint or inhibition imposed on a party to a marriage, under the principles of the denomination of the clergyman or minister who has solemnized the marriage, by reason of the other party's commission or withholding of any voluntary act." In 1992, this law was expanded to permit judges of civil courts to take into consideration a husband's refusal to grant a *get* when deciding the distribution of marital assets. A judge could withhold portions of the assets from the husband until he grants the divorce.[87]

This New York law on divorce, however, has been challenged as unconstitutional. Moreover, other states have refused to adopt such legislation precisely because it compels a party to engage in a religious act on pain of withholding civil relief—a *prima facie* violation of the religion clauses of the First Amendment to the United States Constitution.[88]

The opposition to this solution is not just constitutional in nature. Many Orthodox feminists find the efforts to rely on the secular authorities "insufficient" at best and a *Hillul Hashem* (desecration of God's name) at worst. These women, many of whom have been deeply involved in the struggle on behalf of *agunot*, regard reliance on secular authorities as a concession that Jewish law is incapable of ensuring justice for Jewish women.[89] They also contend that turning to the secular authorities for help is a strange decision

---

[87]Rivka Haut, "The Agunah and Divorce," in Debra Orenstein, ed., *Lifecycles* (Woodstock, 1994), 198.

[88]Dorff and Rosett, *The Living Tree*, 547.

[89]Haut, "The Agunah and Divorce," 199.

for a community that has always believed its legal system to be the keystone of an all encompassing way of life.

Over the years, segments of the Orthodox community have proposed a range of solutions, many of which have not been widely accepted.[90] Recently, the prenuptial agreement, used by couples on an ad hoc basis for years, has been standardized and adopted by the Rabbinical Council of America, the organization of Orthodox rabbis. Under the terms of this agreement, the husband commits to maintain and support his wife until such time as the marriage is properly terminated. Both spouses agree to let the rabbinic court adjudicate any attempts to dissolve the marriage. (That provision protects the husband from a wife who procrastinates in order to be supported.) The major advantage of such an agreement is that it avoids the court as an instrument of religious coercion; the secular authorities are involved only in the enforcement of a civil contract signed by two parties. However, all rabbis must demand that every couple sign such an agreement before marrying, in order for this to serve as an even partial solution. Some rabbis are uncomfortable raising such practical concerns related to divorce with a couple presently planning a life together; some couples even refuse to listen. More significantly, the prenuptial agreement nevertheless requires the woman to hire a lawyer to sue her husband for the conditions stipulated in the contract. This is an expense that, in addition to all the expenses of a divorce, may make the prenuptial agreement of little value for some women in economic distress. Furthermore, this arrangement obviously leaves out all those women who were married without such an agreement but who nevertheless find themselves *agunot*. Thus, this new strategy must be tested over time to see if it will achieve serious results in even a majority of *agunah* cases.

---

[90]For a description of these attempts, see Moshe Meiselman, *Jewish Women in Jewish Law* (New York, 1978), 103–115. Over the years, various halakhic solutions have been offered by rabbinic legal scholars such as Emanuel Rackman, Ze'ev Falk, Shlomo Riskin, and Eliezer Berkovits. See Irwin Haut, *Divorce in Jewish Law and Life* (New York, 1983); Shlomo Riskin, *Women and Jewish Divorce, the Rebellious Wife, The Agunah and the Right of Women to Initiate the Divorce in Jewish Law, A Halakhic Solution* (Hoboken, 1989).

UNDERSTANDING THE JEWISH RESPONSE TO THE AGUNAH

In light of our earlier analysis of human rights, the situation of the *agunah* and the rabbinic responses to her plight point to a disturbing trend in contemporary Jewish law. In a word, contemporary *halachah* has become increasingly Lockean. For much of its formative history, *halachah* had operated with the self-conscious aim of leading the community to a higher plane of mutual respect and concord. It not only anticipated abuses that lay in the technicalities of law and pre-empted them; it also prescribed actions that were deliberately designed to improve the interpersonal relations between men and women, between adults and minors (particularly orphans), and between Jews and non-Jews. To be sure, there were rabbinic enactments that only addressed specific inequities once they had been perpetrated, although the historical extent of these abuses is rarely clear and usually incapable of verification.[91] Nevertheless, the overall trajectory of Jewish law, particularly in the rabbinic period, was to create a covenantal society guided by the revealed law of God and predicated on the infinite worth of the individual who was created in the Divine image. This, as we explained earlier, was in sharp contrast with the Hobbesian-Lockean pessimism regarding human nature.

---

[91]Thus, in connection with Hillel's prosbul, the Babylonian Talmud (*Gittin* 36a) describes the situation that "the people [*am*] had refrained from lending." Whether this was a widespread phenomenon, or merely that some of the people did not lend, remains an open question. Certainly, if Hillel did not act until the abuse was rampant, then there seems to be precedent for the more conservative position that is reluctant to make any sweeping reforms. Two important qualifications to this case must be noted, however. First, Hillel's enactment was to have the practical effect of nullifying a Torah law, viz., the cancellation of all debts in the sabbatical year. Second, in the Babylonian Talmud's formulation, Hillel saw that the people were violating another biblical prescription: not to be close-fisted as the sabbatical year approached and to lend freely (Deuteronomy 15:9–10). Hillel's choice was thus between enacting a measure that would circumvent one law or allow the "rampant" violation of another law to continue. For a discussion of these sources, see *Svara* 2:2 (1991): 61–73.

In recent years, Jewish law has seen its role as primarily reactive, a trend the case of the *agunah* highlights quite well. Rather than preventing abuses that are only theoretically possible, many halakhic authorities wait until a problem reaches a certain intolerable level, and then address it, if at all. Obviously, there are exceptions, such as Rabbi Abraham Kook's *heter mekhirah*, which allowed Jewish farmers to work the soil of Israel during the sabbatical year, a year during which the land is required to lie fallow.[92] However, most rabbinic leaders (across the denominational divide) have allowed certain conditions that they acknowledge as lamentable to continue even as many Jews—usually in the minority—suffer. For instance, families willingly subject themselves to extreme economic hardship in an effort to conduct family celebrations at a level of extravagance dictated by social custom and pressure. The increased affluence among Jews, especially in America but now even in Israel, has created a materialistic bent that imperils the more traditional values of modesty and humility and more seriously forces those less endowed to forgo their dignity and seek assistance just to prevent the greater embarrassment in their own communities of having a substandard affair. Many rabbis address these regrettable social developments in sermons and other exhortatory media, but they remain reluctant to institute measures that could genuinely reverse these disturbing trends.[93] In a liberal, capitalistic environment, where all pursue their own desires unfettered by moral restraints or social considerations, law is seen as interfering in the individual's freedom to spend money as he or she wishes, unless actual aggression or harm is being caused. But this is far from the ideal of nurturing a holy community, the traditional task of *halachah*.

———————————

[92]For a review of the relevant issues, see Yitzchak Gottlieb, "Understanding the Heter Mechira," *Journal of Halakha and Contemporary Society* 26 (1993): 5–57.

[93]For a parallel in the rabbinic period, see Babylonian Talmud, *Ketubot* 8b, where costs of a funeral reached such a prohibitive level that some mourners simply left their dead and fled rather than suffer the embarrassment of a simple funeral. Rabban Gamliel deliberately ordered his own funeral to be as simple as possible, and the populace followed in his footsteps.

Of course, there are many reasons that may account for this passivity: rabbinic authority is, in fact, a small shadow of what it once was, regrettably forcing many rabbis to consider popular opinion before enacting certain rulings; the lack of institutional and social cohesion in the Jewish community makes it very difficult to implement significant changes or monitor their observance;[94] and within Orthodoxy, which has defined itself over and against the Reform and Conservative denominations precisely in its commitment not to change the law, there is self-imposed restraint to implement any far-reaching halakhic changes, as necessary as they may be.[95] Furthermore, we cannot discount that the Jews' very presence in a Lockean system, especially in America, has influenced their views of *halachah*. In defending Jewish law before the bar of contemporary culture, many have adopted the terminology and conceptual apparatus of secular law in their apologia.[96] For most legalists, Jewish law is no different from American law (or any secu-

---

[94]Some ultra-Orthodox communities, which are much more insular and cohesive, have been able to apply some restraint on spending, since affiliation defines the identity of the members. The leaders of some hasidic groups—the Gerrer *rebbe* is perhaps the most noted in apocryphal anecdotes that circulate among the ultra-Orthodox—have enacted some measures to curb the trend.

[95]Jacob Katz was one of the first to point out that "Orthodoxy" is as modern a phenomenon as Reform, and its claims about preserving the old traditions were simply part of its anti-Reform polemic. See Jacob Katz, "Orthodoxy in Historical Perspective," *Studies in Contemporary Jewry* 2 (1986): 3–17. See also Moshe S. Samet, "The Beginnings of Orthodoxy," *Modern Judaism* 8 (1988): 249–69. The reluctance of the ultra-Orthodox in Hungary even to *portray* Judaism as halakhically pluralistic, let alone dynamic and evolving, is well documented by Michael K. Silber, "The Emergence of Ultra-Orthodoxy: The Invention of a Tradition," in Jack Wertheimer, ed., *The Uses of Tradition: Jewish Continuity in the Modern Era* (New York, 1992), 23–84.

[96]One exception is Dr. Isaac Breuer, who insisted on the fundamental differences of Jewish and secular law, which necessarily lead to conflicting implications. See Isaac Breuer "The Philosophical Foundations of Jewish and Modern Law," in Jacob S. Levinger, ed., *Concepts of Judaism* (Jerusalem, 1974), 53–81.

lar, liberal system), and it need only intervene when the level of aggression of one against another becomes intolerable.

While many of these factors are external to *halachah*, it is noteworthy to mention a possible internal cause: the increased codification of Jewish law. When discussing the history of *halachah*, one must be aware that the legal and textual landscape did not remain the same. Aside from the relative social insularity of medieval Jewish communities, the halakhic system itself was extraordinarily pluralistic, with toleration of virtually any opinion that could find support or sanction in the rabbinic sources. In fact, it is not clear that one can refer to a "halakhic system" at all during this period. There was wide latitude within Jewish law, and some rabbis employed this latitude to institute rules and laws that would benefit their communities.

However, during the Middle Ages, there were already attempts to reduce the diversity of *halachah* and to codify only one or two positions on a given subject. Given the multiplication of views, this is quite understandable; limiting options helps to unite a community and to sharpen its self-definition, particularly in the face of schismatic challenges. Codes were also preferred within Islam, inclining those in its orbit to pursue a similar enterprise. Thus, in the twelfth century, Maimonides composed a a major code of Jewish law, partially intended to emulate his Muslim peers and partially intended to delegitimize the Karaites who rejected many rabbinic interpretations of the Torah. The codificatory trend continued (interestingly, in Spain and the Middle East but not in Northern Europe) with the *Arba'ah Turim* of Jacob Ben Asher in the fourteenth century, and the *Shulchan Aruch* of Joseph Caro in the sixteenth century. Due to a variety of reasons, Caro's code, combined with the glosses of Moses Isserless,[97] within a century of its initial printing achieved worldwide acceptance as the authoritative code of Jewish law. On most issues, only one or two positions are cited, thus removing other opinions from the domain of

---

[97]See Isadore Twersky, "Shulchan 'Aruk: Enduring Code of Jewish Law," *Judaism* 16 (1967): 141–58, reprinted in Isadore Twersky, *Studies in Jewish Law and Philosophy* (New York, 1982).

"legitimate," that is, normative, views.[98] Attempting to enact rulings that are not explicitly sanctioned in Caro's code is systemically difficult, inclining contemporary authorities to seek only those solutions that have some basis in the codes. Given the dramatically different set of religious and social circumstances, it is unlikely that an answer will be found that addresses the widespread abuses of the *agunah* in a fundamental way.

Over the last several decades, divorce rates have steadily increased throughout the industrialized world, and the religiously committed community has not been immune to this trend. Unfortunately, in the Jewish case, the legal fallout of this phenomenon has been the widespread use of extortion by the husbands before granting their wives the *get* they so desperately need in order to close this agonizing chapter in their lives and move on. The worst tragedy is the *agunah* who remains in perpetual limbo, married yet single, unable to enter into serious relationships because her prior marriage has not been officially terminated.

The aim of this chapter has not been to offer practical solutions to a clearly vexing problem. We chose not to review the legitimacy of existing legal options or to propose new ones, for that is neither within our expertise nor appropriate to this forum. Rather, in the spirit of this project, we have sought to shed light on a contemporary crisis within the Jewish community by informing an otherwise insular discussion with the philosophical reflection and comparative analysis that a meeting of scholars affords. For only by greater insight and deeper understanding will Jacob be able to ascend the ladder hitherto reserved for angels alone.

---

[98]On the normative preference the ultra-Orthodox gave the *Shulchan Aruch* precisely because it generally codified only one opinion, see Silber, "The Emergence of Ultra-Orthodoxy," 48ff.

4

RELIGIOUS HUMAN RIGHTS
IN THE STATE OF ISRAEL

Asher Maoz

Tel Aviv University[1]

The Israeli approach to religious human rights is inherently eclectic. It combines traditional and new theories, communal and individual rights, freedoms from religion and religious coercion, freedoms of religion from state intervention, and equality among religions and differential treatment of them. These eclectic principles are rooted in historical, theological, political, and national grounds. Perhaps the most significant factor contributing to the complexity of religious human rights in the State of Israel is that this part of the world—the Holy Land—is the birthplace of monotheism. The Holy Land has been the subject of several "holy wars." It occupies a central place in the theology of many religions, including the three main monotheistic religions, and each religion has its own view of the relationship of state and religion, which views sometimes come into conflict. Moreover, the principles and practices of previous regimes that governed the Holy Land still work their influence, even though today Israel is predominantly Jewish in culture and religion.

---

[1]I would like to extend my gratitude to the many individuals and institutions who furnished vital information for the preparation of this chapter. I would also like to thank Tal Arbel, my research assistant.

RELIGIOUS DEMOGRAPHY AND STRUCTURE OF ISRAEL

The population of the State of Israel at the end of 1974 consisted of 5,473,100 people, 81.15 percent (4,441,300) of whom were Jewish. The population at the end of 1993 was about the same (5,327,600), with 81.37 percent Jewish, 14.1 percent Muslim, 2.85 percent Christian, and 1.68 percent Druze and others.[2]

Jews

The Jewish religious population in Israel is overwhelmingly Orthodox. Although a Conservative congregation of German Jews has worshiped in Jerusalem since 1937, the non-Orthodox streams are fairly new in Israel. They were generally founded by recent immigrants from Anglo-Saxon countries, mainly from the United States, and by Israelis who have been exposed to their practices when spending prolonged periods of time there. Although non-Orthodox groups are spreading in Israel, their numbers are still fairly small. Possibly, the social functions performed by these groups abroad are either not viewed as relevant by most Israelis or are regarded as functions being taken care of by other institutions in Israel.

Even many Israelis who are nonobservant still identify Judaism with Orthodoxy.[3] The Orthodox stream is divided into the National Religious and the Haredi ultra-Orthodox. The latter is subdivided into dozens of sects, each concentrated around a rabbi. In general, the difference between the National Religious movement and the ultra-Orthodox is expressed in their attitude toward the State of Israel. The National Religious movement is Zionist in its concepts, intermingles with the nonreligious population, and fully participates

----

[2]These figures are provided in the Central Bureau of Statistics. It is easy to get data on religious affiliations of Israeli subjects, since, under the provisions of the Population Registry Act of 1965, the religious affiliation of each subject is noted.

[3]See Ephraim Tabory, "Religious Rights as a Social Problem in Israel," *Israel Yearbook on Human Rights* 11 (1981): 256, 262.

in national projects. The ultra-Orthodox groups tend to live a segregated life and are non-Zionist, even anti-Zionist, in their philosophy; the most extreme of these groups do not even recognize the legitimacy of the State of Israel and shun its authorities and institutions. However, both the National Religious and the ultra-Orthodox movements (except for the most extreme Haredi sects) take an active part in Israel's political life. They are represented, through their own political parties, in its House of Representatives, the Knesset, and participate in its coalition governments.

There are various estimates of the number of religious Jews living in Israel.[4] Whatever the exact number, only a minority observes the precepts of Jewish religion, the *halachah*, in daily life. Nevertheless, it is wrong to regard Israeli society as secular. In a recent comprehensive study conducted among the adult Jewish population in Israel,[5] only 24 percent of the respondents regarded themselves as "totally nonobservant," and only 7 percent described themselves as "anti religious." Moreover, when asked about observance of specific precepts of religion, even the figure of 24 percent seems high. For example, over 70 percent of those who regarded themselves as "totally nonobservant" still viewed the celebration of the *bar mitzvah* as "important" or "very important," and half of them favored its celebration in synagogue. Again, 70 percent of those same respondents regarded religious circumcision as "important" or "very important," and 56 percent percent of them thought similarly with regard to wedding ceremonies

---

[4]In the 1992 elections to the Knesset, the religious parties scored 345,177 votes out of 2,615,159 valid ballots (13.2 percent) and are represented by 16 out of 120 members of the Knesset. However, it is futile to base an estimate of the proportion of religious people within Israeli society upon religious representation in Parliament. Not only are the elections to the Knesset boycotted by the extreme Orthodox, but many religious Jews vote also for nonreligious parties. It is equally futile to base this estimate on school enrollment, for "traditional," and even religious, parents sometimes send their children to nonreligious schools, and nonreligious parents send their children to religious schools in order to get a "Jewish" education.

[5]Shlomit Levy et al., *Beliefs, Observance and Social Interaction among Israeli Jews* (Jerusalem, 1993) (Hebrew).

being performed by a rabbi. Indeed, 4 percent of the "totally nonobservants" nevertheless regarded themselves as "traditional." A survey conducted on the eve of Yom Kippur in 1995 reveals a similar attitude—79 percent of the adult Jewish population declared their intention to fast on the Day of Atonement.[6]

There are several possible explanations for this seeming contradiction of religious identification and affiliation, on the one hand, and persistent religious observance and practice, on the other. An important factor is the national character of the Jewish religion. To be part of the Jewish people is, implicitly, to be part of the Jewish religion. The identification with religion is not restricted to the Jewish population. Indeed, religious adherence is most common.

Karaites

The Karaites ("people of the Scriptus") are a Jewish sect that departed from the mainstream of Judaism ("Rabbinical Judaism") in the eighth century c.e. They observe only the Commandments of the Torah, and disregard post-biblical *halachah*. They are a small group, with estimates as high as 25,000 people, though judging by statistics of marriage and divorce, the correct number seems to be about half that amount. The Karaites have their own synagogues and religious institutions. They are Jewish, although rabbis of *Askenazi* (European) origin will not marry them to Jews, while rabbis of *Sefardi* (Oriental) origin tend to be more lenient on the matter. This difference in treatment may be historically based: the Jews in Egypt enjoyed a good relationship with the Karaites, while their brethren in Eastern Europe disconnected themselves from the Jews. The Karaite religious leadership also opposes intermarriage with "Rabbinical Jews."

Samaritans

The origin of the Samaritans is somewhat obscure. They follow numerous Jewish customs in their religious practice, yet they are not regarded as Jewish. Today there are about 600 Samarites,

---

[6]Per a poll conducted by Dahaf Institute, with a possible 4 percent error.

half living in the Israeli township of Holon, and half in Nablus in Samaria, near the holiest site of their religion, Mount Grizim. They are led by priests headed by the elder priest, called the Great Priest.

Muslims[7]

Most of the Muslims in Israel adhere to the Sunnite rite. Out of the four schools of faith within Sunnite Islam, the Shafi'i mazhab is most common among rural Muslims, the Hanafi mazhab is prominent in urban areas. The Shar'ia religious courts of the Muslims follow the Hanafi mazhab school. Most Muslims in Israel are Arabs, though the Circassian community, which is of Caucasus origin, are also Muslims of the Sunnite rite. Unlike Arab Muslims, members of the Circassian community are enlisted in the Israeli army, as are the Bedouins, as well as the Druze who are not Muslims. Another non-Arabic sect is the Ahmedans, of Punjab origin, with some 300 adherents in Israel. Their Middle Eastern center is in Haifa. They engage in missionary work, but they oppose religious coercion and the spread of Islam through "holy war" (*jihad*). Many of the Muslims in Israel live in villages. There are also Arab towns with large Muslim populations. There are a few mixed Jewish-Arabic townships. The Muslims live within a traditional community and are characterized by strong religious feelings, which might have been strengthened by nationalistic motivations. They have not been immune to the recent fundamentalist tides in the Muslim world. A political religious movement called "The Islamic Movement" has been created, which combines religious fundamentalism with nationalistic ideology. The movement has gained strength, and encouraged by its success, the leadership of the movement is considering standing for elections to the Knesset.

---

[7]See Odi Stendel, *The Minorities in Israel: Trends in the Development of the Arab and Druze Communities 1948–1973* (Jerusalem, 1973); id., *The Arab in Israel: Between Hammer and Anvil* (Jerusalem, 1992) (Hebrew); Aharon Layish, ed., *The Arabs in Israel: Continuity and Change* (Jerusalem, 1981) (Hebrew).

Christians[8]

In spite of their relatively small number, Christians in Israel are divided into some thirty-five different churches and denominations. This variety of churches should be of no surprise, given the central role of the Holy Land in Christianity and the vast number of holy Christian sites in Israel. The largest churches are Greek Catholic and Greek Orthodox, each comprising nearly one-third of the Christian population. Another large community is the Roman Catholic Church. The Maronite Church has considerably fewer followers. Other churches have a rather small number of followers, in some cases no more than a few dozen members. The Chaldean Church, for example, is headed by a clergyman, himself a former Presbyterian, who has virtually no community. Besides the locally established churches, there are representatives of several overseas churches. The number of Christians and of Christian churches has grown substantially since the 1967 War and the unification of Jerusalem under Israeli rule. Most of the Christians in Israel are Arabs.

Today, Catholic Churches, collectively, claim the largest number of Christians in Israel. These include the Latin Church with some 20,000 followers; six Unitarian Catholic Churches; the Greek Catholic Church, which considers itself the descendent of the first Christians in the Holy Land, with some 45,000 members; the Maronites with 2,000 members; and four other Catholic Churches. The Greek Orthodox Church is the largest among the Orthodox churches with some 45,000 members. Other Orthodox churches include the Russian Orthodox Church. Prior to 1967, this Orthodox Church was associated solely with Russian Mission representing the Russian Orthodox Patriarchate of Moscow (the "Red Russian Church"); after the 1967 War, the new occupied territories brought into Israel churches and convents associated with the Russian Church in exile situated in New York (the "White Russian Church"). The Rumanian Orthodox Church is also represented

---

[8]See Saul A. Colbi, *Christianity in the Holy Land* (Tel Aviv, 1969); id., *Christian Churches in Israel* (Jerusalem, 1969); A. Roy Eckardt, ed., *Christianity in Israel* (New York, 1971).

through the Rumanian Orthodox Mission. Israel also is home to the Monophysite Churches. These are pre-Chalcedonian churches, which emerged in the fifth century after the theological split within the Western Church regarding Christ's nature. They comprise four churches: the Armenian (Orthodox or Gregorian) Church with over 2,000 believers; the Coptic Church and the Syrian-Jacobite (Orthodox) Church with about 1,000 followers each; and the Ethiopian Church with about 100 members. Alongside these are more than twenty Protestant Churches, of more recent origin, including the Church of England, Lutheran Church, Scottish Presbyterian Church, Society of Friends, Baptists, Pentecostals, Seventh Day Adventists, and Mennonites—all claiming some 4,000 members. Given their late arrival to Israel, they are not in possession of holy places. In 1959 the Israel-American Institute of Biblical Studies was founded as a seminar for Protestant clergy.

The Druze[9]

The Druze community stems from the Isma'alia, an extreme sect of Shi'ite Muslims, yet they are not Muslim. The basics of the Druze faith are secret and are not known even within the community. The Druze do not accept converts. Most of the Druze are concentrated in Syria (350,000), in Lebanon (300,000), and in Israel (90,000) where they constitute 1.7 percent of its population. They live mainly in villages, in five of which they constitute the entire population. Following the death of the veteran leader of the Druze community in Israel, Sheikh Amin Tarif, heated disputes broke out regarding the nomination of a new leadership. These disputes suggest that they are attempts to liberalize and modernize the Druze community.

The Baha'i Faith

Like the Druze, the Baha'i faith originated in Islam, but disconnected itself from it. The international headquarters of the community is situated in Haifa, where the religious leadership convenes.

---

[9]See Stendel, *The Minorities in Israel*; id., *The Arab in Israel*; Layish, ed., *The Arabs in Israel*.

In Israel, there are some 300 Baha'is, most of them foreign citizens who serve in the community's institutions.

LEGAL STATUS AND ORGANIZATION OF RELIGIOUS COMMUNITIES[10]

The policy of the State of Israel toward religion and its relationship to the state must be understood in its historical context. The basic structure of church–state relations was established during the Ottoman era, which preceded the British occupation of Palestine. During that period, Islam was the established religion of the Empire. Muslim religious law, the *Shari'a*, was applied by Muslim religious courts, particularly in the area of family law. Muslim law drew a distinction between "heathens" and the Jewish and Christian religions that were based on the Sacred Book (the *Kitabaia*). While heathens were severely restricted, the Turkish Sultan adopted a "millet" system for "religions of the Book," which afforded them organizational autonomy and jurisdiction in matters of personal status. Jewish and Christian communities were not automatically recognized; they were required to procure a special charter from the Sultan; this charter would define the legal status of the community[11] and the jurisdiction of the courts.

This Ottoman structure of church–state relations was largely preserved by the British. The Palestine Order in Council of 1922, as amended, granted eleven religious communities autonomy in matters of personal law and communal jurisdiction—Muslims, Jews, and nine Christian Churches.[12] Interestingly, in spite of the power conferred upon them, the Palestinian Government did not

---

[10]See Edoardo Vitta, *The Conflict of Laws in Matters of Personal Status in Palestine* (Tel-Aviv, 1947).

[11]Frederic M. Goadby, *International and Inter-Religious Private Law in Palestine* (Jerusalem, 1926).

[12]These are the Eastern Orthodox, Roman Catholic, Gregorian Armenian, Armenian Catholic, Syrian Catholic, Chaldean Uniate, Greek Catholic Melkite, Maronite, and Syrian Orthodox.

grant recognition to the Anglican Church, nor to any other religious communities during the Mandate era. (The Israeli Government, by contrast, extended its recognition to the Druze, evangelical Episcopal, and Baha'i communities.) The Palestine Order in Council assured these communities full autonomy in their internal affairs, subject to any future enactments. Recognized communities were given exclusive jurisdiction over their internal constitution and their administration of religious endowments foundations (*wakfs*). Muslim religious courts no longer served as state courts, though they continued to enjoy broader jurisdiction than Jewish and Christian courts.

In practice, the Palestinian Government dealt differently with each of the recognized religious communities. All Christian communities were organized on an internal basis, and were largely left alone.[13] The Jewish community was more closely regulated by the High Commissioner, which allowed the rabbinical court to operate only over persons who had voluntarily subjected themselves to its jurisdiction by registering in the register of the Jewish Community. On the other hand, Muslim as well as Christian religious courts exercised jurisdiction over all members of their communities. By special order, the Supreme Muslim Council was formed in 1921 and was in charge of the religious affairs of the Muslim community as well as over administration of Muslim *wakfs*. When irregularities occurred in the election of the members of the Council, the High Commission came to appoint members to the Council, and the administration of *wakf* funds was placed in the hands of a specially appointed committee.

Upon its establishment in 1948, the State of Israel adopted this Mandatory law, save for modifications resulting from the establishment of the State.[14] The entire traditional system of personal law and religious jurisdiction was retained. The most important change related to the Jewish community. Rabbinical courts now operated

---

[13]With the exception of the Greek Orthodox community, which was regulated by Ottoman Imperial regulations dating back to 1875 as well as further Mandatory ordinances. All of these ordinances were abolished in 1936.

[14]See section 11 of the Law and Administration Ordinance, 1948.

not only over those who voluntarily accepted their jurisdiction, but over all who belonged to the Jewish people.[15] In 1957, the Druze community was recognized; under a 1962 statute, the same jurisdictional principle relating to rabbinical courts applied to their religious courts.[16] At present, all religious courts have exclusive jurisdiction over members of their respective communities in matters of marriage and divorce. In other matters of personal status, some courts enjoy exclusive jurisdiction, while others exercise concurrent jurisdiction with the civil courts. Moreover, the Knesset has removed several matters from the application of personal law and has applied civil law to them. It is interesting to note that, although Israel is a Jewish state, the Muslim religious court retained its status, which is still wider than that of the Rabbinical or the Christian courts.

While there were no major changes in the traditional jurisdiction of religious communities, substantial changes took place in the organization and administration of the Muslim and the Jewish communities. As for Muslims, the communal organization inherited from the Mandate era collapsed in 1948 when members of the Supreme Muslim Council and of the special committee for administration of *wakfs*, as well as the Qadis of the religious courts, fled the country during the war of independence. The Knesset thereafter abolished the Council, and no new members were appointed to the special committee that, as a result, also dissolved. In their place, the Knesset appointed committees of trustees in the five towns with substantial *wakf* assets. The Custodian of Absentee Property, who is in charge of this property, is vested with full ownership of the *wakf* assets. He must either transfer them to those committees, who must use their profits for the benefit of the Muslim population, or else must use the profits himself for that purpose. The Minister of Religious Affairs has recently expressed his intention to re-establish a religious Muslim Council comprised of Muslim clergymen recommended by Muslim heads of local councils and by the minister.

---

[15]Another significant modification included the imposition of Rabbinical jurisdiction on permanent residency as an alternative to citizenship, as was the case under Mandatory law.

[16]Druze Religious Courts Law, 1962.

The Minister of Religious Affairs has recently promulgated regulations for the internal organization of the Druze community. According to these regulations, a religious Druze council will be established consisting of thirty Druze clergymen, twelve members who are recommended heads of Druze local councils, and twelve members who are appointed by the Minister following his consultation with Druze clergymen and leaders. The Council will represent the Druze community in all religious matters, will engage in religious instruction and the development of religious sites and places of worship as well as religious communal centers, and will decide on all religious non-judicial matters.

By establishing the Druze religious council as well as the Muslim religious Council, the institutional structure of both communities will become, in principle, similar to the institutional structure of the Jewish Community, though on a more centralized basis. Judges of the rabbinical, as well as the Muslim and Druze, religious courts are appointed by the President of the State, upon the recommendation of nomination committees similar to the committee for the selection of Civil Court judges. The committees are headed by the Minister of Religious Affairs and most of their members are appointed by bodies other than the relevant religious community. Only religious courts are under the responsibility of the Minister of Religious Affairs. No statute governs procedures, administration, or appointment of judges to Christian religious courts. Such matters are left to the discretion of each Christian community.

The law sets the structure of Jewish religious institutions. The legal structure and authority of the Chief Rabbinate is set in the Chief Rabbinate Law of 1980. Another statute provides for the establishment of Jewish Religious Councils and defines their powers.[17] The form of electing the Chief Rabbis of the State, the Council of the Chief Rabbinate, the Religious Councils, and City Rabbis is provided for by statutory law. The electing bodies consist of members suggested by the Ministry of Religious Affairs, the local coun-

---

[17]See Jewish Religious Services Law (Consolidated Version, 1971). See Asher Maoz, "Constitutional Law," in Itzhac Zamir, ed., *Introduction to Israeli Law* (Jerusalem, 1995). See David Kretzmer, "Constitutional Law," in Amos Shapira, ed., *Introduction to Israeli Law* (Amsterdam, 1995), 39.

cil, and the local Rabbinate. Moreover, according to an Israeli Supreme Court ruling, candidates for these religious councils do not need to conform to halakhic requirements since the councils govern matters such as marriage for the entire Jewish community, not merely for religious Jews.

ISRAEL AS A JEWISH STATE[18]

Israel was established as a Jewish state. The Declaration of the Establishment of the State of Israel (the "Declaration of Independence") specifically states that Israel will be "a Jewish state in Eretz Israel." This comports with the Balfour Declaration of 1917 and the Resolution of the League of Nations of 1922 calling for the establishment of "a national home for the Jewish people" in Palestine, as well as the U.N. General Assembly Resolution of 1947 (the "Partition Resolution") concerning the establishment of independent Arab and Jewish states in Palestine. Although initially the Declaration of Independence had no constitutional status, it has always expressed "the aspirations of the people and their basic credo"[19] and has served as a vital instrument in interpreting Israel's laws and in introducing extra-legal principles. In 1994, this Declaration was raised to a constitutional level, when two of Israel's Basic Laws, which eventually will form its constitution, were amended and declared that "[h]uman rights in Israel . . . will be safeguarded in the spirit of the principles contained in the Declaration of Independence." Moreover, these Basic Laws, the only ones dealing with human rights, specifically provide that "the values of the State of Israel as a Jewish and Democratic State" are the basis of human rights in Israel. Moreover, in accordance with Basic Law, the Knesset in the Political Parties Law, 1992, enjoined any group whose aims or actions negate the existence of

------

[18]See David Kretzmer, "Constitutional Law," in Amos Shapira, ed., *Introduction to Israeli Law* (Amsterdam, 1995), 39.

[19]*Yardor v. Knesset Central Election Committee* (1965), 19(3) Piskey Din (Law Reports of the Supreme Court of Israel) 365 (Hebrew).

the Israel as "the State of the Jewish People" from registering as a political party and running for the Knesset.

The Jewishness of the State of Israel is reflected in its legislation. The best example is the Law of Return, which confers upon every Jew the right to emigrate to Israel. Such an emigrant (*oleh*) receives automatic Israeli citizenship. The law further recognizes the central role of Zionist institutions in the immigration of Jews to Israel and in Jewish settlement in Israel. Moreover, "principles of freedom, equity, and peace of Israel's heritage" serve as a source of positive law in Israel.[20] The Jewish character of the State is further reflected in its national days of rest and festivals and in State education. The national flag, the State emblem, and the anthem are all packed with Jewish symbols.

The Jewishness of the State of Israel is a matter of sharp controversy, with positions on the question ranging from the strictly religious to the highly democratic. It is obvious, however, that when declaring Israel to be a Jewish State, the Knesset certainly did not have in mind a halakhic state. After all, the Zionist movement, which led to the establishment of the State, emerged as a reaction to traditional life in the Diaspora. When speaking of Jewish values, the Knesset has in mind the national values of Judaism. But these national values cannot be separated from their religious origin. Judaism is a national religion. National and religious components of Judaism are inseparable. A Jewish State divorced of religion is an impossibility.[21] It is no coincidence that the Zionist Movement chose the traditional prayer shawl as its flag, just as it seems only natural that the founders of the State chose the seven-branched candelabra of the Second Temple as the State emblem.

Nothing in Israeli law, however, confers upon the Jewish religion the status of a State religion. There are no provisions for the preferable treatment of the Jewish religion as such. It is of significance, in this regard, that the separation between state and religion, between state business and religious matters, is alien not only to Judaism but also to Islam, the second largest religion in Israel.

---

[20]See The Foundation of Law Act, 1980

[21]See Asher Maoz, "State and Religion in Israel," in Menachem Mor, ed., *International Perspectives of Church and State* (Omaha, 1993), 239.

The Jewishness of the State of Israel does not contradict its democratic nature. Israel has, from the start, been both a Jewish state and a democratic state, dedicated to equality and basic freedoms. This synthesis of the national, religious, and democratic natures of the State poses some difficulties. Yet, as the Supreme Court has repeatedly stated,[22] these values are not necessarily contradictory, and every effort must be made to enable their co-existence.[23]

Israel, therefore, does not fit easily into any common category of religion–state relations. It is most accurately classified as a multi-religious state, where various religions are recognized, yet none enjoys the status of official state religion.

FREEDOM OF RELIGION AND FREEDOM FROM RELIGION[24]

The Declaration of Independence proclaims that the State of Israel "will guarantee freedom of religion and conscience, of language, education and culture." It further undertakes to "safeguard the Holy

---

[22]See *Neiman v. Chairman of the Central Election Committee to the 12th Knesset* (1988), 42.

[23]See Asher Maoz, "The Values of a Jewish and Democratic State," *Iyunei Mishat* 19 (1994–1995).

[24]See Itzhak Englard, "Law and Religion in Israel," *American Journal of Comparative Law* 35 (1987): 185; id., "Religious Freedom and Jewish Tradition in Modern Israeli Law: A Clash of Ideologies," in Edwin B. Firmage et al., eds., *Religion and Law: Biblical-Judaic and Islamic Perspectives* (Winona Lake, 1990), 365; Ariel Rosen-Zvi, "Freedom of Religion: The Israeli Experience," *Zeitschrift für auslandische öffentliches Recht und Volkerrecht* 46 (1986): 213; Norman L. Cantor, "Religion and State in Israel and the United States," *Tel-Aviv University Studies in Law* 8 (1988): 185; Maoz, "State and Religion in Israel"; Amnon Rubinstein, "Law and Religion in Israel," *Israel Yearbook on Human Rights* 3 (1973): 223; Shimon Shetreet, "Some Reflections on Freedom of Conscience and Religion in Israel," *Israel Yearbook on Human Rights* 4 (1974): 194, 241; Simha Meron, "Freedom of Religion as Distinct from Freedom from Religion in Israel," *Israel Yearbook on Human Rights* 4 (1974): 219; S. Zalman Abramov, *Per-*

Places of all religions." Since these principles were incorporated in the recent Basic Laws, they should be regarded as enjoining entrenched constitutional status.

Israeli Penal Law includes a whole section dealing with offenses against religious and traditional feelings. It imposes a penalty of three years' imprisonment on a person who disturbs religious worship or assaults a worshiper. A similar sanction is imposed for trespassing on a place of worship with the intent to hurt religious people or to revile their religion. One year's imprisonment is imposed on a person who publishes, or voices in a public place, words calculated to outrage the religious feeling or belief of other persons. Further provisions deal with the promotion of ill will between different sections of the population, seditious publications, and racial incitement. A group that incites racism may not be registered as a political party and is deprived of the right to be elected to the Knesset. A bill now pending in the Knesset provides that an offense committed out of racist motives is punishable with double sanctions.

Israeli legislation supports the exercise of religious freedoms in a number of ways. Religious education, for example, which fulfills the requirements of compulsory education, is heavily supported by the state. Various regulations enable non-Jewish believers to carry on their religious practices without suffering any disadvantage.

Israeli courts also encourage freedom of religion. The Supreme Court has interpreted the term "freedom of religion" to include freedom of worship and not merely the freedom of belief; thus, a public authority that permitted social activities in its halls must also permit use of the hall for religious worship.[25] During the Gulf War,

---

petual Dilemma: Jewish Religion in the Jewish State (Rutherford, NJ, 1976); Donna E. Arzt, "Religious Freedom in a Religious State: The Case of Israel in Comparative Constitutional Perspective," Wisconsin International Law Review 9 (1990): 1; Ruth Lapidoth et al., "Freedom of Religion in Israel," in Alfredo M. Rabello, ed., Israeli Reports to the XLV International Congress of Comparative Law (Jerusalem, 1994).

[25]Peretz v. Head of Local Council of Kfar Shmaryahu (1963), 17 Piskey Din 2101.

the Supreme Court made it clear that when supplying gas masks the government should endeavor to supply men who grow beards out of religious conviction with special masks.[26] Many more examples can be cited.

Freedom of religion may be curtailed on the grounds of pressing public interest.[27] One example of such regulation concerns religious conversion. Each individual enjoys the right to change his or her religion. However, since such a change may affect the personal law and family law governing the neophyte, the rights of other members of the neophyte's family are given special protection.[28] Moreover, the religion of a minor may not be changed against the wish of either parent, save with the court's approval. And, while missionary work and proselytizing are legal, using material inducement to conversion constitutes a criminal offense.[29] A second example may be found in the statutory prohibitions against bigamy or polygamy. Even though polygamy is common among Muslims and to some extent with Jewish newcomers from Arab countries, the Supreme Court upheld the prohibition. The Court was of the opinion that polygamy was a privilege, not a religious precept of Islam.[30] Though the Court's position has been criticized as an infringement of the freedom of religion, it is aimed at protecting the public order. A third example concerns regulation of marriage. The Knesset has declared that the severance of marriage, without a court order, against the wife's wishes constitutes a criminal offense. The Knesset also imposed a minimal marriage age for women, which was substantially higher than was customary among Muslims, especially Bedouins, as well as among several Jewish groups. The Supreme Court declared the

---

[26]See *Miller v. Minister of Defence* (1991), 45(2) Piskey Din 293.

[27]In the absence of a written constitution, there is no formal obstacle for the Knesset to infringe this freedom—subject to the entrenched Basic Laws—for whatever reason it may deem fit. The courts, however, will try to interpret such legislation in accordance with civil liberties.

[28]See Religious Community (Change) Ordinance, 1927. Thus, the unilateral change of one's religion will not affect the validity of one's marriage and the applicable law in matters of marriage, divorce, and alimony.

[29]See Penal Law Amendment (Enticement to Change Religion), 1977.

[30]See *Milchem v. Shari'a Court* (1954), 8 Piskey Din 910.

banning of women from serving on Jewish Religious Councils illegal, though the banning was based on religious grounds.[31]

Freedom *from* religion, being rooted in guarantees of freedom of conscience, seems to stand on an equal footing with freedom *of* religion. Yet, in the Israeli legal system, the protection of the freedom from religion seems weaker than the protection of freedom of religion. From a Jewish religious point of view, even demanding this freedom may be regarded as illegitimate. Those ultra-Orthodox Jewish groups who do recognize the legitimacy of the State of Israel demand it to be instituted on the law of the Torah. The more liberal Orthodox approach demands the imposition of religious behavior, or at least the prevention of anti-religious behavior, in public. Orthodox Jews have a genuine problem with freedom from religion, since under the *halachah* every Jew is responsible not merely for his own behavior but also for that of his fellow Jew. Moreover, religious people do not regard the clash between freedom of religion and freedom from religion as a conflict of ideologies, but as a conflict between ideology and convenience.

This latter approach finds support in some decisions of the Supreme Court. Thus, when the Rabbinical Court, consistent with *halachah*, refused to marry a male of priestly origin (a Cohen) with a divorcée, the Supreme Court recognized the validity of their wedding ceremony, which had been conducted in private. On the other hand, when a secular couple wished to marry in a private ceremony in order to avoid the presence of a rabbi at their wedding, the Supreme Court refused to intervene.[32] Yet the courts, notably the Supreme Court, have sought to soften the effect of religious legislation by giving maximum interpretation to civil liberties. Moreover, the Supreme Court has ruled that no administrative authority may act to further religious interests unless specifically authorized to do so by the legislature. This impediment has also been applied to subordinate legislation. These judicial tactics are of major significance in the protection of civil liberties, especially the freedom from religion.

---

[31]*Shakdiel v. Minister of Religious Affairs* (1988), 42(2) Piskey Din 221, abridged in *Israel Law Review* 24 (1990): 128.

[32]*Segev v. Rabbinical Court* (1967), 21(2) Piskey Din 505.

Religiously motivated legislation in Israel is not limited to enabling religious people to observe the precepts of religion. It is also intended to impose a religious way of life in the public arena, thereby affecting the freedom of the nonobservant civil subject. Some writers have attempted to justify this intrusion on the freedom from religion with arguments respecting freedom of religion. Thus, it has been suggested that nonobservance of the Shabbat by the public in general will impede the rights of the observant Jew, who will not be able to compete in the marketplace. He will also be deprived of the social and cultural activity of Israeli society if that takes place on Shabbat.[33]

It must be stressed that the beliefs of ultra-Orthodox Jews may require them to attempt to impose religious norms upon the nonobservant. Since religious political parties are traditional partners to governmental coalition, this leads to a wide range of religiously motivated legislation and administrative activities. These initiatives do not necessarily stop at the door of private homes. For example, the Israel Land Administration, which owns some 85 percent of the land in Israel, used to impose on its lessees a duty to abstain from doing work in their private homes on Shabbat and religious festivals. Only judicial intervention ended this procedure.[34]

The recent Basic Laws provide a source of freedoms for each religion. Particularly the provisions in the Basic Law on Human Dignity and Freedoms are phrased in broad terms that lend themselves to broad interpretation. Sections 2, 4, and 7 of this law specifically protect human dignity, the right to privacy, and personal confidentiality. These guarantees, coupled with the guarantee of freedom of occupation in the other Basic Law, provide ample protection for each religion. The identical purpose clause in both Basic Laws, that their purpose is to entrench the values of the State of Israel as a Jewish and a Democratic State, is certainly a provision

---

[33]See Simha Meron, "Freedom of Religion as Distinct from Freedom from Religion," 223.

[34]*Oman v. Israel Land Administration* (1969), 67 Psakim Mehoziim (Law Reports of the District Courts), 284 (Hebrew).

upon which both freedom of religion and freedom from religion may be based.[35]

Judicial intervention in the area of religious freedoms entered a new phase with the enactment of the Basic Laws. The Supreme Court declared that legislation that would prohibit the import of nonkosher meat would violate the provisions of Basic Law: Freedom of Occupation and is therefore invalid. Judicial intervention is sometimes frustrated by Knesset future legislation, as happened in the case of the import of nonkosher meat when the Basic Law itself had been amended, yet in most cases the rulings are respected. Moreover, the rejection of religiously motivated activities of the administration drastically reduces the incidences of state intervention with freedom from religion.

GROUP RIGHTS AND THEIR EFFECT ON RELIGIOUS FREEDOMS

As was mentioned previously, wide religious autonomy is accorded to religious communities in Israel. These communities enjoy special legal status and have jurisdiction, inter alia, in matters of marriage and divorce. This religious autonomy substantially affects the rights of nonobservers, for religious law and jurisdiction in family matters apply also to observers and nonobservers alike. Marriage in Israel may take place only according to religious law[36]—although the Supreme Court has recently limited the scope of religious law and enlarged the application of civil law in mat-

---

[35]This possible interpretation is somewhat ironic, since the Knesset has not, to date, adopted a comprehensive bill of rights, given the firm religious opposition to it. Religious political parties feared that a bill of rights may hamper existing and potential religious legislation on grounds that it violates basic rights of nonbelievers.

[36]It should be pointed out that a nationalist justification has been asserted in support of this practice, viz., to avoid splitting the nation over the issue.

ters connected with marriage.[37] The Supreme Court of Israel has sought to alleviate the hardships of such religious laws for non-observers by recognizing a whole range of alternatives to religious marriages—marriages performed abroad even via proxies, private religious ceremonies celebrated in Israel between spouses who have been rejected by the rabbinate, and even simple *de facto* marriages.[38]

The autonomy granted to the Orthodox Jewish community, in particular, infringes the freedom of non-Orthodox Jews. Jewish religion in Israel is usually identified with Orthodoxy. Thus, for example, an attempt to force the Minister of Religious Affairs to authorize Reform rabbis to perform marriages has failed.[39] Here, too, the Supreme Court has removed some of the worst discrimination. The Court ruled, for example, that a person who underwent conversion "in any Jewish community abroad" will qualify for registration as Jewish under the Population and Registration Law.[40] This decision opened the way for Reform and Conservative converts to immigrate to Israel and register as Jews. The Court also ruled that Reform and Conservative members cannot be disqualified from being appointed to Religious Councils[41] and ordered a local council to make a public hall available for the Reform community services during the High Holidays.[42] The Court also ordered that state funding be accorded applicable religious institutions of both the Reform and the Conservative movements.[43]

------

[37]See the recent landmark ruling in *Bavli v. Bavli* (1992), not yet published.

[38]See, generally, Amnon Rubinstein, "The Right to Marriage," *Israel Yearbook on Human Rights* 3 (1973): 233.

[39]See *Progressive Judaism Movement v. Minister of Religious Affairs* (1989), 43(2) Pisky Din 661, abridged in *Israel Law Review* 25 (1991): 110.

[40]See *Shas Movement v. Minister of Interior,* 40(4) Piskey Din 436. See also *Miller v. Minister of Interior* (1986), 40(40) Piskey Din 436. A petition to recognize the legal effect of reform conversion performed in Israel is pending before the Supreme Court.

[41]See *Hofman v. The City Council of Jerusalem,* not yet published.

[42]*Peretz v. Head of Local Council of Kfar Shmaryahu,* 17 Piskey Din 2101.

[43]See *Hebrew Union College v. Minister of Religious Affairs,* not yet published.

The status of the Karaites, let alone unrecognized religious communities, is even more problematic. As Jews, the Karaites are subject to the jurisdiction of the rabbinical courts. Yet their entire religious conviction is based on the rejection of rabbinical teachings. The Ministry of Religious Affairs sought to solve this problem by appointing a marriage registrar from within the community and by recognizing the validity of divorces performed by the Karaite religious court. Yet, since this court has no binding legal status, it may try divorce suits only if both parties are willing to accept its jurisdiction and even then the legal effect of its rulings is questionable. Even more unsatisfactory is the governance of marriage and divorce in unrecognized religious communities. They have their marriage registrars, yet they do not have their own religious courts and must instead apply to the courts of recognized communities.

The special legal status conferred upon Jewish religious institutions and communities, however, invites intrusions not only on the religious freedom of others, but also on the religious freedom of the Jewish religious community. The price these religious institutions must pay for having a state legal status is the intervention of state authorities into their activities. Christian tribunals, which lack such legal status, have no state interference in appointments to their tribunals; such matters are left to the total discretion of the communities. Rabbinical courts, by contrast, are constituted by law. Therefore, secular state institutions have a say in the way religious judges are elected. The same goes for other Jewish religious institutions, such as the Chief Rabbinate and the Religious Councils.

State intervention is not limited to elections of officials to statutory religious bodies. The entire operation and decisions of these bodies are subject to judicial review, mainly by the Supreme Court of Israel. A case in point is *Raskin v. Jerusalem Religious Council and the Chief Rabbis of Jerusalem*.[44] The Chief Rabbinate of Jerusalem granted a *kashrut* certificate to wedding halls only if such weddings did not include "immoral performances," such as belly dancing. This condition was not without halakhic basis; moreover, no court

---

[44]44(2) Piskey Din 673, abridged in *Israel Law Review* 26 (1992): 77; Jerusalem Post Report, 150. See also Maoz, "State and Religion in Israel," 239.

of law in a country committed to freedom of religion would seemingly have intervened in such matter. Yet the Supreme Court of
Israel declared the rabbinate's demand illegal and ordered it to
grant an unconditional certificate. The court did so, since the rabbinate was acting under the authority conferred upon it in the 1983
Kashrut (Prohibition of Deceit) Law, which provides that "in issuing a *kashrut* certificate, the rabbi shall have regard to the *kashrut*
laws only."

Such review of the activities of religious institutions—particularly those of the Chief Rabbinate,[45] supposedly the highest religious authority in the state—has raised much criticism among
religious Jews. Legally, however, in carrying out functions imposed by law, the Chief Rabbinate simply functions as an administrative agency of the state, and as such is subject to judicial
review.[46] It should be noted, moreover, that the Supreme Court
demonstrates more readiness to intervene when Jewish religious
institutions are involved than when the petitions concern other
religious communities.

RELIGION IN THE MILITARY

From the time of their establishment, the Israeli Defense Forces
have insisted that there will be no separate units for religious soldiers.[47] Instead, conditions had to be set in all army units in order

---

[45]Itzhak Englard, "Die Stellung des judischen Rabbinats im Rahmen
des Staat Israel," *Festschrift zum 70. Geburtstag von Werner Kagi*
(Tübingen, 1979), 101. It should be noted, moreover, that the status of
the Chief Rabbinate results from the Law of the Knesset. Unlike Christianity, Judaism does not recognize any hierarchy among rabbis. The
status of each rabbi is determined by the number of his followers and
by their devotion.

[46]See, generally, Asher Maoz, "The Rabbinate and the Rabbinical
Courts between the Legal Hammer and the Halakhic Anvil," *Shenaton
Ha-Mishpat Ha-Ivri* 16–17 (1990–1991): 289 (Hebrew).

[47]There are, however, several *yeshivot* (schools of higher halakhic
education) that combine religious studies with active military service.

to enable religious soldiers to serve without affronting their religious commandments. Indeed, one of the first enactments adopted by the Knesset was the Kosher Food for Soldiers Law of 1949. Similar regulations were passed to enable a religious soldier to worship and not to desecrate the Holy Shabbat and Jewish festivals. Such regulations, however, often came at the cost of interfering with nonobservers' rights to be free from religion. Thus, on Shabbat no canteens are open in army units, and no driving is permitted. Before the High Holidays, a "spiritual revival project" takes place in all units, and all soldiers are required to listen to lectures by chaplains on "the values of the High Holidays."[48] These regulations and practices have been rationalized as being based on the nationalistic nature of Judaism and as being useful to maintain national identification and uniformity within the ranks. The latter rationale is also used to justify the traditional religious rites of funerals; only in recent years has the army honored individual family requests for nonreligious funerals.

The Army chaplaincy, which is Orthodox, is a standard military unit headed by the Chief Chaplain at the rank of General, who is also a member of the General Staff. Given this, and the army's almost exclusively Jewish character,[49] it may be said that Orthodox Judaism is the religion of the Israeli Defense Forces. A manual issued by the Chief Chaplaincy, for example, states that it has two aims: to enable soldiers to preserve religion while in service and "to ensure maintenance of religious, spiritual, and moral values, based on the Jewish Torah, by all soldiers and units, as this is the basis for a unified Jewish character for the army, and according to it, it would be feasible to maintain a unified forum in which all Jewish soldiers of whatever religious convictions may live together."

---

[48]Until recently, nonmilitary religious believers, such as the Lubavitch missionaries, were allowed to conduct religious ceremonies and to deliver lectures in army camps.

[49]Minorities who are drafted into the army, such as Druze and Circassians, usually serve in separate units and care is being taken of all their religious needs. Formally, the Chief Rabbinate is in charge of non-Jewish soldiers, but, practically, they are handled by a special staff officer.

STATE FUNDING OF RELIGIOUS INSTITUTIONS

Religious institutions in Israel enjoy wide state financial support—
in the form of both direct funding and tax exemptions. Both forms
of state support are not uniform with regard to the various religious
communities and lack clear criteria to ensure equal support for all
religions. State funding for religious institutions has not developed
on a systematic legal basis. It should be noted that, to some extent, discrimination in one area of state funding for religion may
be offset by preferential treatment in another. Thus, although Christian churches seem to enjoy less direct state funding, they enjoy
tax exemptions to a substantially larger degree than other communities, including Jews and Muslims.

Direct State Funding

Religious institutions are supported by the state. Jewish, Muslim,
and Druze religious courts, which are established under state law
and constitute state organs, are fully financed by the state, as are
other courts of law. The judges of these courts are paid salaries
on a par with the judges of other state courts of law.

Jewish religious needs are furnished by the Jewish Religious
Services Law, 1971, which states that the entire budget of the Religious Councils, as approved by the local council or by the Ministry of Religious Affairs, shall be funded by the government and
by the local council. The state also pays the salaries of the Chief
Rabbis of the state and of local rabbis who are elected according
to law. The Ministry of Religious Affairs provides specific funding
for various needs of religious life, such as participation in the construction of synagogues, cemeteries, and ritual baths, or the supplying of prayer books and other ritual articles. The Ministry
allocates special funding for religious instruction and education,
maintenance of cemeteries, cultivation of ties with Jews in the
Diaspora, and care for the religious needs of new immigrants.

Within the Ministry of Religious Affairs, special departments deal
with Christian, Muslim, Karaite, Druze, and Samarite communities.
This arrangement is apparently designed to enable the Ministry
to tailor its services to the distinct needs of each minority commu-

nity—though some consider this to be a form of preferential treatment of the Jewish community. Since none of the religious services of these minority religious communities operate according to law, a fact that as shown before has its advantages, their budgets are not fully funded by the state.

The Druze community enjoys full financing of its religious courts as well as state funding for other communal activities. This includes state subsidies for the salaries of clergy, operating expenses, and building and maintenance of places of worship.

Muslim religious courts are state courts and are likewise fully financed by the government. The Ministry of Religious Affairs pays the salaries of some three hundred clergy connected with mosques, notably *imams* and *muezzin*. The Ministry also allocates funds for Muslim religious services, as well as for the construction, renovation, and maintenance of mosques and cemeteries. Another important source of income for the Muslim community is the revenue derived from various *wakfs*, now administered by the Custodian of Absentee Property. Representatives of the Muslim community have criticized this arrangement and demanded that the *wakf's* assets be placed in the control of the Muslim community. They have further criticized the seemingly preferential treatment accorded Christians, whose assets are exempt from the Absentee Property Law. The state has replied that Christian properties, unlike Muslim properties, are exempt since they were in 1948 and are now still registered in the individual names of the Archbishop and clergymen, who themselves were not absentees, and not in the corporate names of the church,[50] and that they had an organized church structure within recognized Christian communities, which could administer these properties.[51] This explanation has not satisfied the Muslim leadership. Present govern-

---

[50]The Greek Catholic community was registered in the name of an archdiocese belonging to Archbishop Hakim, who had left Palestine during the 1948 war and was considered technically an absentee. As a result the community's assets were seized by the Custodian. Upon the Archbishop's return to Israel, the assets were released.

[51]Aharon Layish, "The Muslim *Waqf* in Israel," *Asian and African Studies* 2 (1966): 41, 60.

ment guidelines indicate that a special committee of Muslims will be established to administer the *wakf* for and within the Muslim communities.

As mentioned, Christian institutions, which are not state institutions, receive little direct funding but ample tax exemptions. Christian communities do, however, benefit directly from the funding of several important historical sites in Israel. These include the $2 million renovation of the *Via Dolorasal* in the old city of Jerusalem—the last journey of Jesus crossing fourteen stations, from his trial until his crucifixion—as well as the construction of a modern facility for baptizing in the Jordan River near the lake of Galilee and the construction of a special road to an isolated monastery in the Judea Desert. The Israeli administration in Judea and Samaria is also participating in the reformation and construction of other Christian holy sites. The Ministry of Religious Affairs announced its intention to prepare festive celebrations for the second millennium of the birth of Jesus.

Besides the direct funding of religious courts and religious services, the State of Israel supports various religious institutions. These allocations were, in earlier times, openly partisan and not according to legal provisions. The Supreme Court has had to criticize more than one such allocation scheme, leading to reforms and interventions by the State Comptroller. In recent years, such state funding has been more fairly distributed, though Israel still lacks a clear, comprehensive scheme that would equally distribute state funding among the various religious communities and the different sects within each community.

In the past, such state funding came from the general budgets of the different ministries, not from designated resources. This practice was challenged in a 1971 petition to the Supreme Court, when organizers of a music festival where church music was to be played were denied financial support by the Ministry of Education.[52] The Ministry stated that it was not its duty to support the performances of church music. The majority of the court, though expressing discontent with the ministry's decision, ruled that courts

-----

[52]*Abu Gosh v. Ministry of Education and Culture* (1971), 25(2) Piskey Din 821, (1972); *Israel Yearbook of Human Rights* 2 (1972): 336.

are not authorized to intervene in the distribution of funds, which are not regulated by law. The minority opinion by Justice Cohn, however, paved the way for later reform. Justice Cohn disqualified the ministry's considerations, although he was sympathetic to its reservations about funding a performance of *St. John's Passion*, which treats the Jews as being responsible for Jesus Christ's crucifixion. Such considerations, he said, illegitimately discriminate against the artwork of minority religions. Although the law provided no criteria for allocation of funds, content-based discrimination was illegitimate, Justice Cohn concluded, and the ministry's decision should be overruled.

Such decisions notwithstanding, Jewish religious institutions generally enjoy substantially more state funding than do other religions, and most of that funding goes to Orthodox institutions. This is not only a function of demography, that is, the vast preponderance of (Orthodox) Jews in Israel. National, historical, and political factors have all contributed to this disparity as well. Israel, as the homeland of the Jewish people, has assumed as one of its major tasks the maintenance and development of Jewish culture and tradition, which naturally have religious dimensions. Moreover, following the Holocaust, which destroyed the world centers of Jewish learning, Israel assumed the task of replacing those centers in Israel and rebuilding the institutions of learning that were destroyed in Europe. Israel continually strives to maintain the chain of Torah learning and to establish a Torah center in place of the one destroyed. The state thus allocates substantial financial support to *yeshivot* (Jewish religious academies). This policy has won the approval of the Supreme Court in the 1984 case of *Watad v. Ministry of Finance*. In upholding this policy, the Court stressed "the unique and special place of Torah studying among the Jewish people and the place of *Yeshivot* and of the Torah students."[53] Students pursuing traditional study of the Torah were thus worthy of state support. The Court stated, however, that similar allocations should be granted to non-Jewish religious educational institutions, which are parallel to the *yeshivot* when established.

---

[53]*Watad v. Ministry of Finance* (1984), 38(3) Piskey Din 113; *Israel Yearbook of Human Rights* 17 (1987): 267.

Debates over state funding for religious institutions has brought on several rounds of rulings. In a 1983 Supreme Court case, *Central Tomchei Tmimim v. The State of Israel*, the Lubavich movement argued that a state scheme of funding educational institutions discriminated against the movement.[54] In response, the Knesset made allocations of funds to specific religious institutions. Due to parliamentary sovereignty, the Court could not enjoin this Knesset policy, but it did sharply criticize the practice of allocating funds to favored institutions and without objective criteria. It did not regard the remedial proceedings pending in the Knesset as an obstacle to trying the case, and ordered that thereafter no funds could be allocated without "clear, relevant, and equal criteria."

Following the Court's decision, the Attorney General issued directives for governmental support of public institutions. According to the new policy, state money may be allocated to public institutions only in accordance with just and equal criteria. Direct allocation of funds to named institutions on an unequal basis is strictly forbidden. The Foundations of Budget Law was also amended to provide that annual budget laws must specify the state subsidy for each category of public institution and promulgate in the official Gazette the objective criteria and application procedures used for its distributions. Various ministries have, in response, published detailed criteria for the allocation of State funding on an objective and equal basis. Funding for Jewish institutions, as a consequence, is no longer automatic. For example, a recent application by a religious Zionist institution for grants allocated for Orthodox cultural activities was denied by the Ministry of Religious Affairs, and the applicant's appeal was dismissed by the Supreme Court.[55]

The debate on the issue of state funding for religious institutions is far from closed, however. Not only has it been difficult to set objective guidelines, but state funding has remained subject to constant political pressure and preferences. Orthodox and ultra-Orthodox movements traditionally take part in Israeli political life

---

[54] *Central Tomchei Tmimim v. The State of Israel* (1984), 38(2) Piskey Din 273.

[55] *Ma'ale, Religious Zionist Center v. The Minister of Education and Culture and others* (1992), 46(5) Piskey Din, 590.

and were usually part of its coalition governments. Representatives of these movements sponsor allocations that support their own institutions and that discriminate against various non-Orthodox groups in Judaism or against unfavored sects within Orthodoxy. Non-Orthodox Jewish groups, in particular, have often not qualified for funding according to the criteria published by the Minister of Religious Affairs. This has led to further litigation before the Supreme Court. In response, the Ministry of Religious Affairs included a category of "support for other Jewish religious institutions," which provides allocations to institutions affiliated with the Reform and the Conservative movements.

Muslim and Druze religious institutions are allocated even fewer funds by the Ministry—even though Muslim groups receive additional distributions from *wakfs*. Recently, high officials within the Ministry have admitted to discrimination against these groups, and special funds have been distributed in an attempt to bridge the gap. The present Government has declared its intention to rectify the funding of these communities and to treat them equally henceforth. It also made a commitment to integrate the Arab and Druze communities in Israel into areas of state life, to shore up their support for education, welfare, industry, housing, and health services in these communities, and to absorb Arabs and Druze holding academic degrees into the civil service. A progress report published recently by a nonpolitical association for the advancement of equality of opportunity shows considerable progress in this area in recent years.[56] Thus, the state funding of Muslim religious sites in 1994 exceeded twenty times the funding in 1993. The newly appointed Minister of Religious Affairs published a platform in which he pledges commitment to full equalization of financial support for all religions. This reform includes the establishment of a center for the development of religious services and structures for the Muslim community, which will be duly financed and will take care of the existing Muslim holy sites as well as building new mosques and cemeteries. Within this program all existing buildings of the Shari'a Courts will move into new buildings by the end of 1996.

---

[56]Sikkuy, The Association for the Advancement of Equal Opportunity, Annual Progression Report (1993–94).

An administration for Muslim religious services will be established, which will take care of the entire religious services for Muslims, will administer the Muslim clergy, and will take care of Muslim shrines. Ample independence will be conferred upon this administration, which will promote religious services for the Muslim community. Specific care will be taken for the appointment of sufficient Muslim clergymen and in their status and conditions.

This entire policy of state funding of religious organizations is the subject of a special report by the State Comptroller on the Ministry of Religious Affairs.[57] In her report, the State Comptroller sharply criticized both the criteria and their implementation. Following the report, the incoming Minister of Religious Affairs established a public committee that examined the entire matter and offered its recommendations. The Minister adopted these recommendations and in July 1995 published new criteria for allocation of funds. Those criteria were formulated on objective considerations to ensure that no preference may be conferred upon certain institutions. Moreover, the new criteria establish a tight inspection mechanism to insure the equal allocation of funds and their spending in accordance with the criteria.

Besides direct funding by the Ministry of Religious Affairs, religious institutions are eligible for funding from bequests made in favor of the State of Israel, according to the Ministry's recommendations. According to the guidelines published by the Ministry, equal criteria will be applied to Jewish and to non-Jewish institutions and projects. Moreover, funding will be made available to assist the pilgrimages of Muslims to Mecca and Christians to the Holy Land. Special funds will be made available for the encouragement of understanding among Jews, Christians, and Muslims and other religions. The Ministry is also contemplating the establishment of public committees for the advancement of interreligious understanding and of religious tolerance.

Tax Exemptions

Various tax enactments exempt from taxation those public institutions that engage in social and cultural activities, including nonprofit

---

[57]State Comptroller, 45th Annual Report (1994), 236–289.

religious institutions. The Municipal Ordinance, 1938, exempts religious communities from urban property tax on buildings owned by them and used for worship, hospitals, orphanages, religious courts, or clerical housing. The Land Appreciation Tax Law, 1963, exempts from sales tax transfers of real estate without consideration to religious institutions, among others. The Property Tax and Compensation Fund Law, 1961, exempts from income tax religious institutions that yield no income or have all their income devoted to religious purposes. The Income Tax Law, 1985, exempts public institutions with religious objectives from paying income tax. The Value Added Tax Law exempts from taxation nonprofit organizations, which in practice includes religious institutions.

Beyond these exemptions, which are available to all religious communities, a number of extra-legal exemptions are granted to Christian communities. These exemptions are, in fact, a continuation of the capitulation system that operated during the Ottoman .era. Shortly after the establishment of the State of Israel, the Israeli Government, via Ambassador Fischer, and the French Government, via the Deputy Director of the Ministry of Foreign Affairs, Chouvel, exchanged a series of confidential letters on this subject. This correspondence, now known as the Fischer-Chouvel Agreement, exempts from customs and local taxes all goods—religious and other kinds—imported for the use of French and Italian churches, hospitals, hostels, and other affiliated institutions. This agreement also exempts the heads of these churches from customs on their import of vehicles devoted to official use.[58] This special agreement on exemptions applies only to the French and Italian Christian churches. Other Christian churches are either

---

[58]The exchange of the Fischer-Chouvel missives is highly classified and reviewing them is not permitted. It should be noted that Israel holds that this exchange of letters is not a binding agreement but rather represents an understanding to negotiate a detailed agreement. Despite its stand, Israel, in practice, operates in line with the French version, namely, that the exchange of letters constitutes a binding agreement in itself. By and large, the exemption accorded by the Fischer-Chouvel agreement is similar to that provided for foreign embassies in Israel. In 1975 the Government decided to extend these exemptions to all other Christian churches.

refunded for the customs they pay, or they may ask the Ministry of Religious Affairs to pay their customs directly. Other churches also have narrower exemptions: their goods are exempt from customs, but they are exempt from only 30 percent of the urban property tax.

There is no legal basis for these exemptions granted to Christian communities. Indeed, they may even be infringements of the law, since only Christians and Baha'is receive them, not Jews, Muslims, or other religious groups. This disparity of treatment is all the more striking, since Christian churches refrain from incorporating according to state law, and are thus formally prohibited from all exemptions.

Nonetheless, Article 10 of the Fundamental Agreement between the Holy See and the State of Israel signed in 1995 "reaffirm[s] the right of the Catholic Church to property" and provides that a comprehensive agreement will be worked out "on unclear, unsettled, and disputed issues concerning property, economic, and fiscal matters relating to the Catholic Church generally, or to specific Catholic communities or institutions." Such a comprehensive agreement, once reached, will reify these privileges even further, not only for the Catholic Church, but for all Christian churches.

EDUCATION AND RELIGION

Jewish State Education[59]

When the State of Israel was established in 1948, four forms of Jewish education were available, each associated with a political movement—liberal, labor, national religious, and ultra-Orthodox non-Zionist respectively. The State Education Law, 1953, sought to transform the education system to the state. It integrated the existing system into two education systems—the religious state education system and the general state education system—a classic example of the non-separation between state and religion in Israel.

____

[59]See S. Goldstein, "The Teaching of Religion in Government Funded Schools in Israel," *Israel Law Review* 1 (1990): 36–64.

The State Education Law provides that both religious and non-religious schools must teach the values of Jewish culture and the loyalty of the Jewish people. Religious state schools may further give religious content to their way of life, curriculum, teachers, and inspectors. A Council of Religious State Education supervises these state religious schools, setting standards for the hiring and dismissal of teachers and other staff. Teachers are required to be religiously observant, both in public and private life, in order to be models for their students. Teachers whose beliefs or practices prevent them from communicating religious values to their students cannot be part of state religious education.

Not only the teachers, but also the families of teachers are regulated. The Council of Religious Education requires that spouses of teachers observe the precepts of Orthodox Judaism. It further requires that teachers in the religious education system send their children to state religious schools—not general state schools that teach no specific religious values, nor private Orthodox schools that are often non-Zionist, sometimes even anti-Zionist. Failure to abide by these regulations may lead to dismissal of the teacher.

While teachers and other employees in state religious schools must be religiously observant, students need not be. State religious schools may encourage students' families to observe a religious way of life, so as to avoid confusion of the students, but they may not impose these demands on them in activities that are not connected with school life. Nonreligious students may thus freely attend religious state schools; indeed, a survey conducted a few years ago indicated that up to 25 percent of the students in state religious schools do not come from observant families. Even nonreligious parents seem to want to give their children the basics of Jewish tradition and religion.

Though nonreligious in character, the curriculum of the general state schools includes many subjects relating to Jewish learning. Bible lessons form a major part of their timetable at all levels. In elementary schools, more curricular hours are devoted to Bible studies than to any other subject. The object of teaching Bible in state general schools, however, is to transmit cultural, historical, and aesthetic values rather than to teach specific religious precepts of Orthodox Judaism. Little time is devoted to teaching halakhic religious literature, which is a subject of great emphasis in the religious schools. The school routine includes daily prayers.

The State Education Law provides parents with ample opportunity to influence the curriculum of state schools. Where three-quarters or more of the parents request a unique supplementary program, such a program may be approved by the Minister of Education. In some cases, parents have used this right in order to strengthen the religious education of general state schools. By and large, these supplementary religious classes are more in line with Conservative Judaism, thus expanding the types of religious education within the state system.

Non-Jewish Religious Education

While Arab students may choose to attend state schools in Jewish residential areas, a separate Arab State Education System operates in quarters with large Arab populations. The main language of study is Arabic, and Arabic subjects are taught. These are not religious schools, yet they adapt their curriculum and routine to the religion of the student body, be it Muslim or Christian (of whatever sect). The State Education Law provides that in non-Jewish educational institutions, the curriculum should be adapted to the special conditions thereof. In accordance with this provision the Minister of Education provided that "State education in the Arab sector in Israel will be based on the values of Arab culture, the yearning for peace between the State of Israel and its neighbors, the love of the country common to all citizens of the state, loyalty to the State of Israel, while emphasizing the common interests of all the citizens of the state as well as the special character of the Arabs of Israel. . . ."[60]

Recognized Schools

The State Education Law allows for "recognized" schools that are not state schools. The majority are religious schools. They include ultra-Orthodox Jewish educational institutions, known as the Inde-

---

[60]See the Arab Citizens of Israel, *Relationships between Jews and Arabs in Israel*, intermediate ed. (Jerusalem, 1984), 86.

pendent Education System, and the new "El Ha'Ma'ayan" school system, which was established by a political party of Oriental Jews. They also include a non-Orthodox primary and secondary school in Haifa affiliated with the Reform World Union of Progressive Judaism, many church schools that belong to the Greek Catholic Church, and several new schools of the Latin Patriarch and the Anglican Church, which are in the process of being granted recognition. Recognized schools are financed by the Ministry of Education, though not necessarily at the same level as state schools. There are two exceptions to this rule: the Independent Education System dating back to the period preceding the state schools, as well as the El-Ha'Ma'ayan Schools, receive state funding equal to state schools. There are also several nonreligious schools that receive no state financial support. However, the attendance of children in these schools does satisfy the requirements for Israel's compulsory education law. These schools are autonomous and are not subject to the supervision of the Council of Religious State Education.

Secondary Schools and Schools of Higher Education

Secondary schools are generally maintained by local councils, rather than by the Ministry of Education, yet they enjoy state funding. In non-Jewish sectors, there are high schools operated by local councils, as well as private high schools operated by various churches. In Jewish sectors, Orthodox secondary education includes religious high schools and *yeshivot*. There are national religious and ultra-Orthodox *yeshivot*, the latter usually operating as boarding schools in which students devote most of their time to religious studies. Those studying in *yeshivot* in Israel make up the largest number of yeshivah students in the world. Military service of yeshivah students is delayed until they conclude their study. This exemption, granted by the Minister of Defence, has been endorsed by the Supreme Court. The *yeshivot* of higher education—termed "Great *Yeshivot*"—are budgeted according to the number of students attending them. Their support has risen substantially over the years, and they are now entitled to the same level of state support granted to other institutions of higher education.

In Israel, several institutions are recognized as institutions of higher education. The law confers full autonomy on these institutions in conducting their academic and administrative affairs. Yet, they are prohibited from discriminating in the enrollment of students and in the appointment of teachers on racial, sexual, religious, national, or social status grounds.

The University of Bar Ilan is the only religious university in Israel, with several branches throughout the country. The student body includes a substantial number of nonreligious and non-Jewish students. Graduates of religious high schools are more readily admitted, given the university's emphasis on excellence in the study of Judaism. Also, graduates of Great *Yeshivot* are admitted preferentially to the Law School of Bar Ilan University, which emphasizes instruction in Jewish law. These preferences have been upheld by the Supreme Court.[61] Religious teachers tend to be preferred, although this is not a stated policy of the university. Though the university has sought to maintain a religious atmosphere on campus, the religious character of the university seems to have declined in recent years.

In addition to the University of Bar Ilan, branches of American religiously affiliated universities, such as the Hebrew Union College Biblical and Archeological School and the Jewish Theological Seminary, operate in Israel. These institutions are licensed by their home states, not by Israel, and confer their own academic degrees. They are not recognized as institutions of higher education under Israeli law. Moreover, several Islamic colleges and universities operate in the West Bank. Their numbers have increased significantly under Israeli occupation. Since 1983, two Islamic colleges have operated within Israel. One of these has gained recognition by the Ministry of Education and may grant senior teacher's certificates. These colleges engage mainly in religious studies, with the goal of preparing graduates for religious and judicial leadership in the Muslim community, a goal that the Ministry of Religious Affairs has supported. These Islamic colleges are currently self-funded, but they have applied for recognition by the Ministry of Education; if recognized, they will also receive state

---

[61]See *Dover v. The Council For Higher Education* (1981), 35(4) Piskey Din 263.

funding. With the peace process and the relationship between Israel and its Arab neighbors strengthening, graduates of the Islamic colleges hope to pursue their studies in Arab countries and receive higher diplomas in Islamic studies.

DAYS OF REST AND EMPLOYMENT

The issue of observing Shabbat in the public arena constitutes a central part of the religious struggle for the preservation of the Jewish character of the state. Soon after the establishment of the State of Israel, the provisional council enacted the Days of Rest Ordinance, 1948: "The Shabbat and Jewish festivals . . . shall be the prescribed days of rest in the State of Israel. Non-Jews shall have the right to observe their own Shabbat and festivals as days of rest." In 1951, the Israeli Hours of Work and Rest Law was enacted. It provides that the weekly days of rest include, in the case of Jews, the Shabbat. Non-Jews are given an option to rest on the Shabbat or, alternatively, on Sunday or Friday, whichever day they ordinarily observe as their weekly day of rest. The same rule applies to Jewish and non-Jewish festivals.

These Shabbat regulations were designed to fulfill both social and national religious goals. On the one hand, the prohibition of work on rest days fosters social cohesion and public health. On the other hand, the designation of Shabbat as the weekly day of rest was made with explicit deference to *halachah* and the Jewish tradition. In the words of the Supreme Court of Israel: "It is clear that it is no coincidence that . . . the Hours of Work and Rest Law the legislator instructed that the weekly rest day shall include—in the case of a Jew—the Shabbat, a statement that teaches that he saw the issue of keeping Shabbat in that sense as a national asset of the Jewish people that should be observed in the state of Israel."[62] Unlike America's Sunday blue laws, which must be justified on nonreligious grounds to survive establishment clause scrutiny, Israeli Sunday laws are explicitly rooted in religious national elements of the days of rest.

---

[62]*Simcha Meron v. The Minister of Labour* (1970), 24(1) Piskey Din 349.

Shabbat restrictions are elaborated by city and local councils. The Municipal Corporations Ordinance (New Version) authorizes city councils to regulate the opening and closing of "shops, canteens, and other such places, and of cinemas, theaters, and other places of public entertainment. . . ." The Local Councils Ordinance, 1950, authorizes local councils to define the hours and days of rest and to restrict or prohibit the operation of "every service, undertaking and public institution." In the past, local councils sometimes even enacted bylaws restricting traffic and closing movies and theaters on days of rest and during Shabbat. In 1987, however, the Jerusalem Magistrate Court overruled such local bylaws, declaring that limitations imposed on religious grounds must be enacted by the Knesset alone. The 1950 Law has since been amended to authorize local councils to regulate the opening and closing of businesses on explicitly religious grounds.

The Hours of Work and Rest Law, 1951, prohibits employing workers on days of rest. No work is permitted on the weekly day of rest, unless permitted on an individual basis by the Minister of Labor. The Minister may grant such permissions only if he is content that a full day's interruption of work will jeopardize the defense of the state or the security of persons or property, or seriously prejudice the economy or a process of work or the supply of services that, in the opinion of the Minister, are essential to the public or part thereof. In special cases, general permits to work on a day of rest may be granted by the resolution of a special Committee of Ministers composed of the Prime Minister, the Minister of Religious Affairs, and the Minister of Labor. The volume of permits granted is substantially influenced by the political composition of the Government.

The Employment Service Law, 1959, as amended in 1988, provides further that the State Employment Agency, which is in charge of providing manpower—as well as private employment agencies, private employers, or employment agencies—may not discriminate against candidates on the grounds of their religion, race, nationality, origin, or political views. The Hours of Work and Rest Law provides, moreover, that "a person in need of an employee shall not refuse to accept a person for employment by reason only that on being accepted for employment such person states that in accordance with a prohibition imposed by commandments of his religion observed by him, he does not agree to work on days of rest. . . ." According to this law, only a person who observes the commandments of his religion may refuse to work on the days of rest prescribed by his religion. The Law authorizes an employer to demand such an employee to sign an affidavit attesting to his religious convictions and his observance of the commandments of his religion. He must also attest to his observance of dietary laws and abstention from traveling on the Shabbat. These prohibitions against discrimination on religious grounds do not apply to employers concerning work with public security, hotels, or work connected with the maintenance of essential supplies and services.

Despite the efforts to avoid discrimination on religious grounds, several petitions have been filed in court claiming open discrimination against certain religious employees. This litigation has had mixed results. In response, a private bill, entitled "Prohibition of Discrimination in Work, 1994," was submitted to the Knesset. The bill prohibits direct or indirect discrimination on grounds of religion, views, or beliefs (among other grounds) in admission to work, work conditions, promotion, professional qualification, or severance pay. The bill imposes on the employer the duty to prove that he did not discriminate on these grounds whenever the worker has proved that he seemingly fulfilled the conditions for admittance to work or for promotion. The bill provides, however, that discrimination that is required by the nature of a specific job is not regarded as prohibited discrimination. If passed into law, current prohibitions against religious discrimination in the workplace will be substantially strengthened.

It seems that Shabbat laws, more so than many other religious laws in Israel, have caused divisiveness between the religious and the secular Israeli citizens. The Shabbat laws impose inconveniences on the nonobservers, such as a lack of public transportation on Shabbat.[63] Until recently Israel had a six-day work week, and Shabbat was the only free day for Israelis to pursue their social and recreational activities. Israelis who did not own a car or could not afford a taxi, which does run on Shabbat, had limited options available for their day of rest. Currently, Israel is conclud-

---

[63]The National Bus Carrier Egged is not permitted to run on the Shabbat.

ing a transition to a five-day week, hence this discomfort is eased to some degree.

HOLY PLACES[64]

Some of the most sacred sites of Judaism, Islam, and Christianity are in Israel—the Temple Mount, the Western wall, and the Church of the Holy Sepulchre. Where holy sites are sacred to more than one religion, great disputes arise over control and access, disputes that are not always amenable to rational resolution.

Among Christian holy places, there are more than two hundred churches and chapels of all Christian denominations in Israel. Until the crusades, from 1099 to 1313, the Greek Orthodox Patriarch held principal control over these and other Christian holy places, where other Christians had the right to visit and pray. During the crusades, the Latin Church gained ascendancy. At the time of the Ottoman rule, the Greek Orthodox Church gradually gained control. At the same time, Western powers applied continuous pressure to obtain more concessions for the Roman Catholic Church. In the eighteenth century, disputes among Christians regarding the holy places led to international political pressures on the Ottoman ruler, who, in response, froze the status quo and defined in detail the rights of Catholic and Eastern (Greek) Orthodox Churches to various holy places. This arrangement was confirmed by the Treaty of Vienna in 1858.

At the end of World War I, when General Allenby entered Jerusalem leading the victorious British army, he announced that the British would continue this status quo policy of the Treaty of Vienna. The Mandate writ, by virtue of which Britain gained control over

---

[64]See Itzhak Englard, *The Legal Status of the Holy Places of Jerusalem: Aspects of Law* (Jerusalem, 1973); Stephen J. Adler, "The Temple Mount in Court," *Biblical Archaeology Review* 5 (1991); Walter Zander, "On Settlement of Disputes about the Christian Holy Places," *Israel Law Review* 3 (1978): 331; Walter Zander, "Jurisdiction and Holiness: Reflections on the Coptic-Ethiopian Case," *Israel Law Review* 17 (1985): 245.

Palestine, included an obligation to preserve existing rights and to ensure the requirements of public order and decorum in the holy places. Article 14 of the Mandate writ ordered the appointment of a special commission to study and define the rights and claims of the different religious communities in the holy places. The report of this committee, known as the Cust Report, still governs the area today. The Cust Report defines in detail the rites that may be practiced in each of the holy places by each religion, and the location and permitted times of worship. It relates to traditional places of the crucifixion and the burial of Jesus, which has been an object of Christian pilgrimage since the fourth century. The major area of contention relating to the Holy Sepulchre is *Dier el Sultan.* Other problematic holy places in Jerusalem include the Tomb of the Virgin and the Sanctuary of the Ascension, which is holy to both Muslims and Christians. In Bethlehem, disputes have arisen over the Church of the Nativity, the Grotto of the Milk, and the Shepherd's Field.

From 1948 to 1967, when Jordan controlled East Jerusalem, Muslim and Christian holy places were protected, although Christian rights of access to them were limited. In 1953, Jordan passed laws restricting the right of Christian religious communities to own or purchase property near a holy place. In 1964, Jordan further limited Christian rights by prohibiting churches from purchasing real estate anywhere in Jerusalem.

During the Jordanian control over East Jerusalem, synagogues, *yeshivot* and cemeteries were damaged (intentionally) and sometimes destroyed. The most notorious example was the desecration of graves in the Jewish cemetery on the Mount of Olives and the use of the tombstones for the construction of Jordanian army camps. In this same period, Jews were totally deprived of access to their holy places—in open violation of the cease-fire agreement. Even Israeli Muslims were not permitted to visit their holy places in East Jerusalem.

Following the 1967 war, the holy places in Jerusalem came under Israeli rule, and East Jerusalem was attached to the municipal area of the city of Jerusalem. Since then, Israeli law has guaranteed all residents freedom of religion, including freedom to perform their religious rites, subject to the limitation that they do not disrupt public order. Since this policy was enacted, many historical religious monuments have been discovered and restored by archeological explorations. The Israeli Government has strived to protect the holy places and to maintain public order, while guaranteeing free access and freedom of prayer for all.

Soon after the 1967 War, Israel applied its law, jurisdiction, and administration to East Jerusalem[65] and enacted the Protection of Holy Places Law, 1967. This law provides: "The holy places shall be protected from desecration or any other violation and from anything likely to violate the freedom of access of the members of the different religions to the places sacred to them or their feelings with regard to those places. . . ." The Law declared it a crime to desecrate or otherwise violate a holy place or to impede freedom of access to it. Indeed, it was the need to protect the holy places that served, in part, to justify the Israeli government's application of Israeli Law to East Jerusalem, which practically meant the annexation of it to Israel.

The Basic Law: Jerusalem, 1980, provides that united Jerusalem is the capital of Israel and repeats the provisions of the Protection of Holy Places Law—thus raising the protection of holy places to a constitutional level. The Penal Law, 1977, contains several sections relating to offenses against holy places: A person destroying, damaging, or desecrating a place of worship is liable to three years' imprisonment. Trespassing on places of worship is punishable as a crime. The holy places in the West Bank, which are administered by the Israeli military governor, are protected by an order of the Military Administration.

A 1924 Palestine (Holy Places) Order in Council provides that "no cause or matter in connection with the Holy Places or religious buildings or sites in Palestine or the rights or claims relating to different religious communities in Palestine shall be heard or determined by any court in Palestine." The major ground for this legislation is no doubt the awareness of the difficulty of rulings on these matters using legal tools. For this reason the authority was put in

---

[65]Asher Maoz, "On the Legal Status of the Golan Heights: Application of Israeli Law or Annexation? Application of Israeli Law to the Golan Heights is Annexation," *Brooklyn Journal of International Law* 20 (1992): 365.

the hands of a non-judicial body. Originally, there was an intention to establish a special committee that would deal with these issues; however, such a body has not been constituted. Since Basic Law: Government states that any authority of the State that is not allocated to a specific authority shall be placed under the power of Government, this duty rests with the government.

The intention of the 1924 legislation was to enable legal and even political considerations to be taken into account; however, the Order in Council permits the court to intervene in order to ensure public order and proper conduct in holy places. The Supreme Court ruled that it is up to the courts to determine if the dispute in question involves substantial rights, in which case the matter is not in the authority of the court, or if the issue does not relate to substantial rights and may be tried in court.

The most renowned (and still unresolved) dispute over holy places is the Coptic-Ethiopian case. This conflict began in the Middle Ages, when the Ethiopians moved to the monastery of *Dier el Sultan*. This monastery is situated east of the Church of the Holy Sepulchre. Eventually, a bitter conflict over the monastery arose between the Ethiopian and Coptic churches—the Ethiopians claiming that they were expelled from the church and deprived of their rights to the monastery, the Copts maintaining that the monastery had always been theirs and that they had admitted the Ethiopians merely as their guests. (It should be noted that the Ethiopian Church was derived from the Coptic Church.[66]) At the time the status quo policies of the Ottoman Empire Treaty of Vienna were crafted, Copts held control over the area in dispute. The two rival churches sought, several times, to have Turkish and, later, British authorities resolve their dispute. After the Church of the Holy Sepulchre came under the control of Jordan, the Ethiopians presented a petition to a committee established by the government, which found the Ethiopian claim to be justified. This decision was later, inexplicably, reversed. This was the situation when Israel acquired control over East Jerusalem (and thus the site of the monastery) in 1967.

---

[66]For a detailed history, see Kirsten Peoplessen, *The History of the Ethiopian Community in the Holy Land from the Time of Emperor Teodorus II till 1974* (Jerusalem, 1983).

On Easter night, 1970, while the Coptic monks were praying in the Church of the Holy Sepulchre, the Ethiopians changed the locks of the doors to the passage of *Dier el Sultan* and seized possession. The police refused to intervene, and the Coptic Archbishop submitted a petition to the Supreme Court. The Court considered the Archbishop's claim to be justified in principle.[67] It issued an unqualified *order nisi*, though implementation was postponed in order to enable the Israeli government to deal with the substantive dispute in the manner they deemed fit. Following the Court's ruling, the government appointed a ministerial committee for the purpose of resolving the dispute. After attempting unsuccessfully to negotiate a settlement between the parties, however, the Committee resolved to work toward an atmosphere of peace and trust, in which, ultimately, an agreement might be reached. Unsatisfied with the process, the Coptic Archbishop submitted a second petition to the Supreme Court in 1977.[68] The Court denied the petition and refused to intervene, now arguing that it was up to the Israeli government to act. The Government has still not reached a solution, and apparently the Copts are considering yet another petition to the Supreme Court. The unhappy adventures of *Dier el Sultan* illustrate the intractability of disputes over holy places, and the inherent limitations of judicial and governmental officials to resolve them.

Another source of dispute concerns the registration of church properties in Israel. Since Christian churches are not incorporated, there is no systematic means of registering their properties. In many cases, church property is held and registered in the name of its priest; this leads to disputes within the community and makes it difficult to discharge a priest. In addition, there is a long unsettled dispute between the Russian Delegation of the Moscow Patriarchate and the Russian Church in Exile over churches, monasteries, and other assets belonging to the Russian Orthodox Church.

A source of constant tension between Muslims and Jews relates to the Temple Mount, which is revered by both groups as the site where Abraham offered to sacrifice his son Isaac. This is the Jews'

---

[67]*The Coptic Patriarchate v. The Minister of Police* (1971), 25(1) Piskey Din 225.

[68]*The Coptic Patriarchate v. The Government of Israel* (1979), 33(1) Piskey Din 225.

most holy site, where Solomon's Temple and the Second Temple later stood. Muslims consider this their third most holy site, after Mecca and Medina. The disputes regarding the control of the site, as well as the freedom to hold religious services there, commenced soon after the 1967 war. Muslims claim absolute rights over the site; Jewish activists demand that Israel exercise control of the site, or at least enable Jews to have full access and the right of worship. What renders the dispute even more complicated is that Jewish *halachah* prohibits indiscriminate entrance by Jews onto this holiest of sites. Governmental policy has sought a middle way among these competing concerns. Israeli authorities have allowed the *wakf* to continue their administration of the Temple Mount, while denying full right of access and worship to Jews. When Jewish claimants sued to gain greater access, the Supreme Court was ambivalent: it recognized the validity of the Jewish claim, yet abstained from fully implementing it.[69] On the one hand, the Court recognized that all religious groups must have freedom to worship on Temple Mount—not least, Jews, for whom the Temple Mount was religiously central. On the other hand, the Court opined that it could not intervene while the matter was in the hands of Government regulators. Subsequent appeals to the Court to intervene were repeatedly denied.[70] The *modus vivendi* eventually introduced by the government, and upheld by the Court,[71] was to grant all individuals access to the Temple Mount to conduct their own silent prayers. However, public prayers by Jews are not permitted, nor are individuals allowed to carry with them a prayer book or to wear any religious apparel such as *tefillin* and *tallit*. Such acts, the government reasoned, would provoke Muslims into breaches of public order that might end in tragic results for all parties.[72]

---

[69]*National Circles v. Minister of Police* (1970), 42(2) Piskey Din 141, (1990); *Israel Yearbook on Human Rights* 20 (1990): 376.

[70]See *Shtanger v. Government of Israel* (1981), 35(4) Piskey Din 673.

[71]*Kach Movement v. Minister of Religious Affairs* (1993), 47(2) Piskey Din 1; *Israel Yearbook on Human Rights* 20 (1990): 376.

[72]A few years ago, during a Jewish licensed demonstration against this policy, masses of Muslims fortified in the Temple Mount and a deterioration in the situation led to riots and bloodshed.

Jews and Muslims have also clashed over nonreligious activities on the Temple Mount. Jewish groups have claimed that construction work carried out by the *wakf* on the Temple Mount results in destruction or damage to ancient sites and artifacts. Israeli authorities, however, chose not to prosecute the *wakf* for these acts, given the relatively little damage that had been done. The government's decision was upheld by the Supreme Court on appeal, though the Court ordered the authorities to supervise the site and ensure no such damage occurs in the future.[73] In a similar case, where Jewish parties claimed that Muslim *wakfs* were performing unlicensed construction work on the Temple Mount and desecrating it by allowing Arab youths to hold picnics and ball games there,[74] the Court stated:

> In this petition we are dealing once again with the problem of enforcing Israeli law on the Temple Mount. There is no doubt that the rule of law demands strictness in the enforcing of the law, any law, in all of the area of the state and on all its citizens and inhabitants equally. Nevertheless, the appropriate authorities must exercise their discretion in a manner that will ensure that the enforcement of the law will be made reasonably, bona fide, logically, and seriously. When the issues are related to the Temple Mount, with all the emotional, religious, and political aspects involved, a special caution is demanded.[75]

Similar disputes between Jews and Muslims have broken out over access to the Cave of the Patriarchs, the place of burial of the patriarchs of both Jews and Muslims. Jewish law imposes no restriction on entrance onto this site. During the Jordanian era, however, secular law denied Jews any entrance. After 1967, Israeli law mandated joint use of the cave for worshipers. This led to constant conflicts between the two communities, for Muslims demanded exclusive rights to the cave. At the tragic height of the conflict, a

---

[73] *Temple Mount Faithful Association v. Attorney General* (1993), 47(5) Piskey Din 122.

[74] *The Temple Mount Association v. The Mayor of Jerusalem* (1993), 47(5) Piskey Din 865.

[75] Ibid.

fanatic Jew committed a massacre of Muslim worshipers. A state Commission of Inquiry was established following the event, and it concluded that the massacre was the result of individual initiative.[76] Following this event, the military administration introduced total separation between Jewish and Muslim worshipers, and limited their numbers. Jews are also prohibited from entering the cave on Fridays, when the main Muslim services take place.

These disputes over holy sites clearly demonstrate the inherent limitations of any simple human rights solutions to religious conflict in Israel. The decisions that these disputes have generated also demonstrate Israel's sensitivity to the feelings and aspirations of non-Jewish religions and its dedication to respecting them, even at the price of frustrating seemingly legitimate Jewish claims.

FUTURE DEVELOPMENTS

The future development of religious human rights in Israel will be shaped by at least two related events—the agreement recently signed between the Holy See and the State of Israel and the peace talks with Arab states and the Palestinians.

The fundamental agreement with the Holy See is of historic significance. The agreement marks a dramatic shift from the Church's traditional attitude toward Judaism. From the early dawn of Christianity, the Church regarded the destruction of the Temple and the exile of Jews from the Holy Land as proof of the divinity of Jesus and the abrogation of the Old Covenant in favor of the New. These acts were viewed as divine retaliation against the Jews for their rejection of Jesus. Moreover, the Church regarded itself as a replacement for the Jewish people. Christianity was thus hostile to the Jews throughout the Middle Ages. The Catholic Church, in particular, persecuted the Jews and sought to convert them, forcibly if necessary. Even in the new era, Christianity was not neutral toward Jews.

---

[76]*Report of the Investigation Committee Regarding the Massacre at the Cave of the Patriarchate* (Jerusalem, 1994) (Hebrew).

Particularly tragic was the silence of the Holy See during the atrocities of the Holocaust. It is no wonder that the Church developed a negative attitude toward the Zionist Movement, which was seen as a faint attempt to end God's curse of exile.[77] Note, for example, the reply of Pope Pius X to Theodor Herzel's request for the Church's support of the Zionist cause: "We are unable to favor this movement. We cannot prevent the Jews from going to Jerusalem, but we could never sanction it. The Jews have not recognized our Lord, therefore, we cannot recognize the Jewish people; and so if you come to Palestine to settle your people there, we will be ready with churches and priests to baptize all of you."

The establishment of the State of Israel posed both a theological and political problem for the Vatican. On a theological level, this event meant the revival of the "condemned" people of Israel in the Holy Land. On a political level, the event triggered war between Israel and its neighboring Arab states. Global international interests, as well as concern for the many Arab Christians in Arab countries, forced the Church into silence about Israel. Moreover, the Vatican could not simply disregard the holy Christian sites that fell within the jurisdiction of Israel. A special problem was presented by the most holy places in East Jerusalem,[78] which came under Israeli control after 1967. The State of Israel would have to be dealt with.

The appointment of Pope John XXIII signified a radical change in the attitude of the Church toward the Jews. The document known as the *Nostre aetate*, issued in 1965 by the Second Vatican Council, officially rejected the idea of Jewish responsibility for the death of Jesus. This document enabled the Church to accept a Jewish State and provided the cornerstone for building a new relationship between the two parties. In 1985, the Vatican Commission for Religious Relations with the Jews issued a document stating the importance of the State of Israel for the Jewish people. After the promulgation of this document, the present pope, John Paul II, made several declarations condemning anti-Semitism and recog-

---

[77]D. Rosen, "Vatican–Israel Relations: The Jewish Perspective," *Justice* 3 (1994): 22.

[78]A. Macchi, "Vatican–Israel Relations: The Catholic Perspective," *Justice* 3 (1994): 26.

nizing the centrality of Israel for the Jews. Moreover, the Middle Eastern peace process, starting with the peace treaty between Egypt and Israel and continuing with peace negotiations with other Arab countries and the PLO, paved the way for the normalization of the relations between the Vatican and the State of Israel.

The current pope has dramatically changed the Holy See's theological stance toward the Jews, spurning the Church's traditional negativism and aloofness. Until recently, his relations with Israel were based on a de facto recognition of Israel; the only visit of a pope to Israel was purely private. Since that visit, there was extensive talk of visits by other high clergy to the Holy Land; these never matured, possibly because of the political embarrassment they might cause. Although there were no official visits, there were meetings between representatives of the State of Israel and the Vatican. These eventually led to the signing of the Fundamental Agreement between Israel and the Holy See on December 30th, 1993, in Jerusalem and at the Vatican.

This agreement was, in part, a product of the emerging peace process in the Middle East. Most Catholics in Israel and the territories administered by Israel identify themselves as Palestinian; they had opposed any relations between Israel and the Vatican until Palestinian political claims were satisfied. The peace talks between Israel and the PLO removed this obstacle to Vatican–Israeli relations. Moreover, the Catholic Church had substantial interests in Jerusalem and various holy places in Israel, and its representatives did not wish to be left out of any peace treaties between Israel and the Palestinians and other Arab states.

The agreement between Israel and the Vatican does not deal expressly with the problem of Jerusalem. Earlier, the Holy See had supported the internationalization of Jerusalem, a policy recommended in 1947 by the General Assembly of the United Nations. Since the 1967 war, representatives of the Vatican have abandoned this demand, yet formally this is still its official stand. The Agreement is silent on this contentious issue. Instead, it provides a number of provisions concerning the Church's rights in holy places.[79]

---

[79]R. Lapidoth, "Jerusalem: The Legal and Political Background," *Justice* 3 (1994): 7.

Article 5, for example, commits both parties to favoring Christian pilgrimages to the Holy Land. In other articles, both parties agree to maintain the status quo respecting control, access, and use of the Christian holy sites.[80]

The holy places of Jerusalem were subject to additional references in the 1994 Peace Treaty between the State of Israel and the Hashemite Kingdom of Jordan. Article 9 includes a commitment to provide mutual freedom of access to places of religious and historical nature. It further commits Israel to respect Jordan's "special" role in the Muslim holy shrines, which consists of appointing the administration of the Temple Mount and paying their salaries out of the Jordanian Ministry of Religious Endowment, and planning and financing the restoration of the Golden Dome of the Omar Mosque. The same Article has an opaque paragraph stating that "when negotiations on the permanent status will take place, Israel will give high priority to the Jordanian historic role in these shrines. . . ." This language might suggest that Jordan may participate in the negotiations between Israel and the Palestinians, though several commentators have dismissed this suggestion. Other commentators have argued that this provision in the Jordan-Israel treaty is incompatible with the 1993 declaration of principles signed with the PLO, which left the problem of Jerusalem open for future negotiations. Yet Israel has assumed no specific obligations to Jordan in negotiations over the holy places in Jerusalem. At most, Israel has committed itself to adopting a favorable attitude to Jordan's interests.

The agreement with Jordan has aroused much antagonism from Palestinians, as well as criticism from other Arab states such as Morocco, which claim special interests in Muslim holy places in Jerusalem. Representatives of the Russian Patriarch of Moscow have made similar claims and have asked to participate in any

---

[80]Despite this provision, in a letter by Israel's Minister of Foreign Affairs presented to his Norwegian counterpart on October 1993, the role of certain Palestinian institutions in East Jerusalem was recognized, including those relating to the Christian and Muslim holy places. The legal status of this document is unclear and is subject to conflicting interpretations. One of the opinions expressed regards the vagueness of the letter as intentional, thus stressing the idea that it is of no binding authority.

future negotiations for their final settlement. A research group operating within the Jerusalem Institute for Israeli Studies, which is of no official status, has studied the issue and delivered its finding and recommendations to the Israeli Government.[81] From what has been published about this putative secret report, it seems that the team has mapped all the holy sites in Jerusalem and found that there are sixty-five active mosques in East Jerusalem and several cemeteries. The team has also noted that the *wakf* administration is endeavoring to expand the list of Muslim holy places. The team has compiled various different historical proposals for resolution of the problem of Jerusalem.

It seems clear that the present Israeli Government will not consider any solution that leaves any part of Jerusalem beyond Israeli sovereignty. The PLO, on the other hand, demands the withdrawal of Israel from all territories occupied by it during the 1967 war, leaving full control over East Jerusalem to the Palestinians. The Hamas, a fundamentalist Islamic terror movement that enjoys large support within the Palestinian population, has adopted even more radical views. Egypt has expressed its views on the matter in letters attached to the Camp David agreements with Israel. Egypt supports Palestinian control over East Jerusalem and opposes all steps taken by Israel to change the status of the city. Jordan, on the other hand, wishes to regain control over Muslim shrines in Jerusalem and restore its historic role there.[82]

The holy places are the chief stumbling blocks of the current peace talks between Israel and the Palestinians, and they will be

---

[81]M. Hirsch, D. Housen-Couriel, supervised by R. Lapidot, *The Jerusalem Question: Proposals for its Resolution.*

[82]The position of Jordan regarding the status of Jerusalem is of great importance in view of the ties that exist today between Jordan and the city and in light of the peace agreement with Israel. Until 1974 Jordan demanded the restoration of its control over East Jerusalem and the West Bank. Following the Arab summit conference at Rabat in 1974, which affirmed the Palestinian right to self-determination in the territories occupied by Israel, the Jordanian stand toward Jerusalem modified. New Jordanian policy called for the establishment of a federation between the West Bank and Jordan. At present Jordan expresses its desire to regain control over Muslim shrines in Jerusalem and restore its historic role there.

the last item to be negotiated. All parties now have, at least publicly, taken uncompromising stands. If agreement can be reached
on all other matters, thereby making real the possibility of peace
in the region, these conflicting stands may soften.

The word "Jerusalem" (*yerushalayim*) in the Hebrew language
comprises two nouns: peace (*shalom*) and wholeness (*shalem*). Let
us hope that its destiny will be one of an undivided city of eternal
peace.

5

JEWISH NGOS AND RELIGIOUS HUMAN RIGHTS: A CASE STUDY

Irwin Cotler

McGill University

INTRODUCTION

This article is written at a critical juncture in the struggle for human rights in general, and religious human rights in particular. On the one hand, there has been a literal explosion of human rights. Human rights have become an organizing idiom of our political culture, indeed, the new secular religion of our times. At the same time, however, in the dialectics of revolution and counter-revolution in human rights, violations of human rights continue unabated. The homeless of America, the hungry of Africa, and the imprisoned of Asia and the Middle East can be forgiven if they think the human rights revolution has somehow passed them by; while the silent tragedy of the Kurds, the ethnic cleansing in the Balkans, the horror of Sarajevo, and the agony of Angola and Rwanda are the metaphor and message of the assault upon, and abandonment of, human rights in our time.

What is true of the human rights revolution and counter-revolution in general, in this Dickensian era with its best of times and worst of times, is also true of the state of religious human rights. On the one hand, freedom of religion is one of the most fundamental of human rights, anchored and given expression in contemporary international law. It is enshrined in Articles 1(2) and 55(c) of the

UN Charter,[1] Article 18 of the 1948 Universal Declaration of Human Rights,[2] Article II of the Convention on the Prevention and Punishment of the Crime of Genocide,[3] Article 9 of the 1950 European Convention for the Protection of Human Rights and Fundamental Freedoms,[4] Article 1 of the 1950 UNESCO Convention Against Discrimination in Education,[5] Article 4 of the 1965 International Convention on the Elimination of all Forms of Racial Discrimination,[6] Article 18 of the 1966 International Covenant on Civil and Political Rights,[7] Article 12 of the 1969 American Convention on Human Rights,[8] Principle VII of the 1975 Final Act of the Helsinki Conference on Security and Cooperation in Europe,[9] Article 8 of the 1981 African Charter on Human and Peoples' Rights,[10] Article 7 of the International Convention on the Elimination of All Forms of

----

[1]While the UN Charter was being drafted, Chile, Cuba, New Zealand, Norway, and Panama suggested detailed provisions on the right to freedom of thought, conscience, and religion. The suggestion was not adopted. But the UN Charter did become the first international agreement to incorporate the idea of universal human rights, and one of the world organization's principal purposes is to encourage "respect for human rights and fundamental freedoms for all without distinction as to race, sex, language, or religion" (Article 1). The Charter pledges all Member States, jointly and separately, to pursue this goal (Articles 55 and 56). For a compilation of the instruments relevant to freedom of religion or belief and freedom from discrimination based on religion or belief contained in international and regional instruments, see UN Doc. E./CN.4/L. 1417 (197a).

[2]UN G.A. Res. 217(III)(A) (1948), 2 *United Nations Resolutions, Series I*, 135, 138 (D.J. Djonovich, ed.).

[3]For a general text of United Nations human rights instruments mentioned in this article, see *Human Rights: A Compilation of International Instruments*, United Nations (1988). The *Genocide Convention* appears on p. 143 [hereinafter *Human Rights*].

[4]*European Conventions and Agreements* 1:21, 25–26.

[5]Articles 1(1), 3(d), and 5.1(a) of the UNESCO Convention Against Discrimination in Education.

[6]For text, see *Human Rights*, 56, note 3.

[7]*UN Juridical Y.B.* (1966), 178, 184.

[8]*Am. J. Int'l. L.* 65 (1971), 679, 684.

[9]*I.L.M.* 14 (1975), 1292, 1295.

[10]*I.L.M.* 21 (1982), 59, 60.

Discrimination against Women,[11] Article 1 of the 1981 Declaration on the Elimination of All Forms of Intolerance and of Discrimination Based on Religion or Belief,[12] and Article 14 of the 1989 Convention on the Rights of the Child.[13] The special status of freedom of religion in international human rights law is further buttressed by the fact that it is non-derogable even in times of emergency under Article 4(2) of the CP Covenant,[14] as well as Article 27(2) of the American Convention.[15]

Notwithstanding this "critical mass" of protections for freedom of religion in international law, however, freedom of religion remains "the most persistently violated human right in the annals of the species."[16] Indeed, "religious intolerance has generated more wars, misery, and suffering than any other type of discrimination or bias,"[17] and is not unrelated to much of the ethnic, tribal, "civilizational" conflict of our day.

Interestingly enough, this dialectical character of religious human rights—with its consecration in law, on the one hand, and its massive violations, on the other—finds expression in the history of the Jewish religion and the experience of the Jewish people.

On one level, the Jewish religion and Jewish religious rights are at the core, the foundation, of universal human rights as a whole. In a word, if human rights has emerged as the new "secular religion" of our time, then the Jewish religion is at the core of this new secular religion of human rights—the whole symbolized by the normative exhortation in the Jewish religion of *Tikun Olam*—the responsibility to "repair the world."[18] This responsibility, as well as the notion of *B'Tselem*—that we are all created in the image of

---

[11]*Human Rights*, 56, note 13.

[12]UN G.A. Res 36/55 (1981), *Israel Yearbook on Human Rights* 12 (1982), 190, 191.

[13]*I.L.M.* 28 (1989), 1457, 1462.

[14]*UN Juridical Y.B.* (1966), 180.

[15]*Am. J. Int'l. L.* 65 (1971), 688.

[16]Y. Dinstein, *Freedom of Religion and the Protection of Religious Minorities* (American Jewish Committee, 1981), 2.

[17]Ibid.

[18]This moral injunction is found in the Jewish prayer *Aleinu*, which is said three times daily.

God—is the essence of a religion organized around the inherent dignity of the human person and the equal dignity of all persons. Jewish lore has often elaborated on this theme, as reflected in the following story from the Talmud: "What is the most important verse in the whole Bible?" asked a Talmudic sage, Ben Azai. And his answer was, "The verse from the Book of Genesis that says: 'Man was created in the Divine image.'" That verse establishes for Jews the fundamental relationship between one person and another. All were created in the image of God. Therefore, all are entitled to equal respect for their dignity and worth. Similarly, the Talmud provides that when a witness in a capital case comes to the witness stand, he must be admonished in the following words: "A single man was created in order to teach you that if one destroys a single person, it is as though he had destroyed the population of the world. And if he saves the life of a single person, it is as though he had saved the whole world."[19]

And yet, notwithstanding this profound commitment to human rights anchored in the Jewish religion, in the very history of the Jewish people and in the prophetic tradition (or perhaps because of it, as Edmond Cahn put it in his insightful work *Warrant for Genocide*[20]), violations of Jewish religious rights—be they through forced conversions, expulsions, inquisitions, pogroms, or genocide—have been one of the most persistent and enduring hatreds in all of human history.

It is not surprising, therefore, that Jewish Non-Governmental Organizations (NGOs), as legatees of the Jewish past and trustees of the Jewish future, have committed themselves to the pro-

---

[19]*Mishnah, Sanhedrin* 4:5. This "universalist" perspective finds expression in both the *halachah* and *aggadic* literature. For example, the Rabbis say that Adam was made from the dust gathered by God from the four corners of the earth so that no person could say later that he was made from dust gathered only in his part of the world. In another talmudic passage, the Rabbis ask: "Why were there not several Adams and several Eves?" And they answer: "So that it might not be said that some races are better than others." In a similar vein, the Rabbis tell us that the Torah was revealed in the desert in order to make it accessible to all. No man's land was every man's land.

[20]Edmond Cahn, *Warrant for Genocide*.

motion and protection of human rights in general, and religious rights in particular, and to combatting human rights violations in general, and the violations of freedom of religion and Jewish rights in particular.

Defining Jewish NGOs and Their Agendas

A word about definition: In referring to "Jewish" NGOs, I have adopted a definition of the term "Jewish" that is anchored both in an inclusive notion of what being Jewish means, as well as in an appreciation of what Jewish NGOs, in fact, do. More particularly, I have not restricted or limited the term "Jewish" to its religious or sectarian definition of a Jew as a person born of a Jewish mother or who has converted to Judaism.[21] Rather, the term "Jewish" refers here to the intersecting religious, cultural, ethnic, and national identities whose composite defines what it means to be Jewish.[22] This is, in fact, the mosaic that defines Jewish NGOs, or the mosaic by which these NGOs define themselves, and that defines the Jewish agenda or mission statements of the major and mainstream Jewish NGOs reflected in its variegated forms.[23]

---

[21]Yitzhak Englard, "Religion and State in Israel," *Am. J. Comp. Law* (1987).

[22]See, for example, the "multi-issue" public affairs agenda of the National Jewish Community Relations Advisory Council (NJCRAC), the umbrella planning and coordinating body for the organized Jewish community. Its advocacy agenda reflects and represents the Jewish mosaic.

[23]See, for example, the agenda or mission statements of international Jewish NGOs such as the World Jewish Congress, B'nai Brith, American Jewish Joint Distribution Committee, Hadassah, and the International Council of Jewish Women; or those of the major American Jewish NGOs, which are themselves becoming increasingly internationalized, such as the American Jewish Committee, the Anti-Defamation League, the American Jewish Congress, and the Simon Wiesenthal Center; or Canadian Jewish NGOs such as the Canadian Jewish Congress, B'nai Brith of Canada and its League for Human Rights, Hadassah-Wizo, and the National Council for Jewish Women. Even the "single issue" NGOs, such as the National Conference for Soviet Jewry or the Union of Councils for Soviet Jewry, dealt with the Soviet Jewry issue in its religious, cultural, ethnic, and

One way of describing this mosaic—in terms of the category of religion alone and as an example of the multiple configurations involved—is as being composed of the following religious rights: (1) the religious rights of Jews as individuals involved in the free exercise of religion; (2) the religious rights of Jews as a group where the free exercise of religion can be exercised only in community with others; (3) the religious rights of Jews as a community with respect to, inter alia, the responsibilities of Jews as a community or collectivity in the Diaspora; (4) the religious rights of Jews as a culture, referring to the transmission of ideas, heritage, values, norms, morals, and the like that make up the composite of a culture; (5) the religious rights of Jews as a people, where such rights are inextricably bound up with the Jewish right of self-determination; and (6) the religious rights of the Jews as a nation in their homeland Israel, particularly respecting those rights that may be fulfilled only in Israel, and the centrality of Israel to the Jewish people.

Likewise, if one approaches the meaning of the term "Jew" from the perspective not of freedom of religion, but of freedom from discrimination on grounds of religion, that is, Jewishness, a similar configuration emerges. As Natan Lerner put it, "In the case of the Jews, ethnicity, religion, and culture are inextricably interwoven, in the self-perception of the victims of anti-Semitism as well as in the perceptions of the anti-Semites."[24]

____

national dimensions, thereby reflecting and representing this Jewish composite or mosaic of intersecting identities. Indeed, even the religious or sectarian NGOs, like the Union of Orthodox Jewish Congregations of America, or the United Synagogue of Conservative Judaism/Women's League for Conservative Judaism, and the Union of American Hebrew Congregations (Reform) have an agenda that embraces the intersecting religious, cultural, ethnic, and national identities; while the Joint Program Plan of the National Jewish Community Relations Council, the voluntary association of Jewish community relations agencies, is a case study of this inclusive notion of a Jewish NGO.

[24]Natan Lerner, *Group Rights and Discrimination in International Law* (Martinus Nishoff, 1991), 122.

Linking this "typology" of what it means to be Jewish to the "typology" of Jewish NGOs, the universe of Jewish NGOs may be characterized as follows:

1. There are religious or sectarian Jewish NGOs that represent or advocate denominational or sectarian interests only—or even a particular feature of the sectarian or denominational interest. There are, therefore, religiously Orthodox, Conservative, or Reform Jewish NGOs,[25] devoted to the promotion and protection of their particular sectarian interest, for example, the concern of a religiously Orthodox Jewish NGO such as Agudath Israel with the religious rights of observant Jews in the matter of *kashruth*.

2. There are secular and liberal Jewish NGOs—sometimes referred to as Jewish "human rights" NGOs—that concern themselves with the promotion and protection of religious human rights from a constitutional or "rights" perspective, and that, inter alia, use "church–state" litigation as a main prong in their strategic advocacy.[26] This litigation strategy is often deployed more in the defense of non-Jews than in the defense of Jews, on the principle that "there cannot be security and freedom for Jews unless there is security and freedom for persons everywhere."[27]

3. There are Jewish "human rights" NGOs that are particularly concerned with protecting Jews from discrimination in general and from "Jew hatred" in particular. For these groups, Holocaust remembrance is an organizing idiom, Holocaust denial a "clear and

---

[25]It should be noted that the sectarian Jewish NGOs, such as the Union of Orthodox Jewish Congregations (OU), the United Synagogue for Conservative Judaism, and the Union of American Hebrew Congregations— together with their respective public affairs institutes and counterpart women's groups—increasingly pursue a broad domestic and international public affairs agenda, albeit from their particular sectarian perspectives.

[26]For example, the American Jewish Committee, the Anti-Defamation League, and the American Jewish Congress.

[27]Oft-quoted statement of American Jewish Committee President, Jacob Blaustein, cited in J. Shestack, *Judaism and Human Rights* (American Jewish Committee, 1983), 11.

present" danger, and bringing Nazi war criminals to justice a special responsibility.

4. There are "international" Jewish human rights NGOs, such as the World Jewish Congress, which serve as the "diplomatic" arm of the Jewish people and whose mission "is to address the interests of Jews and Jewish communities all over the world."[28] The mission statement of the World Jewish Congress, for instance, is expression and example of the integrative advocacy of international Jewish NGOs organized around the concern for Jews and Judaism in their religious, cultural, ethnic, and national configurations, including the notion of the centrality of Israel to the Jewish people.[29] Indeed, the increasingly intersecting and interlocking nature of what it means to be a Jew—and the increasingly transnational character of this mosaic—is finding enhanced expression even amongst the major "national" Jewish NGOs,[30] whose advocacy is increasingly being internationalized.

5. There are "international" Jewish NGOs, such as the American Jewish Joint Distribution Committee (JDC), whose ongoing mission is the relief, rescue, and reconstruction of Jews and Jew-

---

[28]Mission Statement, World Jewish Congress.

[29]The core component of the mission statement reads as follows: "The World Jewish Congress is an international human rights organization whose mission is to address the interests of Jews and the Jewish communities throughout the world. . . . Towards that end, the World Jewish Congress works:

- to secure the rights, status, and interests of Jews and Jewish communities everywhere and to defend them wherever they are violated, denied, or imperiled.
- to intensify the bonds of World Jewry with Israel as the central creative force in Jewish life . . .
- to act on behalf of its participating communities before governmental, intergovernmental, and other international authorities on matters concerning the Jewish people.
- to cooperate with all peoples on the basis of universal ideas of peace, freedom, and justice."

[30]See, for example, the mission statements and work of the American Jewish Committee, the Anti-Defamation League, the American Jewish Congress, and the Simon Wiesenthal Center.

ish communities in distress, and whose mission statement cites the mishnaic injunction that "to save one person is to save a world."[31] JDC is often joined in its efforts by another international Jewish NGO, the World ORT Union, whose object is "the amelioration of the economic and social status of Jews and other persons through vocational training and technical education in countries where the need exists";[32] and by national networks of "immigrant and refugee rights" NGOs, such as the Jewish Immigrant Aid Services (JIAS) of Canada, which is "dedicated to facilitating the lawful entry of Jewish refugees and immigrants into Canada,"[33] including the protection of their religious rights.

6. There are general purpose, grass roots, mass membership international Jewish NGOs, such as B'nai Brith, the "oldest and largest Jewish service organization in the world."[34] B'nai Brith's name (meaning "sons or children of the Covenant"), its emblem (the seven-branched Menorah), and its motto[35] have a clearly discernible religious motif. Another of the largest grass roots, mass membership, international NGOs is the Women's International Zionist Organization (WIZO), which, like B'nai Brith, enjoys consultative status at the United Nations and engages in a myriad of Israeli-centered educational, cultural, and humanitarian endeavors.[36]

7. One of the oldest NGOs, and the oldest Jewish human rights NGO, is the Paris-based Alliance Israelite Universelle. Founded in 1866, the AIU, together with the Anglo-Jewish Association and the Board of Jewish Deputies, made an important contribution to the early development of international human rights law in general and religious human rights in particular.[37] Over the years, it emerged

---

[31]Mission Statement, JDC, 1994, published on the occasion of the eightieth anniversary of its founding in 1914.

[32]Mission Statement, ORT, 1994.

[33]Mission Statement, JIAS, 1994.

[34]Mission Statement, B'nai Brith, 1994.

[35]Ibid.

[36]For example, WIZO enjoys representation in some thirty countries on five continents.

[37]See, for example, reference to AIU in N. Feinberg, "The International Protection of Human Rights and the Jewish Question (A Historical Survey)" *Israel Law Review* 3 (1968).

as the prototype of an "educational/cultural" human rights NGO, responsible for establishing a network of schools and other institutions for Jewish communities in distress.[38]

8. There are "Jewish" NGOs that are almost exclusively devoted to a universalist agenda, as in the work of those NGOs that operate to alleviate hunger in the developing world,[39] or whose humanitarian work is largely in "countries without Jews," inspired by the injunction of *Tikun Olam*.

9. There are "legal" or "juridical" Jewish NGOs, such as the International Association of Jewish Lawyers and Jurists,[40] which seek to act as "Counsel to the Jewish people," including the promotion and protection of their religious human rights.

10. There are "single issue" or special purpose Jewish NGOs,[41] which have organized themselves around a particular compelling issue, such as the struggle for Soviet Jewry. Indeed, during the period that the Soviet Jewry issue became a major human rights issue on the East–West agenda, NGOs such as the National Conference on Soviet Jewry or the Union of Councils of Soviet Jews had a major impact on the development of a U.S. human rights foreign policy.

11. There are Jewish women's NGOs[42]—of both a national and international character—such as the International Council of Jewish Women, engaged in the struggle for Jewish human rights in general and women's rights and the rights of Jewish women in particular. Some of these organizations, including Jewish religious

---

[38]For example, the "Alliance" School in Damascus engaged in some "Jewish" education on the grounds that the education was defined as "religious."

[39]For example, the American Jewish World Service Organization.

[40]The Association has a growing representation in over thirty countries, including Country Sections in North and South America, Europe, Asia, and Africa.

[41]For example, the National Conference on Soviet Jewry, the Canadian Task Force on Syrian Jewry, and the various organizations organized on behalf of Ethiopian Jewry.

[42]See, for example, mission statements of the International Council of Jewish Women and WIZO.

rights NGOs,[43] have had to challenge violations of Jewish women's rights carried out ostensibly in the name of Judaism itself, such as in the case of *agunot*.[44]

12. Finally, the mission statements of all the major international[45] and national[46] Jewish NGOs include reference, in some form, to the "survival, security, and well-being of the State of Israel." Indeed, an appreciation not only of the mission statements but of the advocacy of Jewish NGOs demonstrates the extent to which Israel has emerged as the "civil religion" for organized Jewry and the existential relationship between Israel and the Jewish people that embraces the panoply of identities and rights described earlier, including religion and religious rights. In this context, mention should be made of the consortium of national and international Zionist membership organizations that are themselves constituent members of the World Zionist Organization, an international, Israeli-centered NGO with consultative status at the United Nations.

Summary of Issues Addressed

Having regard to this preamble, this article will be organized around the following seven themes or questions:

First, what has been the contribution of Jewish NGOs to the development of international law in the matter of religious human rights? I propose to offer a snapshot of the history of Jewish NGO contributions at various historical junctures in the development of international human rights law.

Second, what has been the contribution of Jewish NGOs to the development and critique of domestic constitutional and statutory law? Here I offer a comparative perspective of the involvement of

---

[43]See, for example, mission statements of Emunah and the International Coalition of Agunah Rights.

[44]The term used for Jewish women whose husbands have refused to grant them a *get* (discussed below).

[45]See, for example, the mission statements of the World Jewish Congress, B'nai Brith, the International Council of Jewish Women, and WIZO.

[46]See, for example, the mission statements of any of the major national American, Canadian, or European Jewish NGOs.

Jewish NGOs in the development of constitutional and statutory law in both Canada and the United States, which may be instructive regarding not only their respective perspectives on religious human rights but also their distinctive legal cultures and Jewish sensibilities.

Third, what has been the role of Jewish NGOs in combatting violations of religious human rights in the domestic arena? Here I will identify eight areas where Canadian and American Jewish NGOs have made a significant contribution to the protection against discrimination on grounds of religion, with particular reference to the divergent and contrasting positions taken by these NGOs in church–state issues as well as in the hate speech controversies.

Fourth, what strategies have Jewish NGOs engaged in, and indeed sometimes pioneered, in exposing and combatting violations of religious human rights? Here the paper will focus on the struggle for oppressed Jewry—particularly Soviet Jewry—not only as a case study of the role of Jewish NGOs in the promotion and protection of religious human rights, but as a model for strategic advocacy by NGOs in the matter of redressing violations of religious human rights generally speaking.

Fifth, what has been the role of international Jewish NGOs in the protection against discrimination in the international arena? Here the paper will focus on three case studies—reclamation of Jewish communal property in Eastern Europe and the former Soviet Union, redressing the historic "teaching of contempt" in the context of Christian–Jewish dialogue, and combatting the "new anti-Semitism" in the international arena—and the related founding of three international Jewish NGOs to address these concerns.

Sixth, are there distinctive features of the general panoply of religious human rights protections about which Jewish NGOs are particularly concerned, and how have these concerns shaped their advocacy and activism respecting religious human rights?

Finally, what has the role of Jewish NGOs in the promotion and protection of religious human rights taught us about the importance of religious human rights in the pantheon of human rights, and about the importance of religious human rights to the agenda of Jewish NGOs?

THE CONTRIBUTION OF JEWISH NGOS TO THE DEVELOPMENT OF THE INTERNATIONAL LAW OF RELIGIOUS HUMAN RIGHTS

The following is a snapshot of the contribution of Jewish NGOs in the development of international human rights law before and after World War II. During the nineteenth century and up to World War II, Jewish NGOs were instrumental in the development of five fundamental principles that constitute the foundation of contemporary international human rights law. After World War II, these groups made notable contributions to the creation of important instruments of international human rights law. The role of Jewish NGOs in this process is little known but is a matter of great historical moment in the emergence of the international law of human rights.

From the Congress of Vienna in 1815 to the Paris Peace Conference and the Minorities Treaties in 1921: A Century of Historic Involvement

Although contemporary international human rights law is popularly regarded as a post-World War II phenomenon—"United Nations Law," as it is sometimes characterized—the "historic antecedents"[47] of international human rights, as Thomas Buergenthal put it, are rooted in developments that found expression from the Congress of Vienna in 1815 to the Treaty of Berlin in 1878; from the American intervention on behalf of Romanian Jewry in 1902 to the U.S. intercession in the Kishinev Pogrom of 1905; and from the Treaty of Paris 1919–20 to the Minorities Treaties of 1921.

Admittedly, on the level of Jewish experience during this century, it was yet another century-long example of Jewish persecution, of what Robert Wistrich has called the "enduring hatred"[48] of the Jews. On another level, though, this century constituted—as

---

47T. Buergenthal, *International Human Rights* (St. Paul: West Publishing, 1988), 1.

48R. Wistrich, *Antisemitism: The Longest Hatred* (London: Thames Methuen, 1991).

Professor Feinberg points out in a brilliant but largely unknown article entitled "The International Protection of Human Rights and the Jewish Question"[49]—a historic watershed in the development of international human rights law in general, and religious human rights in particular. Thus, while contemporary international human rights law has met with a "consistent pattern of gross violations of human rights" despite the international human rights legal regime, the century from 1815 to 1921 witnessed the reverse phenomenon: the development of international human rights law in response to the violations of that period.

Indeed, as Professor Feinberg notes, "the oppression, persecutions, and sufferings which were the lot of Jewry in many lands stirred the conscience of the world"[50] and led to the conceptualization of, in particular, five international legal doctrines that became the foundation of contemporary international human rights law, particularly in the area of religious human rights.

The first such doctrine is the *doctrine of humanitarian intervention*—the principle that a state may intervene in the affairs of another state if that other state engages in inhumane or uncivilized conduct that shocks the conscience of humankind. While the moral and legal authority of this doctrine has been gradually undermined or blunted by its manipulation for political purposes, it has been reasserted with uncommon juridical vigor by the United Nations Security Council in the 1990s to authorize humanitarian intervention in Somalia, Bosnia-Herzegovina, Rwanda, and now Haiti.[51] It is a little known but not unimportant datum that the roots of this doctrine can be traced to humanitarian intervention on behalf of Jews and Christians in the nineteenth century—interventions inspired by concern for the religious human rights of Jews and Christians, and, in the case of the Jews, quintessentially and prototypically humanitarian, inspired only by concern for religious human rights and no other political or partisan design. These interventions represented the classical and original conception of the

---

[49]Feinberg, "Human Rights and the Jewish Question."

[50]Ibid., 500.

[51]See, for example, UN Security Council resolutions on these matters, 1992–94.

doctrine of humanitarian intervention as it was meant to be, rather than what it subsequently became.

Moreover, as Feinberg alludes to in the double entendre of the title of his article, not only does the "Jewish Question"—the persecution of Jews—constitute a case study in the violation of international law in general, and religious human rights in particular; but it also represents a historic watershed in the contribution of Jewish NGOs to the development of international human rights law in general and Jewish religious rights in particular. For during this nineteenth-century period, Jews were not only the object of humanitarian interventions, they were at the same time an important factor in moving the great powers to take action on their behalf. Almost every one of the humanitarian interventions for the benefit of Jews was the result of petitions and appeals of Jewish organizations such as l'Alliance Israelite Universelle, the Board of Deputies, and the Anglo-Jewish Association. As Feinberg puts it: "Worthy of special mention is the fact that the most significant achievement in the field of the international protection of human rights in the 19th century was to a very large—perhaps even decisive—extent, the outcome of Jewish endeavors."[52] Feinberg is here referring to the Congress of Berlin in 1878, at which Rumania, Serbia, and Montenegro were granted independence "on the condition that they undertook to eschew discrimination between their subjects on grounds of religion and to guarantee them equal rights and freedom of worship."[53] The guarantee of rights in Serbia, Montenegro, and particularly Russia concerned the Jews above all, and it was the Jews who fought for this issue at the Congress of Berlin.

It was the "Jewish" connection—both as prospective victims of discrimination and as petitioners for redress—that led to a second historic doctrinal development: the principle that *the recognition of the independence of a state is contingent upon that state's guarantee of freedom of religion and eschewal of discrimination on the grounds of religion.* "By defending—and vindicating—the cause of the Jews of Rumania, Serbia, and Bulgaria before the Congress," wrote Saint Vallier, the second French delegate at the Congress,

---

[52]Feinberg, 496.
[53]Ibid.

to l'Alliance Israelite Universelle, "we have defended the cause of justice, humanity, and civilization."[54]

This principle of state responsibility in turn led ineluctably to a third major doctrinal development or principle—*the protection of minorities*—which found expression at the Paris Peace Conference in 1919–20, where the Minorities Treaties were drafted, and which Feinberg describes as a historic step "towards the recognition of human rights as an integral part of international law."[55] He sums up this historical development and the role Jewish NGOs played in it as follows:

> The demand for guarantees of the rights of the Jewish communities in East, Central, and Southern Europe was brought before the Conference by the Committee of Jewish Delegations, set up in Paris in the very days when the Conference was being assembled, and composed of delegates from those communities, and representatives of Jewish communities in the United States, Canada, Palestine, and Italy and representatives of the Zionist Congress and the B'nai Brith Order. It is worthwhile noting that, in its memorandum to the Conference, the Committee did not demand special rights or privileges for the Jews alone; it presented a proposal for the general settlement of the minorities problem, to be applied to all minority groups in all the countries in question.[56]

The fourth doctrinal development, writes Feinberg, is the principle of *universalization of rights*—including religious human rights—and the *very idea of a United Nations.* This principle and idea grew out of the Minorities Treaties themselves. Indeed, in 1926 the Institute of International Law—and in 1927 the International Diplomatic Academy—asked that "a Universal Treaty for the Protection of the Fundamental Rights of Man"[57] be drawn up.

Finally, out of the doctrine of humanitarian intervention—the protection of vulnerable peoples from actions that "shock the conscience" of humankind—emerged a fifth international legal doc-

---

[54]Ibid., 497.

[55]Ibid.

[56]Ibid.

[57]Ibid., 499.

trine, namely, the principle of *accountability for crimes against humanity*, which became the cornerstone of the Nuremberg Principles following World War II. As Henri Rolin put it, the concept of crimes against humanity, from an historical point of view, is "the logical outcome of the humanitarian intervention by States against certain odious acts which rouse the conscience of the civilized world."[58] Adds Albert de la Prudelle: "Where once the law of nations knew only humanitarian interventions—be it that of the United States in Kishinev or the great powers in Rumania—it hereinafter recognized the subjection of those guilty of inhuman persecutions to an [international] criminal jurisdiction."[59]

In summary, five great doctrines, organized around, if not inspired by, religious human rights, emerged from the Congress of Vienna to be reconsidered or reasserted at the Paris Peace Conference, and thereby to comprise the "historic antecedents" of contemporary international human rights law—the doctrine of humanitarian intervention, the principle of state independence conditioned on guarantees of freedom of religion and protection against religious discrimination, the principle of minorities rights (including religious human rights on an individual and collective level), the principle of the universality of rights as the best guarantee for human rights (including religious human rights), which was the forerunner of the United Nations itself, and the principle of accountability for crimes against humanity. As to the role of Jewish organizations in the promotion and protection of human rights in general, and Jewish human rights in particular, Feinberg's comments are particularly relevant:

The oppression, persecutions, and sufferings which were the lot of Jewry in many lands stirred the conscience of the world in the period between the Congress of Vienna and the Paris Peace Conference and prompted the Great Powers to intervene from time to time on their behalf. Throughout that period, and at the Conference itself, the Jews applied all their energy and initiative in the international arena to the struggle against oppression and for the assur-

---

[58]Ibid., 500.
[59]Ibid.

ance of Jewish rights and of respect for Jewish dignity. In doing so, they made a noble contribution to the furtherance of fundamental human rights and Man's basic freedoms, and to the development of public international law.[60]

Post-World War II Developments

Given this moral and jurisprudential legacy, it is not surprising that Jewish NGOs have made a notable contribution to the creation of five important post-World War II international human rights instruments, including, in particular, provisions relating to religious human rights. For reasons of economy, I will but enumerate these agreements and identify briefly the contribution of Jewish NGOs.

The Development of the United Nations Charter (1945)

Jewish NGOs were not only "present at the creation," but played a formative role in the organization of the San Francisco Conference in 1945 and the formulation of the UN Charter itself. As Natan Lerner explains, "the WJC, the American Jewish Conference, and the Board of Deputies of British Jews made joint representations to the San Francisco Conference, while their representatives approached delegations, expressing their concern that an effective system of human rights should be adopted."[61] Indeed, "the fate of the Jews at Hitler's hands was a major impetus for the decision to make the protection of human rights a principal purpose of the United Nations."[62] And so, in the ashes of the Holocaust, and in the wake of the collapse of the special guarantees in the Minorities Treaties and the like, Jewish NGOs were prominent among those organizations that, even before the United Nations founding Conference in San Francisco, joined in publishing in December 1944 a "Declaration of Human Rights" asserting that "an International

---

[60]Ibid.

[61]Natan Lerner, "The World Jewish Congress and Human Rights" (World Jewish Congress, 1978), 7.

[62]S. Liskofsky, "The International Protection of Human Rights," in L. Henkin, ed., *World Politics and the Jewish Condition* (1972), 277.

Bill of Human Rights must be promulgated."[63] In language premoniscent of contemporary international human rights law doctrine, they affirmed that "no plea of sovereignty shall ever again be allowed to permit any nation to deprive those within its borders of those fundamental rights."[64] They affirmed their belief in "the equal and inalienable rights of all members of the human family," and, in the words of Sidney Liskofsky,[65] acted on the credo "that the human rights of Jews would be respected and secured in the degree that the rights of all men were honored and safeguarded."[66]

In a word, for Jewish NGOs the protection of human rights was held out as a principal purpose of a United Nations; the notion of "state sovereignty" was not to be used as an exculpatory defense or immunity for human rights violations; and the United Nations was to be the guardian and protector of universal human rights. Thus, they pleaded for the adoption, together with the Charter of the United Nations itself, of a comprehensive Bill of Rights—with requisite implementation measures.

Regrettably, however, from the outset, the major Western countries, including the United States, as well as the USSR, were reluctant to assume specific legal commitments.[67] Accordingly, while the United Nations Charter declares that one of its purposes is "to promote respect for human rights and fundamental freedoms for all without distinction as to race, sex, language, or religion,"[68] it eschewed a legally binding Bill of Rights. Instead, a nonbinding Universal Declaration of Human Rights was adopted—the first component of a three-part project that was to include the Declaration, a binding Covenant, and a system of implementation measures for the Covenant.

---

[63]Ibid.

[64]Ibid.

[65]Ibid., 278.

[66]Ibid.

[67]Ibid., 283.

[68]Article 1(3), reaffirmed in Article 55(C).

The Universal Declaration of Human Rights (1948)

Because it was generally considered to be without legal force, and perhaps because the Cold War had not yet begun, the Universal Declaration, as "a common standard of achievement for all peoples and nations," was completed and adopted with remarkable speed.[69] Two provisions were included that were and are of particular concern to Jews and to the theme of this paper. The first is Article 12, which recognizes "the right of everyone to leave any country, including his own."[70] This "*Grundnorm*" right, which is intimately bound up with the exercise of all other rights, including freedom of religion, became the moral and juridical clarion call for oppressed Jewry. Accordingly, not only was the inclusion of this right important to Jewish NGOs at the time, but it became the organizing theme of Jewish NGO advocacy in the 1970s and 1980s with respect to oppressed Jewry in general and Soviet Jewry in particular. A second provision of importance to the Jews, found in Article 19 of the Declaration, speaks of the right of everyone, "alone or in community with others, and in public or private, to manifest his religion or belief in teaching, practice, worship, and observance,"[71] This article was the precursor of similar provisions from the C.P. Covenant to the Helsinki Final Act.

The Convention on the Protection and Punishment of the Crime of Genocide (1948)

Just one day before the adoption of the Universal Declaration of Human Rights—and no less inspired by the horrors of the Holocaust—the Genocide Convention was adopted. The document was very much the product of the work of Jewish NGOs such as the World Jewish Congress, and of the unrelenting commitment of a single Polish Jew, Rafael Lemkin. It was Lemkin who named it and Jewish NGOs who helped nurture it to creation. Indeed, a 1947 WJC

---

[69]Liskofsky, 284.

[70]This right is also enshrined in Article 12 of the International Covenant on Civil and Political Rights.

[71]See commentary on Article 18 in N. Robinson, *The Universal Declaration of Human Rights* (New York, 1958), 128.

memorandum "had urged the ECOSOC to outlaw genocide as a non-political crime, whether committed in times of war or peace. Congress urged its affiliates to approach their governments in order to obtain their endorsement of the Convention."[72] Regrettably, the United States took forty years before ratifying the Convention, notwithstanding that its essential juridical and existential core is the right of groups to be protected against acts committed with intent to destroy, in whole or in part, a national, ethnical, racial, or religious group as such. It constitutes, therefore, an existential protection for religious human rights.

The International Covenant on Civil and Political Rights and the International Covenant on Economic and Social Rights (1966)

It took close to twenty years for these two International Covenants to be adopted, during which time, as Liskofsky has written, "Jews stood in the vanguard of those advocating additional human rights laws of general applicability and stronger measures of enforcement."[73] Indeed, during the preparation period, the WJC made oral and written submissions at every single meeting of the Commission on Human Rights, and of the ECOSOC NGOs Committee.[74] In particular, the WJC argued for the inclusion in the Covenants of a nondiscrimination clause, and of a clause prohibiting incitement to national, racial, or religious hatred. It submitted that "no real equality could be achieved unless dissemination of racial or religious hatred and intolerance were prohibited, and freedom of speech was not abused in order to incite hatred."[75]

As well, as soon as the drafting committee of the Human Rights Commission was established in 1947, the WJC urged it to take measures providing for the recognition of the right of petition for individuals and non-governmental organizations, and for the establishment of appropriate machinery to implement substantive principles, such as those relating to discrimination and religious

---

[72]Lerner, 12.

[73]Liskofsky, 287.

[74]Lerner, 8.

[75]Ibid., 7.

human rights. While both Covenants—particularly the International Covenant on Civil and Political Rights—contain express references to religious human rights, the implementation provisions were weakened, with the right of petition made optional and relegated to a separate Protocol.

The International Convention on the Elimination of All Forms of Racial Discrimination (1966) and the Declaration on the Elimination of All Forms of Intolerance and of Discrimination Based on Religion or Belief (1981)

NGOs in general, and Jewish NGOs in particular, were active early on in pressing for action on the prevention of discrimination. As early as 1953, the WJC had asked for a special covenant outlawing the advocacy of national, racial, and religious hatred and intolerance, and was among the promoters of the Geneva Conference of Non-Governmental Organizations interested in the Eradication of Prejudice and Discrimination in 1955, which adopted a number of resolutions relating to discrimination.[76] Following a wave of swastika paintings in 1960 in Germany and elsewhere, the American Jewish Committee and the World Jewish Congress urged the United Nations to draft the appropriate international instruments to address such manifestations. The United Nations decided to split the focus, preparing one instrument on racial discrimination and a second on religious freedom.

The American Jewish Committee, the World Jewish Congress, and other Jewish NGOs were very much engaged in the preparation of these and other UN instruments through convening meetings of legal experts, preparing and submitting proposed draft language to government delegates and independent experts serving on the relevant UN bodies, critiquing new and revised proposals, and advocating adoption of the instruments.[77] Later, they

---

[76]Ibid., 9.

[77]Memorandum on "The AJC and the Right to Freedom of Religion and Belief," by Felice Gaer, Director, The Jacob Blaustein Institute for the Advancement of Human Rights of the American Jewish Committee, dated September 30, 1994, and conveyed to the author.

also assisted in efforts to ensure implementation of the instruments, both by monitoring procedures developed by the supervising body for CERD, and by taking a leadership role in defining and refining ways to implement the Declaration. For example, in the 1980s, the American Jewish Committee commissioned the preparation of a legal commentary (guide) to the 1981 UN Declaration on Religious Intolerance, the principal intergovernmental instrument guaranteeing protection of religious freedom.[78] This commentary, now nearing completion, was the basis for the preparation of a draft "general comment" detailing government responsibilities to assure religious freedom as interpreted by Article 18 of the International Covenant on Civil and Political Rights, to which the United States, Canada, and some 130 other nations are now parties. In an age of growing challenges to religious freedom by religious extremists and governments alike, the adoption, in 1993, of this "general comment" is an important, internationally respected, and authoritative counterweight to the otherwise continued limitations placed on religious freedom by new UN instruments.

Ultimately, volumes could be written, and remain to be written, about the contributions made by Jewish NGOs to the development of international human rights law. Indeed, one could easily write a volume about the differing personalities of these Jewish NGOs themselves, let alone about their respective contributions at any one of these historic junctures in the development of religious human rights. Consider, for instance, Professor Natan Feinberg's text on the contribution of Jewish NGOs to the Minorities Treaties: "La Question des minorités à la Conférence de la Paix de 1919–20, et l'action juive en faveur de la protection internationale des minorités."[79] The next part of this article surveys the contribution of Jewish NGOs to the constitutional law of religious human rights.

---

[78]Ibid., 4.

[79](Paris, 1929), 114–15, cited in Feinberg, 497.

THE CONTRIBUTION OF JEWISH NGOS TO THE DEVELOPMENT AND CRITIQUE OF CONSTITUTIONAL LAW IN THE MATTER OF RELIGIOUS HUMAN RIGHTS

I will now offer a comparative perspective of Jewish NGO involvement in asserting religious human rights in the United States and Canada, which may be instructive regarding not only the legal cultures of the two countries, but their respective perspectives on religious human rights as well.

Jewish NGOs in the United States

The activities of Jewish NGOs in the United States in the formulation of constitutional and statutory law regarding religious human rights have been organized around three basic themes:[80] (1) ensuring guarantees of the freedom to manifest and maintain one's own belief without coercion; (2) ensuring maintenance of the boundaries between religion and politics—that is, the separation of church and state—in accordance with the United States Constitution; and (3) ensuring the right to equality, equal citizenship, and nondiscrimination in matters of religious human rights.

The activities of three major U.S. "Jewish defense organizations"[81] in the promotion and protection of religious human rights—largely, though not exclusively, through the courts and largely, though not exclusively, in relation to issues of separation of church and state—are a case study of the role of Jewish NGOs in the promotion and protection of religious human rights in general. They are a case study, too, of their organizing principle of "promotion and protection"—that is, "that the rights of Jews would only be secure when the rights of people of all faiths were equally secure."[82] Indeed, these three NGOs have filed more *amicus* briefs on behalf of the rights of non-Jews than on behalf of Jews.

---

[80]Gaer, "The AJC and the Right to Freedom of Religion."

[81]The American Jewish Committee, the Anti-Defamation League, and the American Jewish Congress.

[82]Blaustein, (see note 27).

What follows is a snapshot of the advocacy of one NGO—the American Jewish Committee (AJC)—in this regard, offered with three caveats. First, it is a snapshot of a litigation strategy that, while crucial to Jewish NGOs in the protection of religious human rights, is not the only strategy deployed. Second, in many of the cases discussed below, the AJC was joined by the other two major Jewish NGOs—the Anti-Defamation League (ADL) and the American Jewish Congress. Third, more recently, and in the last ten years in particular, the perspectives and litigation strategies of these three Jewish NGOs have increasingly been challenged by religiously Orthodox Jewish NGOs. In particular, the Commission on Law and Public Affairs, which is the litigation arm of Agudath Israel, has filed opposing *amicus* briefs in matters pertaining to the litigation of religious human rights in general, and in matters of separation of church and state in particular.

The first major case in which the AJC, the ADL, and the American Jewish Congress filed a legal brief—*Pierce v. Society of Sisters of the Holy Names of Jesus and Mary*[83]—had nothing to do directly with the religious human rights of Jews. The AJC filed a brief in the *Pierce* case to challenge an Oregon law, inspired by the Ku Klux Klan, that required all children to attend public schools. The real intent—and ultimate prospective effect—of the law was to put Catholic parochial schools out of business. There were no Jewish parochial schools in Oregon, and one might wonder what the "nexus" was between this case and a Jewish NGO. But this case was to emerge as a "defining moment" in the litigation strategy of the AJC and of its associated sister organizations. It was through this case that these Jewish NGOs were to declare and establish the underlying theme of their litigation strategy—that the religious rights of Jews would be secure only if the religious rights of people of other faiths were equally secure. Hence, even though there were no Jewish parochial schools in Oregon at that time, AJC filed its brief on the side of the Catholic schools. The Supreme Court unanimously struck down the law, holding that, inter alia, it interfered with the liberty of parents to educate their children as they wished. This decision, as Samuel

---

[83]268 U.S. 510 (1925).

Rabinove, legal counsel to the AJC, put it, "has been termed the Magna Carta of Parochial Schools."[84]

The *Pierce* case was the first of a series of cases in which the AJC upheld religious rights, freedoms, and practices for people of all faiths. For example, in the 1943 case of *West Virginia v. Barnette*,[85] the compulsory "flag salute" case, the AJC supported the right of Jehovah's Witness children, in accordance with their parents' religious convictions, to refuse to salute the flag in public school. Justice Robert Jackson, speaking for the Court, directly addressed the constitutional guarantee of religious freedom and pluralism: "If there is any fixed star in our constitutional constellation, it is that no official, high or petty, can prescribe what shall be orthodox in politics, nationalism, religion, or other matters of opinion, or force citizens to confess by word or act their faith therein. If there are any circumstances which permit any exception, they do not occur to us."[86]

In the 1963 landmark case of *Sherbert v. Verner*,[87] the AJC filed a brief in support of the right of a Seventh Day Adventist to receive unemployment compensation benefits when she had refused to accept employment requiring her to work on Saturday. The Supreme Court held that for the state to disqualify Mrs. Sherbert for such benefits solely because she refused to work on Saturday—a decision based squarely on her religious beliefs—imposed an unconstitutional burden on her free exercise of religion. As Justice Brennan, writing for the majority, put it: "To condition the availability of benefits upon this woman's willingness to violate a cardinal principle of her religious faith effectively penalized the free exercise of her constitutional liberties."[88]

In a remarkably similar case in 1987, *Hobbie v. Unemployment Appeal Board of Florida*,[89] the AJC filed an *amicus* brief, together

---

[84]S. Rabinove, "How—and Why—American Jews Have Contended for Religious Freedom: The Requirements and Limits of Civility," *Journal of Law and Religion* 8: 1 and 2 (1989): 141.

[85]319 U.S. 624 (1943).

[86]Ibid., 642.

[87]374 U.S. 398 (1963).

[88]Ibid., 406.

[89]480 U.S. 136 (1987).

with the Baptist Joint Committee on Public Affairs and the Christian Legal Society, on behalf of Mrs. Hobbie, who had converted to the Seventh Day Adventist faith during her employment. The Supreme Court's tough standard, articulated in *Sherbert*, requiring "strict scrutiny" of state actions that infringe on religious liberty unless the state can show a "compelling interest" in so doing, was significantly reinforced by its decision in the *Hobbie* case.

In *Wisconsin v. Yoder*[90] in 1972, the AJC joined Jewish and Christian groups in supporting the right of Amish parents to limit their children's education to the eighth grade, in conflict with Wisconsin's compulsory school attendance law, requiring attendance until age sixteen. Similarly, in 1986, in *Witters v. Washington Department of Services for the Blind,*[91] the AJC supported Witters in his claim for government aid to the handicapped, which he had chosen to use for training to become a Christian minister. The U.S. Supreme Court unanimously held that the state program of aid to the handicapped clearly had a secular purpose, that is, to aid a particular category of persons not defined by religion to become productive citizens.

More recently, however, in a series of cases in which secular and liberal Jewish NGOs joined conservative and sectarian ones in filing *amicus* briefs in support of the free exercise of religion, the decisions of the Supreme Court have raised some serious and as yet unanswered questions about the nature, scope, and efficiency of the Free Exercise clause. For example, in the case of *Goldman v. Weinberger,*[92] also in 1986, where the AJC joined with the Christian Legal Society in upholding the right of an Orthodox Jew in the Air Force to wear his yarmulke indoors while on duty, the Court held that the denial of this right was not a breach of the Free Exercise clause. In *Lyng v. Northwest Indian Cemetery Protective Association,* the Court held that the Free Exercise clause does not prohibit the construction of a road through a sacred site revered for centuries by Indians. And in *Oregon Department of Human Resources v. Smith,* the Court eroded the threshold prin-

---

[90]406 U.S. 205 (1972).
[91]474 U.S. 481 (1986).
[92]475 U.S. 503 (1986).

ciple established in the *Sherbert* and *Yoder* cases that the government may not restrict a person's free exercise of religion absent a demonstrable and compelling state interest. The decision sent "shock waves"[93] through the Jewish community, and while its effects were mitigated somewhat in the *Lukumi*[94] case (in which the Jewish NGOs also filed *amicus* briefs), it required a Congressional statute, the *Religious Freedom Restoration Act* (discussed below) to remedy the adverse fall-out from the *Smith* decision.

While the AJC and its sister NGOs have been "vigorous proponents of the free exercise of religion,"[95] they have opposed, no less vigorously, any state "entanglement" with religion "or breach in the wall of separation between Church and State,"[96] be it by way of religion in the public schools, government aid to religious schools, or religious symbols on public property. For example, the AJC filed *amicus* briefs in a series of cases involving state-sponsored organized prayer and bible reading in public schools.[97] These cases are compelling examples not only of the church–state "separation" controversy in the United States, but of the adherence of the major liberal and secular Jewish NGOs to the "separationist" ideology. The issue came to a head in the landmark cases of *Engel v. Vitale*[98] and *Abington School District v. Schempp,*[99] in which the Supreme Court held that such state-sanctioned conduct violates the Establishment Clause. While in *Engel* the Court struck down a state-composed prayer for public school use, *Schempp* went fur-

---

[93]Conversations with Marc Stern, Director, Commission on Law and Social Action, American Jewish Congress, and Nat Lewin, Counsel, Commission on Law and Public Affairs, Union of Orthodox Jewish Congregations.

[94]936 F.2d 586 (1991), rev'd. 508 U.S. 520 (1993).

[95]S. Rabinove, "Separationism for Religion's Sake," in *First Things* (1990).

[96]"Wall of Separation" principle (*Everson v. Board of Education*) cited by S. Rabinove, "The Supreme Court and the Establishment Clause" (American Jewish Committee, 1994), 1.

[97]See, for example, AJC briefs in *Zorach, Engel, Schempp,* and *Weisman* cases.

[98]370 U.S. 421 (1962).

[99]374 U.S. 203 (1963).

ther to rule that state-sponsored recitation of *any* prayer, or devotional reading from the Bible, breaches the Establishment Clause. The decisions, which caused a furor at the time and were widely denounced as being anti-religious, anti-Christian and un-American, engendered a backlash against the Jewish NGOs, which were accused, along with the Supreme Court, of trying to remove God from the classroom. While subsequent attempts during the Reagan and Bush administrations to amend the First Amendment to permit organized school prayer have not been successful, the recent Republican "Contract with America," supported by a Republican-controlled Congress, might make it a reality. Jewish NGOs are once again at the forefront of the opposition.

As for government aid to religious schools, just as there are those who believe that the Establishment Clause does not prevent state-organized prayer in the public schools, there are also those who believe that it does not bar a state from subsidizing parochial schools, even if the purpose of these schools is to propagate a religious faith. Indeed, the Supreme Court has upheld certain kinds of state aid to religious schools, in the form of bus transportation (the *Everson*[100] case), secular textbook loans (the *Allen*[101] case), and services for the health and welfare of the student (the *Wolman*[102] case), provided the performance of these services is essentially secular.

Equally, however, the Court has said, and the three Jewish NGOs have argued, that it is not a proper function of government to advance the religious mission of parochial schools, and so it has struck down state attempts to fund specific educational activities within parochial schools.[103] As the AJC has put it, "the predominant view of the Jewish Community is that all religions will flourish best if government keeps its hands off, neither to hinder nor to help them." In the 1993 case of *Zobrest v. Catalina Foothills School District*,[104] however, the Supreme Court ruled five to four that the

---

[100]330 U.S. (1947).

[101]392 U.S. 236 (1962).

[102]433 U.S. 229 (1977).

[103]Rabinove, "Separationism for Religion's Sake."

[104]509 U.S. 1 (1993).

Establishment Clause does not bar using government money to pay for a sign language interpreter to accompany a deaf student in a parochial school. This decision marked the first time that the Court has allowed a public employee to be part of a religious school's instructional program.

It now appears that the major "parochiaid" battleground in the years immediately ahead is likely to be the issue of tax-dollar vouchers for parents to enroll their children in any school they may wish, including denominational schools. The AJC, the ADL, the American Jewish Congress, and NJCRAC are opposed to such vouchers for religious schools as well as for private schools, both on constitutional and public policy grounds. COLPA, the litigation arm of Agudath Israel, and other Orthodox religious Jewish NGOs, are in favor. The Supreme Court has never ruled squarely on the constitutionality of such tax-funded vouchers for religious schools, but with the various initiatives now pending, it may be just a matter of time before one is passed and a litigation challenge to vouchers for such schools reaches the Court. As a review of the cases indicates, each side in this battle can cite case law in its favor; and each side will be supported, if not led, by Jewish NGOs.

In the matter of religious symbols on public property, and following on the "separationist" theme, the AJC in *Lynch v. Donnely* (1984)[105] joined other Christian and Jewish groups in filing *amicus* briefs opposing government-sanctioned religious symbols on public property. The Supreme Court upheld five to four the constitutional right of a city to erect a Nativity scene as part of its annual Christmas celebration. The result, in the eyes of some Jews, was so insensitive to any religious sensibility that they said it was a mistake for the ACLU to have brought this "hard" case in the first place—and an even greater mistake for Jewish organizations to have participated in it. But in 1989 the ACLU—joined by the Jewish NGOs—was back in court again, in the dual case of *County of Allegheny v. ACLU,*[106] this time to challenge not only the display of a crèche in a courthouse, but also a *Menorah* display, which was provided by Chabad, a branch of Lubavitch hasidic movement.

---

[105]465 U.S. 668 (1984).
[106]492 U.S. 573 (1989).

The secular and liberal Jewish NGOs challenging the displays were opposed by Chabad and Orthodox Jewish NGOs, which supported them, in a pattern that is increasingly going to characterize church–state litigation in the United States. In an ambivalent five to four ruling the Supreme Court declared the Nativity scene unconstitutional ("endorsement of religion"), but upheld the *Menorah* (which had been placed alongside a Christmas tree) as a "secular expression."

Jewish NGOs in Canada

The Canadian experience, and the role of Canadian Jewish NGOs in the matter of religious human rights, contrasts sharply with the situation in the United States. This contrast reflects not only the different "rights cultures" of the two countries, but the different "rights perspectives" of Jewish organizations in the United States and Canada. These differences find expression in the manner in which, both through litigation strategy and otherwise, Jewish NGOs in the two countries have adopted dramatically different, if not opposite, principles and policies. Indeed, the "constitutionalist" and normative perspectives of Canadian Jewish NGOs invite one to ask some serious questions about the seemingly "self-evident truths" held out by the American Jewish organizations.

Canadian Constitutional Law Prior to the Canadian Charter of Rights and Freedoms

First, a word about constitutionalism and context. It should be noted that, for the first 115 years of the Canadian constitutional experience, Canada, unlike the United States, did not have an entrenched Bill of Rights. Indeed, any inquiry into the Canadian constitutional process from 1867 to 1982 would reveal a continuing preoccupation instead with the powers of government, at the expense of the rights of people. More particularly, traditional constitutional analysis and reform revolved around the division of powers between the federal government and the provinces, otherwise known as "legal federalism," as distinct from the American preoccupation with limitations on the exercise of power, whether federal or state, otherwise known as "civil liberties." The result was that the powers of government tended to precede, if not obscure, the rights of people, when the rights of the people ought to have preceded the powers of government. The outcome was a political or legal theory in which the constitutional discourse was about federalism or "power," and not about "rights" or people.

In a word, constitutional law developed in Canada as a "powers process," a battle of "sovereign jurisdictional rivalry" between the federal government and the provinces, with the courts as the arbiters of that process, rather than as a "rights process" with the courts as the guardians of those rights. It is not surprising, therefore, that while in the United States the popular metaphor of the American Constitution—"life, liberty, and the pursuit of happiness"—is a rights-oriented, people-oriented metaphor, the popular metaphor in the Canadian constitution—"peace, order, and good government"—is a power-based, government-oriented metaphor, with a clear federalist, if not centralist, orientation. Professor Bora Laskin, before he went on to become the Chief Justice of the Supreme Court of Canada, summed up this constitutional experience in one pithy sentence: "The basic constitutional question was which jurisdiction should have the power to work the injustice, not whether the injustice itself should be prohibited."[107] As he otherwise put it, "the constitutional issue is simply whether the particular suppression is competent to the Dominion or the Province, as the case may be."[108]

This historical obsession with the division of powers not only obscured the claims to protection of civil liberties, but very often determined the disposition of the claims themselves. That is, ironically, legal federalism became the "looking glass" for the determination and disposition of civil liberties issues. Whenever a federal or provincial statute appeared to offend against civil liberties, the central question for judges became, "Is the alleged denial of civil liberties within the legislative competence of the denying legislature?" Sometimes this "jurisdictional" technique worked, but more

---

[107]P. Hogg, *Canadian Constitutional Law*, 3d ed. (Toronto: Carswell, 1992).

[108]B. Laskin, *Canadian Constitutional Law*, 2d ed. (Toronto: Carswell, 1960), 939.

often it did not. If it did not work, that was the end of the matter, however much this analysis may have obscured, let alone denied, the civil liberties issue. Even when it worked, it left the disturbing inference that if the same offensive legislation had been passed by the competing, yet competent, legislative jurisdiction, that legislation would necessarily have been held to be valid.

And so it was then, that legislation offending religious human rights was either upheld or invalidated on jurisdictional grounds only, that is, not on the grounds that the legislation was offensive, but that the wrong legislature enacted it. Accordingly, in the *Saumur*[109] case, a Quebec City bylaw that effectively prohibited Jehovah's Witnesses from distributing their religious tracts was struck down on the grounds that it trespassed on federal jurisdiction in relation to criminal law. Similarly, a long line of cases held the enactment of "Sunday Observance" legislation to be within the exclusive federal criminal law jurisdiction.

Freedom of Religion under the Charter

With the adoption of the Canadian Charter of Rights and Freedoms in 1982, and the constitutionalization of rights in Canada, any law affecting freedom of religion became vulnerable to challenge under section 2(a) of the Charter, which guarantees to everyone the fundamental freedom of "freedom of conscience and religion." In 1985, the Supreme Court of Canada in *R. v. Big M Drug Mart*[110] struck down the Lord's Day Act, the federal Sunday Observance legislation that mandated store closings on Sundays and other Christian holidays on religious grounds. For seventy-five years, this statute had withstood constitutional challenge. In striking down the law, Chief Justice Dickson offered the following definition of freedom of religion: "The essence of the concept of freedom of religion is the right to entertain such religious beliefs as a person chooses, the right to declare religious beliefs openly and without fear of hindrance or reprisal, and the right to manifest religious belief by worship and practice or by teaching and dissemina-

---

[109]*Saumur v. Quebec*, [1953] 2 S.C.R. 299.
[110][1985] 18 D.L.R. (4th) 321.

tion."[111] In 1988, in the *Zylberberg*[112] case, the Ontario Court of Appeal struck down an Ontario regulation mandating religious exercises, including prayer in the public schools, on the grounds that it "imposed Christian observances upon non-Christian pupils, and religious observances on nonbelievers."[113] In 1990, in *C.C.L.A. v. Ontario,* the same court struck down another regulation, requiring a public school to devote two periods per week to religious education, on grounds that this was "Christian" education.[114] The Canadian Jewish Congress had intervened in both cases to challenge the Ontario legislation. The Ontario government did not appeal either decision.

In a word, the Charter has effectively wrought a constitutional revolution in Canada, to the point that, as Madam Justice Claire L'Heureux-Dubé of the Supreme Court put it in 1987, "the Court has stretched the cords of liberty more in five years than the U.S. Supreme Court has in 200." However, the protection of religious human rights—and the role of Jewish NGOs in this protection— has been remarkably different in Canada compared to the United States.

First, while American Jewish NGOs have gone to court to challenge government sanctioned religious symbols on public property, Canadian Jewish NGOs have avoided controversial "crèche" cases. On the contrary, they have supported, for example, the building of a *Sukkah* (symbolic shelter marking the Jewish holiday of Sukkot) at City Hall in Toronto, and of a *Chai Menorah* on the grounds of the Manitoba Legislative Assembly to mark the holiday of Hanukkah, while being singularly unconcerned with a Christmas tree in a City Hall Plaza.[115]

Second, while American Jewish NGOs have challenged any government aid to Jewish education, Jewish NGOs have supported such government assistance in Canada. Indeed, Jewish NGOs such

----

[111]Ibid., 336.

[112][1988] 52 D.L.R. (4th) 577.

[113]Ibid., 654.

[114][1990] 71 O.R. (2d) 341 (C.A.).

[115]M. Prutschi, "Church–State Separation in Canada," *Reconstructionist* (Jan.–Feb. 1986): 17.

as the Canadian Jewish Congress have even gone to court to secure government support for Jewish education precisely on the grounds that the absence of such support constitutes an infringement of both the "freedom of religion" and the "equality" provisions of the Charter. In this sense, then, Jewish NGOs in Canada have interpreted the promotion and protection of religious human rights in the matter of government aid to education in a manner exactly opposite to that of their counterparts in the United States.

Third, Jewish NGOs in the United States have been steadfast in limiting government aid to public schools only and have eschewed, on both constitutional and policy grounds, any government recognition of a state-supported private school system. Jewish NGOs in Canada, on the other hand, have sought equal standing for Jewish schools within, for example, the Quebec school system—on the grounds that the public school system in Quebec under the Canadian constitution is effectively confessional, that is, it authorizes government aid to Catholic and Protestant denominational schools. In other words, rather than challenge the constitutionality of the "confessionality" principle in the Quebec public school system, Canadian Jewish NGOs have sought to be recognized as another component of it. Similarly, in Ontario, Jewish parents supported by the Canadian Jewish Congress have recently gone to court to secure standing and assistance for Jewish parochial schools in Ontario, not unlike the "constitutional practice" in Quebec.

Fourth, while American Jewish NGOs have filed *amicus* briefs challenging a variety of breaches of the "wall of separation" between church and state, Canadian Jewish NGOs have not espoused any constitutional principle of "separation." Indeed, section 29 of the Charter, which expressly incorporates the "confessionality" principle from section 93 of the Constitution Act, 1867, effectively constitutionalizes the role of the state in religion. Canadian Jewish NGOs are now seizing upon this principle—and the equality rights principle in section 15 of the Charter—to seek support for government assistance to Jewish schools.

Why the difference in the approach of Jewish NGOs to the protection of religious human rights in the United States and Canada? The answer may well lie in the different political and legal cultures of these two countries. First, the United States is organized around an "individual rights" theory and culture, while Canada is organized around "group rights" and communitarian sensibilities as well as individual rights—a culture reflected in the provisions protecting group rights and individual rights in the Canadian Charter of Rights and Freedoms, as well as in the case law interpreting and applying the Charter.[116] Second, the United States eschews any relationship between church and state. For the mainstream U.S. Jewish rights organizations, this notion of "separationism" emerges as much as an article of faith as a principle of constitutionalism. In Canada, the Charter of Rights acknowledges the relationship or commingling of the two—certainly at least as far as denominational rights in education are concerned—and the Supreme Court of Canada has upheld this relational principle.[117] Third, the socio-cultural image of the United States has been that of a "melting pot" or, at least, of a legal culture uncomfortable with the recognition of multiculturalism as a cultural, let alone juridical, norm. In Canada, the socio-cultural image has been that of a "mosaic," while multiculturalism is entrenched as a constitutional norm in section 27 of the Charter.[118] Fourth, the United States Constitution makes no reference to God, while the Canadian Charter, in its opening Preamble, speaks of a Canada founded upon principles that recognize the "supremacy of God and the rule of law."[119] Fifth, as sociologists like to point out, the organizing idiom of American constitutionalism is that of "the right to life, liberty, and the pursuit of happiness," while the organizing idiom of Canadian constitutionalism—if not of Canadian culture itself—is that of "peace, order, and good government," reflective, as Edgar Friedenberg points

---

[116]See, for example, sections 16–23 of the Charter of Rights, protecting minority language rights in education; section 25 respecting aboriginal rights; section 27 respecting multiculturalism; section 28 respecting women's rights; and section 29 respecting denominational rights in education.

[117]See, for example, Bill 30 (Ontario Separate School Funding) [1987] 1 S.C.R. 1148.

[118]Section 27 reads: "The Charter shall be interpreted in a manner consistent with the preservation and enhancement of the multicultural heritage of Canada."

[119]The Preamble reads, in full: "Whereas Canada is founded upon principles that recognize the supremacy of God and the rule of law."

out, of Canadian "deference to public authority," at least in pre-Charter culture. Finally, Americans, born of revolution and having endured the ravages of a Civil War, tend to regard their government as more adversary than ally. Canadians, products of a Parliamentary system and spared the fallout of revolution, tend to regard their government as more ally than adversary, though the new rights culture appears to be modifying that notion.

Leaving different constitutions and legal cultures aside, there are also, in Canada and the United States, different Jewish sensibilities regarding religious human rights. For example, in the United States, the notion of separation of church and state not only protects Jews from "established" religion, but protects them from their own inner religious establishment as well. In Canada, Jews have been more generally responsive to a traditional religious sensibility, which influences their approach regarding religious human rights as a whole. Furthermore, in the United States, Jewish NGOs have been largely activist secular organizations, and even religiously Jewish NGOs have been predominately associated with Reform Judaism. In Canada, Jewish NGOs, while also secular activist organizations, tend to have a more "traditionalist" sensibility, while religious Jewish NGOs tend to be more Orthodox.

THE ROLE OF JEWISH NGOS IN COMBATTING RELIGIOUS DISCRIMINATION IN THE UNITED STATES AND CANADA

For purposes of economy, I will summarize, rather than elaborate upon, eight areas of Jewish NGO activity in combatting discrimination on the grounds of religion in the United States and Canada. While the previous description of the Jewish NGO contribution to the development of constitutional and statute law in the promotion and protection of religious human rights focused largely on the role of the American Jewish NGOs, with contrasting references to Canada, this discussion will focus mainly on the role of Canadian Jewish NGOs, with contrasting references to their American counterparts.

The Origins of Antidiscrimination Law in Canada: The Role of Jewish NGOs

The first human rights case[120] in Canada in which any NGO was accorded standing to intervene was one involving religious discrimination—the 1945 case of *Re Drummond Wren*. The first NGO ever to be given standing in a Canadian court was a Jewish NGO, the Canadian Jewish Congress (CJC), one of the oldest Canadian human rights NGOs.[121] The case concerned a challenge to an Ontario restrictive covenant purporting to prohibit "the sale of land to Jews or persons of objectionable nationality."[122] The Ontario High Court, invoking the UN Charter's commitment to the protection of individuals from discrimination on grounds of religion, and citing pronouncements of political leaders such as Roosevelt, Churchill, and de Gaulle condemning anti-Semitism, held that the covenant was void because it offended public policy. This was the first Canadian case to grant relief from discrimination on grounds of religion—in this case to those of "Jewish nationality"[123]—and it appears that the outcome of the case was not unrelated to the intervention by a Jewish NGO. The condemnations by world leaders of anti-Semitism, and the reference to the UN Charter as exemplary of public policy, were contained in the submissions of the CJC, and the reference by the High Court to the horrors of the Holocaust and the dangers of racism were not unlike the argument made by the CJC itself.

If the intervention by a Jewish NGO helped bring about the first case ever in which a Canadian court awarded relief from religious discrimination, Jewish NGOs also had played a role in the conception, drafting, and enactment of the first antidiscrimination statute to be passed in Canada, the Ontario *Racial Discrimination Act* of

---

[120][1945] 4 D.L.R. 674.

[121]The CJC was founded in 1919. It commemorated its seventy-fifth anniversary in 1994 by convening a major conference on "NGOs and Human Rights."

[122][1945] 4 D.L.R. 675.

[123]Ibid.

1944. Indeed, the Court in *Inre Drummond Wren* had relied partly upon the prohibitions contained in this legislation in voiding the discriminatory restrictive covenant at issue in the case. The Act prohibited the publication, display, or broadcast of anything indicating an intention to discriminate on the basis of race or creed. It was designed to remedy the "Whites Only," "Gentiles Only," or "No Jews or Dogs Allowed" signs that once littered beaches and shop windows in Ontario. Not surprisingly, Jewish NGOs lobbied for the enactment of this legislation, as well as for the statutes respecting fair employment and accommodation that came into force in some provinces in the 1950s.

The real revolution in the protection of religious human rights in Canada, however, came with the enactment of comprehensive Human Rights Acts, which provided for, inter alia, full-time human rights commissions. The first such statute was the Ontario Human Rights Code of 1962, which prohibited discrimination on the grounds of race, creed, color, nationality, ancestry, or place of origin. Today, all Canadian provinces, the Northwest Territories, the Yukon Territory, and the federal government have enacted similar antidiscrimination legislation. Jewish NGOs, particularly in Quebec, Ontario, and Manitoba, advocated, lobbied for, and otherwise helped bring about this legislation.

Constitutionalizing Freedom of Religion and Protection against Religious Discrimination in Canada: The Role of Jewish NGOs

Canadian Jewish NGOs played a formative role in the adoption of the Canadian Charter of Rights and Freedoms, and the constitutionalization thereby of both the principle of "freedom of conscience and religion" in section 2 of the Charter, and the prohibition against discrimination on grounds of religion (including a provision for affirmative action) in subsections 15(1) and (2) of the Charter. The adoption of the Charter was heralded by the then federal Justice Minister, Mark MacGuigan, as "the single most significant legal development in Canada and in the second half of the 20th century." The Chief Justice of Canada, Antonio Lamer, speaking on the occasion of the Charter's tenth anniversary, likened the addition of the Charter to a "revolutionary" act, "comparable to the discoveries by Pasteur in science."[124]

The CJC, having a prescient sense of the revolutionary character of those changes—and of what it might portend for Jews as well as others—developed a strategy designed to maximize the Jewish voice in the conception, drafting, and enactment of the document. First, the CJC established, in May 1980, a Select Committee on the Canadian Constitution, composed largely of leading Canadian constitutional law scholars, and presided over by one of Canada's most distinguished scholar-advocates, Professor Maxwell Cohen, former Dean of Law at McGill University and Judge Ad Hoc of the International Court of Justice. Second, it authorized the Select Committee to review the various drafts and related *travaux préparatoires* of the proposed Charter of Rights and to engage in a clause-by-clause analysis. Third, it requested the Committee to identify the areas and issues of particular concern to Jews and to report back to the CJC, both as to the Committee's overall conception of the Charter and its recommendations respecting prospective CJC submissions on particular subject areas. Finally, the Committee was asked to invite submissions from Canadian Jewry, which would be factored into its analysis and recommendations.[125]

In November 1980, pursuant to the decision of the Supreme Court to uphold the constitutionality of the "people's package"— the federal government's proposals for constitutional reform, including its centerpiece, the Charter of Rights—the draft Charter was submitted to a newly established Joint House-Senate Committee on the Constitution for a clause-by-clause review. Submissions were invited from interested members of the Canadian public. Although the time frame for preparing and making such submissions was less than a month, hundreds of organizations lined up to make written and, when permitted, oral submissions on the pro-

---

[124]Cited in G. A. Beaudoin, ed., *The Charter Ten Years Later* (Cowansville: Yvon Blais, 1992).

[125]The establishment of the Select Committee on the Canadian Constitution was one of the first decisions taken by the newly elected CJC executive in May 1980.

posed Charter. The parliamentary hearings were packed, the atmospherics heady, the media coverage intense. There was a felt sense by all participants that they were partaking of a great historical drama.

In what was characterized as a "historic CJC forum on the Charter,"[126] the Canadian Jewish Congress set aside a full day to discuss whether, through the Select Committee, it should make any submissions to the Joint House-Senate Committee on the Constitution, and if so, what those submissions might be. After protracted and heated debate, the CJC voted to authorize the Select Committee to make a comprehensive submission on the whole of the draft Charter, with specific support for the following inclusions: First, in the area of fundamental freedoms or political rights, the inclusion of references to freedom of conscience and religion and freedom of expression, and the specific exclusion of hate speech from the ambit of expression; second, the inclusion of a clause constitutionalizing the domestic prosecution of war criminals; third, the inclusion of a clause constitutionalizing equality rights and protection against discrimination, with particular reference to discrimination on grounds of race, religion, or gender; fourth, and the subject of particular debate at the CJC meeting, the inclusion, with respect to equality rights, of a clause constitutionalizing the legitimacy of affirmative action programs; fifth, the inclusion of a clause affirming minority language rights in education; sixth, the inclusion of a clause entrenching the principle of multiculturalism; and finally, the inclusion of a clause requiring that any purported limits on the guaranteed rights be "reasonable, prescribed by law, and demonstrably justified in a free and democratic society"—the overarching balancing principle of section 1 of the Charter,[127] and the contemplated analogue to the American "strict scrutiny" principle.

---

[126]Professor Maxwell Cohen, describing the unprecedented decision by the CJC.

[127]The original draft of section 1 had authorized limits on the guaranteed rights, provided they were "reasonable, and generally acceptable in a parliamentary democracy." The final draft was a far more stringent justificatory standard.

The CJC was one of the first NGOs invited to appear before the Parliamentary Committee, to which it submitted a written brief and made oral argument in support of the above recommendations. Ultimately, the final draft of the Charter incorporated all the recommendations made by the CJC, save for the recommendation that hate speech be excluded from the ambit of protected expression, and these recommendations were to prove to be of further importance in the historic case-law interpreting and applying the Charter. However, while the CJC made an important and, indeed, historic contribution to the adoption of this revolutionary rights Charter, its involvement in court challenges under the Charter—in the "litigation of the values of the nation"—was less involved and sustained, for a number of reasons.

First, the mandate of the CJC Select Committee was not renewed after a new CJC administration was elected in 1983, reflecting a change in the perceived purposes and priorities of the CJC. More particularly, the CJC was prepared to consign "human rights" advocacy to other human rights NGOs, confining itself to a more narrow and limited role in Charter litigation, becoming involved primarily in cases raising a direct "Jewish nexus." Effectively, the CJC eschewed the principle that guided American Jewish NGO involvement in religious liberty cases, namely, the principle that the human rights of Jews would be respected and secure to the extent that the rights of all people were safeguarded and respected. Second, by absenting itself from human rights litigation where it did not discern a Jewish nexus, the CJC unsuspectingly acquiesced in the "adverse impact" of this litigation for matters of Jewish concern, such as in equality rights litigation. Third, and perhaps most important, the CJC did not appear to have a clear strategy on these issues. There were times when the CJC did not intervene in cases even where a Jewish nexus was discernible—such as in the historic "Sunday Observance" cases, which had a direct interest for Canadian Jewry—yet it did intervene to challenge religion in the public schools and to support government aid to Jewish education.

To be fair to the CJC, it, like any NGO, had to adjust commitments to capacities. In the absence of a legal department, such as exists within the American Jewish NGOs, involvement was much more restrained. And while the CJC did not appear to map out its interventions in the matter of equality rights and religious liberty as part of an overall strategy—as did, for instance, the Women's Legal Education and Action Fund (LEAF) on equality and gender issues—it did make an important contribution in cases and areas where it did intervene. In particular, mention must be made of two areas where it did intervene in the major litigation engaging these areas, namely, hate speech and the bringing of Nazi war criminals to justice.

Hate Speech as a Discriminatory Practice: The Constitutionality of Anti-Hate Speech Legislation

If there is a single issue that has galvanized Canadian Jewish NGOs, it has been the right of minorities to protection against group vilifying speech. While the proximate cause of the passage of hate propaganda legislation in Canada was the report of the Special Committee on Hate Propaganda (hereinafter the Cohen Committee), demands by Jewish NGOs for legislation of this kind predated the establishment of the Cohen Committee. Indeed,

> it is fair to say that the Canadian Jewish Congress (CJC) was the leader in bringing the problem of hate propaganda, particularly anti-Semitic literature largely originating in the United States, to the attention of the government authorities, and requesting remedial legislation. For the CJC was convinced, following a careful analysis of existing Criminal Code provisions, that there was no legal basis to fight hate propaganda in the criminal courts, and for years, beginning in the early 1950s, and through the 1960s, it lobbied for legislative reform.[128]

During this period, a series of events converged in support of the enactment of anti-hate legislation.[129] First, a growing human rights movement had mobilized across Canada and attracted considerable public support for the passage of remedial legislation

---

[128]W. Kaplan, "The Special Committee on Hate Propaganda," in W. Kaplan, ed., *Law, Policy and International Justice: Essays in Honour of Maxwell Cohen* (Montreal: McGill-Queen's Press, 1993), 244.

[129]Ibid., 244–45.

to combat discrimination of various kinds. Second, international treaties were being signed committing signatory states, including Canada, to the enactment of measures against racist hate speech. Third, a number of foreign states had turned their attention to the problem of hate propaganda and were enacting anti-hate legislation, while in Canada there was a growing belief—and supporting evidence—that the dissemination of hate propaganda was on the rise. As William Kaplan states,

> the mass dissemination of vituperative materials appeared to accelerate in early 1964, and in March of that same year the *Toronto Star* editorialized about the "stream of violently anti-Semitic and anti-Negro material . . . circulating through the mails in Toronto," including the notorious Nazi newspaper, *Der Sturmer,* containing an account of "Jewish ritual murder." At the same time, and from across the country came demands from organizations as diverse as the Manitoba Bar Association, the Canadian Federation of University Women, and the National Convention of the Royal Canadian Legion for government action to halt the attacks. Some commentators called for a "test case" to deal with the use by hate propagandists of the mails, while Jewish NGOs felt the time was propitious to enact anti-hate legislation.[130]

It was the dramatic findings contained in the unanimous 1965 Report of the Cohen Committee—and the prestige of its membership[131]—that became the catalyst for action. In the words of the Cohen Committee, later invoked by the Supreme Court of Canada in upholding the constitutionality of the anti-hate legislation, "[t]he potential for psychological and social damage of hate propaganda, both to a desensitized majority and to sensitive minority target groups, is incalculable. As Mr. Justice Jackson of the United States Supreme Court wrote in *Beauharnois v. Illinois,* such 'sinister abuses of our freedoms of expression . . . can tear apart a society, brutal-

------

[130]Ibid., 245.

[131]The Committee included civil libertarians and former law professors Pierre Elliot Trudeau and Mark MacGuigan, who were later to become, respectively, Prime Minister and Minister of Justice of Canada.

ize its dominant elements, and persecute even to extermination, its minorities.'"[132]

Accordingly, the Cohen Committee recommended in 1965, and the Canadian Parliament in 1970 ultimately enacted, anti-hate legislation closely modeled on the CJC recommendations of the 1960s. In particular, the legislation prohibited the advocacy or promotion of genocide, the communication of hatred against an identifiable group in a manner likely to lead to a breach of the peace, and the willful promotion of hatred in a public place against an identifiable group. It established also a series of defenses to safeguard the rights of the accused.[133]

In a major forum on "Freedom of Expression and Hate Propaganda" at McGill University in 1987, Professor Maxwell Cohen, in a retrospective on the Report, summed up the dilemmas faced by his Committee—and subsequently by the Canadian courts—as follows:

> The Report on Hate Propaganda was published in November of 1965—twenty-two years ago. It dealt with the classic dilemmas in this field. "Sticks and stones may break my bones but names will never hurt me" had become, in the light of the increasing sensibilities of people everywhere, an impossible cliché with which to live. It may have suited an older, fairy-tale time; it was impossible in the post-Nuremberg generation in which we lived. So, we faced the classic philosophical dilemma of determining the limits on free speech, when speech is not directed to a serious political debate as such, but is directed to race or to religion in some unpleasant, intentionally hurtful way.[134]

All of the major Canadian Jewish NGOs supported the enactment of the anti-hate laws—as they had supported earlier federal and provincial antidiscrimination legislation—perceiving the anti-hate legislation as part of the genre of legislation protecting against

---

[132]Cited in *R. v. Keegstra,* [1991] 3 S.C.R. 697.

[133]Section 319(2) of the Criminal Code of Canada.

[134]M. Cohen, "Words That Maim," in I. Cotler, ed., *Nuremberg Forty Years Later: The Struggle Against Injustice in Our Time* (Montreal: McGill-Queen's Press, 1995).

AMERICAN	CANADIAN
1 Free speech issue	Equality issue—discriminatory practice
2 Absolutist approach: all hate speech is protected speech—no limits	Balancing approach—Competing right: the right of minorities to protection against group vilifying speech
3 Individual rights	Group rights—rights of minorities
4 Content neutral	Context relevant
5 Ahistorical: no reference to Holocaust, to Jews as victim, or to historical oppression of Jews	Historically grounded: reference to Holocaust and "catastrophic effects of racism," to Jews as target, and as historically oppressed group
6 Political speech: government as censor—establishment as target	Abhorrent speech—Parliament as protector—minority as target
7 Underlying values of free speech—marketplace of ideas, democratic participation, individual self-realization—need to be promoted and protected	Agreement on promotion and protection of underlying values of free speech; but hate speech regarded as "assaultive" on each of these values
8 No reference to international law—U.S. not even a State Party to International Convention on the Elimination of All Forms of Racial Discrimination (CERD)	International law as "relevant and persuasive authority"; Canada as State Party to both ICCPR and CERD, which prohibit hate speech as a discriminatory practice
9 No reference to international jurisprudence	Reference to international jurisprudence prohibiting hate speech
10 No comparative perspective—no reference to legislative and judicial experience of other "free and democratic societies"	Reference to comparative jurisprudence of other free and democratic societies; courts uphold anti-hate legislation in order that, inter alia, such societies remain free and democratic

11	No reference to United States as a multicultural society, or to multiculturalism as a normative referent	Canada held out as multicultural society, multiculturalism as a constitutional norm, and hate speech as an assault on multiculturalism
12	No "harms-based rationale" regarding injury caused by hate speech	"Harms-based rationale" for limiting hate speech regarded as injurious to members of the target group, to the target group itself, and to society as a whole
13	Anti-hate legislation will lead us inevitably down the slippery slope into censorship	Danger of different "slippery slope" not into censorship but into hate—"a swift slide into a marketplace of ideas, in which bad ideas flourish and good ideas die"
14	The value/virtue of tolerance	The more that hate speech is tolerated, the more it is likely to occur—the "paradox of tolerance" is that it breeds more intolerance
15	The answer to hate speech is more speech	More speech is desirable and always possible, but hate speech silences its victims

religious discrimination. Further, they have intervened in support of the constitutionality of the legislation in every hate speech case that has come before the Supreme Court of Canada, including supporting the constitutionality of the criminal law "group libel" legislation prohibiting the public and willful promotion of hatred against an identifiable group, the federal antidiscrimination remedy in the Canadian Human Rights Act that prohibits the repeated use of telephonic communications for the propagation of hatred against an identifiable group (which is defined as a discriminatory practice), and provincial antidiscrimination remedies such as those found in the Quebec Charter of Human Rights and Freedoms,[135] whose provisions are even broader than those in the federal Act.

American Jewish human rights NGOs might be surprised to learn that their Canadian counterparts were largely responsible for the enactment of Canada's anti-hate legislation to begin with, let alone the intervention of Canadian Jewish NGOs in all the "hate speech" cases in support of the constitutionality of such legislation. Unlike the Canadian NGOs, all the major American Jewish NGOs regard hate speech as protected speech under the First Amendment, and have filed *amicus* briefs in support of the constitutionality of hate speech, or have challenged legislation seeking to combat it. What follows is a comprehensive snapshot of the contrasting positions of American and Canadian Jewish NGOs in hate speech litigation, using Holocaust-denial hate speech directed against Jews as a case study. What emerges are deeply divergent views not only from a legal or "rights" perspective, but also from a cultural-religious or Jewish one.

Hate Crimes Legislation:
Combatting Bias-Motivated Crime

While American Jewish NGOs eschewed any support for the criminalization of hate speech, they have been at the forefront of national and state efforts to counter hate-motivated crimes. In particular, from the time the Anti-Defamation League (ADL) conceived, drafted, and proposed model hate crimes legislation for adoption some fourteen years ago, the response has been nothing short of dramatic.[136] More than half of the states have now enacted laws based on, or similar to, the ADL model, and almost every state has some form of legislation that can be invoked to redress bias-motivated crimes. The United States Congress has also taken steps to enact a federal hate crime statute, with both the House of Representatives and the Senate recently voting to include a penalty-enhancement provision in their respective versions of an omnibus crime bill.

------

[135]Charter of Human Rights and Freedoms, R.S.Q. c.C-12.

[136]Anti-Defamation League, *Hate Crimes Laws: A Comprehensive Guide* (New York: Anti-Defamation League, 1994).

Furthermore, in a landmark decision in the struggle against bias-motivated criminal conduct in June 1993, in Wisconsin, the U.S. Supreme Court in a unanimous decision[137] upheld the constitutionality of Wisconsin's penalty-enhancement hate crimes statute, which was based on the ADL model.

The ADL had filed an *amicus* brief in support of hate crimes legislation before both the Wisconsin and United States Supreme Courts, where it described the compelling need for such legislation, and explained how the Wisconsin law was consistent with the First Amendment. The brief maintained that the core of the legislation is a "penalty enhancement" concept whereby the defendant is subject to an enhanced penalty if his crime is motivated by an intent to harm based on the victim's race, religion, or similar characteristics—thereby harming the entire community as well as the victim. As the brief put it, "enhancing the penalty also serves to give a message as to the seriousness with which society judges bigotry that takes the form of criminal conduct directed toward certain groups, and acts as a deterrent to such conduct."[138] The brief affirmed that the statute was not criminalizing hate speech, which was protected by the First Amendment; it merely enhanced the penalty for crimes where bias was the principal motivating factor.

The ADL model statute also includes an institutional vandalism or "religious rights" section, which increases the criminal penalties for vandalism aimed at houses of worship, cemeteries, schools, and community centers, and seeks to deter attacks against the most common targets of vandalism: churches, synagogues, and religious schools. The statute requires knowledge of the character of the property, but does not require proof of motive for the vandalism, making convictions easier to obtain. Another provision of the model legislation creates a civil action for victims. While these activities might presently be actionable in a common law tort suit, the provision makes the remedy explicit. The section also provides for additional forms of relief, that is, recovery for actions by mi-

---

[137]*Wisconsin v. Mitchell*, 113 S.Ct. 2194 (1993).

[138]Anti-Defamation League, *ADL in the Courts: Litigation Docket 1993* (New York: Anti-Defamation League, 1993).

nors, which is generally not permitted under most states' common law tort actions. These additional forms of relief can have a significant deterrent value and should also encourage victims to consider bringing civil suits. The ADL model legislation also includes a section on bias crime reporting and training. Experience has shown that accurate, comprehensive, and comparative data concerning the number, location, and types of bias crimes are essential to combat hate crimes. The enactment of the federal Hate Crime Statistics Act in 1990 demonstrated widespread recognition of the necessity of gathering data on crimes motivated by bigotry and prejudice in order to be able to combat hate crimes.

As for Canada, as set forth previously, Canadian Jewish NGOs such as the CJC and B'nai Brith have been at the forefront of advocacy for anti-hate laws to protect minorities against group villifying speech, which, unlike their American counterparts, Canadian Jewish NGOs characterize as a "hate crime." They have appreciated, however, that "other forms of hate crime are not caught by Canada's anti-hate laws. These are Criminal Code offences motivated by hatred against an identifiable group which do not involve hate propaganda. Such offences can range from mischief, to the most vicious assault, to murder."[139]

Accordingly, and not unlike the ADL in the United States, CJC and B'nai Brith have been the principal advocates in Canada of recently passed legislation that directs a comprehensive reassessment of the sentencing regime in Canada. Canadian Jewish NGOs argued successfully for the inclusion of "hate motivation" as an aggravating factor in the sentencing regime, in their briefs before the Parliamentary Committee considering the legislation. In the words of one CJC submission, "sentencing can have an important impact in dealing with hate crimes. Specifically, this aspect of the legislation sends out a strong message that hate-motivated offences constitute a unique category of crime requiring the special attention of the judicial system. Sentence enhancement will complement existing Criminal Code provisions in this regard." The CJC pointed

---

[139]Canadian Jewish Congress, *CJC Submission to the Standing Committee on Justice and Legal Affairs Regarding Bill C-41* (Montreal: Canadian Jewish Congress), 1–2.

out that hate crime of this type continues to rise in a most dramatic fashion, particularly in the urban areas of Canada. Its submission referred to a report in August 1994 by Detective Sergeant Wayne Cotgreave of the Metropolitain Toronto Police Hate Crimes unit, in which he noted that there had been a 51 percent increase in hate crimes reported in the Metro Toronto area compared with the previous reporting period. Tragically, two-thirds of the perpetrators investigated were under the age of twenty-five. Similar statistics have been gathered by police forces in other urban areas in Canada and the United States.

Regrettably, the law has traditionally viewed hate crimes such as synagogue desecrations as simple mischief, without paying due regard to the intense emotional pain suffered by members of the entire targeted community. However, in a landmark 1990 decision, the Ontario Court of Appeal in *R. v. Lelas*[140] recognized this perspective of hate crime. The accused in *Lelas*, a member of the Ku Klux Klan, who described himself as a racist, spray painted anti-Semitic symbols and slogans on a synagogue, on a Hebrew school building, and on an automobile. He was charged with mischief to property worth over one thousand dollars. At trial, the accused was sentenced to six months' imprisonment, with two years' probation. Upon appeal by the Crown, the Ontario Court of Appeal recognized hate as an aggravating factor in the crime. In his ground-breaking judgment, Mr. Justice Houlden increased the accused's sentence from six months to one year. As Mr. Justice Houlden wrote:

> In spray painting the synagogue and Hebrew school, Lelas was not merely intending to cause damage to property; rather, to use his words, he wanted to enrage the Jewish community. His acts were done to strike fear and terror and to cause emotional upset in the Jewish community. When mischief is racially or religiously motivated and is done to cause emotional injury or shock to a particular segment of Canadian society, it calls for a far more severe penalty than mischief which is done merely to damage property.

The CJC brief, citing from the Houlden judgment, concluded that "when crime of any type is motivated by hate against an identifi-

---

[140][1990] 74 O.R. (2d) 552.

able group, such crimes are committed to cause emotional injury or shock to that particular segment of Canadian society and thus call for more severe penalties."[141]

Combatting Discrimination in Employment on Grounds of Religion: Developments in Canadian and American Law and the Role of Jewish NGOs

In June 1994, in an important case[142] involving "adverse impact discrimination," the Supreme Court of Canada reversed a lower court ruling upholding the refusal of a Catholic School Board to compensate Jewish teachers for loss of pay for not working on Yom Kippur. In doing so, the Court relied on a line of precedents[143] and principles in antidiscrimination law in the matter of religion that Canadian Jewish NGOs had helped establish through their interventions in the cases. In particular, the Court held that adverse impact discrimination will arise where an employer, for genuine business reasons, adopts a rule or standard that is on its face neutral and that will apply equally to all employees, but that has a different and discriminatory effect upon another employee or group of employees based on the prohibited ground of religion. This principle and proposition can be expected to guide the court in cases of this kind.

In the United States, Title VII of the Civil Rights Act of 1964 prohibits discrimination in employment on the basis of religion. Section 70(j) was added to Title VII by amendment in 1972. It defines "religion" as follows: "The term 'religion' includes all aspects of religious observance and practice, as well as belief, unless an employer demonstrates that he is unable to reasonably accommodate to an employee's religious observance or practice without

---

[141]*CJC Submission to the Standing Committee*, 3.

[142]*Commission scolaire régionale de Chambly v. Bergevin*, [1994] 2 S.C.R. 525.

[143]*Ontario Human Rights Commission and O'Malley v. Simpson Sears Ltd.*, [1985] 2 S.C.R. 536; *Central Alberta Dairy Pool v. Alberta (Human Rights Commission)*, [1990] 2 S.C.R. 489; *Central Okanagan School District No. 23 v. Renaud*, [1993] 2 S.C.R. 970.

undue hardship on the conduct of the employer's business (42 U.S.C. Section 2000e(j))."

The U.S. Supreme Court has interpreted this provision narrowly,[144] so as to place relatively little restraint on an employer's ability to refuse to provide religious accommodation. Regrettably, the Court has tended to interpret the legislation through the lens of the "Establishment" clause rather than the lens of the "Free Exercise" clause of the First Amendment. Indeed, the Court appears to ignore that the principle of disestablishment of religion is itself rooted in the Free Exercise Clause, and that "the spirit, if not the letter of this clause points to the conclusion that Title VII should be interpreted to afford meaningful protection against religious discrimination."[145] The Court's interpretation is inconsistent with the principle that religious discrimination—or lack of accommodation—should be treated as seriously as any other type of discrimination. Since the Court's activity in this area involves interpretation of legislation, rather than constitutional doctrine, the matter is susceptible to correction by the Congress, and Jewish NGOs are now engaged in helping to draft legislation to provide greater protection against religious discrimination for observant members of all faiths. It is not without some irony, however, that these same NGOs helped develop the very "separationist" disestablishment jurisprudence that has been used to inhibit the Free Exercise clause.

Combatting Transnational Discrimination by Foreign Governments in U.S. Courts: The Arab Boycott as a Case Study

In 1977, the Report of the Commission on Economic Coercion and Discrimination[146] exposed a pattern of compliance and complicity with the Arab Boycott in Canada in both the private and public sectors. It concluded that the notion of an "Arab Boycott" was a

---

[144]*Trans World Airlines v. Hardison*, 432 U.S. 63 (1977).

[145]Ibid.

[146](Montreal: Centre for Law and Public Policy, McGill University, 1977).

misnomer. What really was taking place was a "Canadian boy-cott"—the acquiescence by Canadian corporations in the extra-territorial application of foreign law to Canada, purporting to dictate, through a restrictive covenant, the terms of commerce between Canada and a friendly state, the terms of commerce between Canadian corporations themselves, and, worst of all, the terms of employment in Canada on grounds of religion. In other words, Canadian corporations, as a condition for doing business with an Arab country, had to undertake not to do business with Israel (secondary boycott) or with another Canadian corporation that did business with Israel (tertiary boycott) and not to employ or promote Canadians of the Jewish religion. The evidence in the Commission's Report established that both Crown corporations and leading Canadian private corporations had knowingly com-plied with both the secondary and tertiary boycotts, and in some instances, had refused to hire or promote Canadians specifically because they were Jews.

While these dramatic disclosures were taking place in Canada, and Canadian Jewish NGOs were seeking to get anti-boycott, anti-discrimination legislation enacted, similar revelations in the United States had already resulted in: (1) U.S. Congressional Hearings on the impact of the Arab boycott in America; (2) the enactment of comprehensive federal anti-boycott legislation mandating dis-closure of requests to comply with the boycott, while prohibiting actual compliance itself; (3) the establishment of a "Boycott Watch" monitoring unit and newsletter by the American Jewish Congress; (4) the initiation by American Jewish NGOs of a Business Round-table with leading American corporations to secure their support for a strong anti-boycott stance; and (5) the authorizing of a "right of action" in U.S. courts for American citizens to seek redress for any damages caused through the discriminatory application of the Arab boycott in America.

The ADL filed *amicus* briefs[147] in support of a private right of action in American courts for victims of the Arab boycott. The briefs document the inception, expansion, and growing impact of the Arab boycott of Israel, the methods by which the boycott had been

---

[147] *ADL in the Courts*, 36.

enforced by the Arab League, its discriminatory effects on companies and individuals, and the enactment of the federal anti-boycott provisions, which Congress enacted primarily to deal with the unfairness and discrimination implicit in these restrictive covenants. In particular, as the briefs demonstrate, the anti-boycott legislative provisions were intended to protect the civil rights of a special class—people discriminated against on the basis of race, religion, sex, or national origin; nationals, residents, and business concerns of boycotted countries; and American Jews as well as U.S. companies employing American Jews or supporting Jewish organizations, indicating the clear nexus to discrimination on grounds of religion. The briefs conclude by recalling that "the EAA's anti-boycott provisions were intended to protect victims of the Arab boycott, both by permitting them judicial redress and by prohibiting any further participation in the boycott. These purposes can only be served by recognition of a private right of action under the EAA."[148]

But while Jewish NGOs in the U.S. helped secure the enactment of comprehensive anti-boycott legislation, filed *amicus* briefs in support of victims of the Arab boycott seeking redress in American courts, and were instrumental in a host of initiatives as set forth above, Canadian Jewish NGOs were markedly less successful in developing parallel initiatives in Canada. Part of the reason was that all this was taking place in the pre-Charter era, before a "rights culture" had taken hold in Canada. A more important reason, which demonstrates the importance of rights-based arguments, was that the advocacy for anti-boycott legislation and related measures in Canada was being advanced by the Canada-Israel Committee (CIC), the lobby group for Israel in Canada, rather than by Cana-

---

[148]The only two reported decisions that deal with this issue reached opposite conclusions. In *Bulk Oil (Zug) v. Sun Company, Inc.*, 583 F. Supp. 1134 (S.D.N.Y. 1983), *aff'd without op.* 742 F2d 143 (2d Cir. 1984) the court ruled that there was no implied private right of action under the EAA, and in *Abrams v. Baylor College of Medicine*, 581 F.Supp. 1570 (S.D. Tex. 1984), *aff'd in part and rev'd in part*, 805 F.2d 528 (5th Cir. 1986) the court determined that there was indeed an implied private right of action. ADL participated as *amicus curiae* in both cases.

dian Jewish human rights NGOs such as the CJC and B'nai Brith. In other words, the advocacy by CIC took a Canadian rights issue of antidiscrimination law and made it appear to be a political issue related to the Arab-Israeli conflict. In contrast, the advocacy by major American Jewish human rights NGOs—in concert with American civil liberties groups—resulted in the issue in the United States being perceived for what it was, namely, a human rights issue involving discrimination on one or more prohibited grounds of discrimination. As a human rights, antidiscrimination issue, it resonated in the court of American public opinion; as a perceived political, Middle East issue in Canada it never seriously got off the ground.

Use of Domestic Courts to Enforce International Human Rights Norms against Persecution on Grounds of Religion in a Foreign Country: The Siderman[149] Case as a Case Study

Siderman v. Argentina concerned the confiscation of property and acts of torture committed against the Siderman family in Argentina by the Argentine military junta that seized power in 1976. The Sidermans were among the many victims of the Argentine military, whose rule from 1976 to 1983 was characterized not only by a virulent anti-Semitism, but also by kidnappings, torture, and the "disappearances" of thousands of Argentine citizens. Jose Siderman was a prominent Argentine Jew who survived being kidnapped, beaten, and tortured. After he and his family fled to the United States—where they found a safe haven—their assets, including the largest hotel in northern Argentina and other significant real estate holdings, were confiscated. When their initial efforts to obtain redress in Argentina failed, the Sidermans initiated a lawsuit in the United States. At that time, the ADL supported their complaint in federal district court with an *amicus* brief that detailed a pattern of anti-Semitism in Argentina and argued that U.S. courts have jurisdiction to redress injuries such as those the Sidermans suffered.

---

[149]965 F.2d 699 (9th Cir. 1992), cert. denied, 113 S.Ct. 1812 (1993).

In 1984, the U.S. District Court issued a default judgment in favor of the Sidermans. However, the judgment was vacated a year later when a representative of the Argentine government appeared in court for the first time in the case and invoked the Foreign Sovereign Immunities Act. The Sidermans chose not to appeal the District Court's decision immediately. Instead, they again sought to obtain redress in Argentina, where the military was no longer in power. However, after several years their efforts proved fruitless, prompting a decision to return again to the U.S. courts.

In the ADL's brief supporting the Sidermans' appeal to the Ninth Circuit, the focus again was on anti-Semitism in Argentina, both historically and specifically under the rule of the military junta. In addition, the ADL brief argued that the facts of the *Siderman* case brought it within an exception to the Act of State doctrine, and that consequently the District Court erred in applying that doctrine. The judicially created Act of State doctrine allows U.S. courts to abstain from deciding a case involving an international transaction on the grounds that one of the actors in the transaction is a foreign state. However, what has come to be known as the *Bernstein*[150] exception to the doctrine precludes its application by the courts if the U.S. State Department informs the court that the executive branch has determined application of the doctrine to be unnecessary. In its brief, the ADL contended that *Bernstein* stands for the general proposition that the Act of State doctrine does not bar claims in U.S. courts for property seized by a foreign government as a result of religious discrimination. Furthermore, the brief pointed out that the Sidermans' property was confiscated by a regime no longer in power, and that therefore "it can hardly be argued that a court's consideration of this case could embarrass the Executive's conduct of foreign affairs." Finally, the brief noted that the treatment of the Sidermans was also a violation of international law that U.S. courts should redress.

Judgment in the case is still pending. But the importance of the case lies in the principle that U.S. domestic courts may be resorted to for the enforcement of international human rights against a foreign government in matters of religious discrimination—demon-

---

[150]*ADL in the Courts*, 39–40.

strating again the importance of religious discrimination as a matter of *jus cogens* in international law.

Gender-based Discrimination under the Cover of Religion

Canadian Jewish NGOs have challenged attempts to use religion as a defense to a gender-related human rights violation, for example, where the country of origin supports the practice of female genital mutilation as a "religious" responsibility. Jewish NGOs have also gone to court to support claims for refugee status on grounds of gender-specific persecution.

In a landmark immigration ruling,[151] Canada has granted refugee status to a Somalian woman who fled her country with her ten-year-old daughter because she feared that her daughter would face ritual genital mutilation. In one of the rare occasions that any Western nation has specifically cited the threat posed by this ancient custom, widely practiced in Africa, as a reason for granting asylum, a panel of the Immigration and Refugee Board said the daughter's "right to personal security would be grossly infringed" if she were forced to return.

A similar case came up recently in the United States, when a federal immigration judge ruled in March 1994 that a Nigerian woman living illegally in Portland, Oregon, would not be deported to her native country because her two young daughters would probably face genital mutilation if they accompanied her.[152] The Portland judge's ruling was not so sweeping as that of the Canadian panel—the judge, Kendall Warren, did not grant a request for asylum, which would have broken new ground, but merely annulled an expulsion order—but both the American and Canadian decisions have put foreign governments on notice that religion will not avail as a cover for human rights violators. Jewish NGOs in

---

[151]See N. Mawani, "Canada Gives a Somali Refuge from Genital Rite," *New York Times* (July 21, 1994): A-14.

[152]"Violations of the Rights of Women in Refugee Context," *Human Rights Research and Education Bulletin* 26 (1994): 1–8.

Canada and the United States have been active in securing the enactment of guidelines that would authorize the conferral of refugee status on the basis of gender-related persecution on grounds of religion.

Holocaust Remembrance and War Crimes Justice: The Right to Memory as a "Religious" Right

Being Jewish has been described as an exercise in "collective memory." Indeed, for Jews, memory itself is almost a religion, and Holocaust remembrance a religious right, and even a duty. For the Holocaust, as Nobel Laureate Elie Wiesel has reminded the world again and again, was a war against the Jews in which not all victims were Jews, but all Jews were victims. *Zachor*[153]— "remember"—has become for Jewish NGOs not only a moral exhortation, but a "right to memory,"[154] a religious commandment. Holocaust denial is regarded by these NGOs not only as an assault on memory, on truth, but as the "killing of the victims a second time"—the ultimate assault on Jewish sensibility; while bringing Nazi war criminals to justice is seen as much as a matter of fidelity to Holocaust remembrance as it is fidelity to the rule of law.

Thus, for American, Canadian, European, and Latin American Jewish NGOs, fidelity to Holocaust remembrance, combatting Holocaust denial, and bringing Nazi war criminals to justice is seen as the ultimate protection of religious human rights—the Jewish NGO sword and shield against defamation, the existential antidote to injustice. It has also been a centerpiece of the work of international Jewish human rights NGOs such as the World Jewish Congress, and national human rights NGOs such as the ADL, just as it is the *raison d'être* of the Simon Wiesenthal Centre, the fastest

---

[153]Indeed, "ZACHOR" is also the name of a Jewish NGO devoted to Holocaust remembrance.

[154]E. Wiesel, "Witness," in I. Cotler, ed., *Nuremberg Forty Years Later*, 21.

growing Jewish human rights NGO of the past decade.[155] It has been the inspiration behind the building of Holocaust Memorials such as the Simon Wiesenthal Centre Museum of Tolerance in Los Angeles, the U.S. Holocaust Museum in Washington, and the Holocaust Memorial Centre in Montreal.

For Canadian Jewish NGOs, these issues have not only been priorities on the "Jewish" rights agenda, but the NGOs have sought to make them priorities on the Canadian justice agenda. Accordingly, these NGOs have played a crucial role in the enactment of anti-hate legislation to combat Holocaust-denial and protect the integrity of memory; in the enactment of war crimes legislation to authorize the domestic prosecution of Nazi war criminals in Canada;[156] and in having included in the Canadian Charter of Rights and Freedoms a provision constitutionalizing prosecution of war criminals, in the sense of insuring that "retroactivity" shall not avail as a defense against prosecution.[157] Moreover, Jewish NGOs have appreciated that these issues are inextricably bound up one with another. For those NGOs then, the first order of justice is combatting racist incitement, while every time the NGOs bring a Nazi war criminal to justice, they strike a blow against the Holocaust-denial movement.

Canadian Jewish NGOs have not only played a crucial role in public advocacy on these matters, but they have gone to court to secure the application of these laws, having intervened in every major war crimes case before provincial appellate courts and the Supreme Court of Canada. For the Jewish human rights NGO for whom memory is itself almost a religion, Holocaust remembrance and bringing Nazi war criminals to justice are regarded as profound statements—and actions—in the promotion and protection of religious human rights.

---

[155]In the sixteen years since its founding, the Simon Wiesenthal Centre has amassed close to 500,000 members, most of them in the last decade alone.

[156]The Canadian Jewish Congress and B'nai Brith Canada were instrumental in the enactment of s.7(3.71–3.76) of the Canadian Criminal Code.

[157]Section 11(g) of the Canadian Charter of Rights and Freedoms.

STRATEGIES AND MODELS OF ADVOCACY BY JEWISH NGOS IN THE PROMOTION AND PROTECTION OF RELIGIOUS HUMAN RIGHTS: THE STRUGGLE FOR SOVIET JEWRY AS A CASE STUDY

There is perhaps no single religious human rights issue around which Jewish NGOs coalesced more than the situation of oppressed Jewry. Indeed, the plight of Soviet Jewry in the 1970s and 1980s and, somewhat belatedly, that of Syrian and Ethiopian Jewry in the 1980s, dominated the Jewish and human rights agendas of every major Jewish NGO, while spawning single-issue Jewish NGOs dedicated to the struggle for Soviet, Syrian, and Ethiopian Jewry. Some of these single-issue Jewish NGOs, such as the National Conference on Soviet Jewry and the Union of Councils for Soviet Jewry, became major Jewish and human rights NGOs in their own right, helping to influence the course and conduct of both American foreign policy and the Helsinki process throughout most of the 1970s and 1980s, as the situation of Soviet Jewry was a watershed issue in East–West relations.

What follows is an identification of the role played, and strategies deployed, by Jewish NGOs in addressing and seeking to redress violations of religious human rights, using Soviet Jewry as a case study. What emerges is a prospective model for strategic advocacy by religious NGOs, and by human rights NGOs generally speaking, in the matter of redressing violations of religious human rights and human rights at large.

Fact Finding and Human Rights Monitoring

One of the most important, indeed crucial, NGO functions—and one indispensable to the promotion and protection of religious human rights—is the investigation, documentation, exposure, and denunciation of violations of religious human rights and of the violators themselves. As Professor John Humphrey put it,[158] the

---

[158]John Humphrey, *Human Rights and the United Nations: A Great Adventure* (Dobbs Ferry, N.Y.: Transnational Publications, 1984).

"mobilization of shame against human rights violators" is the ultimate sanction. Or as Professor Mullerson has said, "monitoring is the very essence of human rights enforcing."[159] The knowledge that "the whole world is watching" tends to concentrate the minds of human rights violators wonderfully.

Accordingly, whether we are speaking about the human rights of Jews in the Soviet Union, Syria, or Ethiopia, the evidence is compelling that this fact-finding function is crucial to the promotion and protection of human rights. Indeed, governments themselves have become increasingly dependent on the fact finding of NGOs, while the inter-governmental machinery, such as the UN Commission on Human Rights, and the Human Rights Committee under the International Covenant on Civil and Political Rights, would be "virtually incapacitated"[160] in the absence of NGO briefs, petitions, documentary evidence, legal analysis, and written and oral interventions.

But if fact finding and human rights monitoring by NGOs is crucial to the promotion and protection of human rights generally, the "mobilization of shame" by Jewish NGOs against the Soviet Union's violations of the rights of Soviet Jews is dramatic evidence of the efficacy of this fact-finding and monitoring NGO strategy. It was the exposure of the Soviet Union's systematic denial to Soviet Jews of the right to emigrate that led to the enactment of the Jackson-Vanick Amendment, conditioning the conferral of U.S. trade benefits on the rate of Jewish emigration from the USSR. It was the documentation of the Jewish Prisoners of Conscience in the USSR—people who, like Josef Begun, were fired from their job for desiring to emigrate, and then charged with parasitism for not having a job—that exposed the full brutality of the Soviet Union and isolated them in the court of world public opinion. And it was the massive

---

[159]R. Mullerson, in an unpublished paper at the Canada-Soviet Conference on "Ending the Cold War," Simon Fraser University (June 20–22, 1990).

[160]See, for example, David Weissbrodt, "The Contribution of International Non-Governmental Organizations to the Protection of Human Rights," in Theodore Meron, *Human Rights in International Law: Legal and Policy Issues*, vol. 2 (Oxford: Clarendon Press, 1984), 403–438.

evidence[161] of the corresponding denial of the religious rights of Soviet Jews—the right to the free exercise of their religion, the right to teach and learn the Hebrew language and the basic tenets of their faith and culture, the right "to worship or assemble in connection with a religion or belief,"[162] the right to visit and be visited by their co-religionists abroad—that culminated in the "shame" that is the international community's chief enforcement weapon. The denial of these religious rights, coupled with the denial of the right to emigrate—regarded as tantamount to the denial of the right to life itself—led to the international sanctions regime, including the "linkage" under the Helsinki Final Act.

Legislative/Advocacy Role

It might seem paradoxical to attribute a legislative role to NGOs, but increasingly, in the international arena in particular, NGOs are playing a formative role in the initiation, drafting, interpretation, and application of international human rights agreements and standard-setting generally.[163] Thus, whether it be the International Covenant on Civil and Political Rights, the International Covenant on Economic Social and Cultural Rights, the International Convention on the Elimination of All Forms of Racial Discrimination, the Convention on the Elimination of All Forms of Discrimination Against Women, or the recent Convention on the Rights of the Child, the NGOs have played an important legislative role.

What is true of the legislative role of human rights NGOs, in general, is particularly evident in the legislative contribution of Jewish NGOs in the matter of religious human rights in particular. It was Jewish NGOs that were responsible for the inclusion of the

---

[161]For example, the Soviet Jewry NGOs compiled compelling documentary evidence and witness testimony regarding the denial of religious rights.

[162]See, on this point, Y. Dinstein, "The Human Rights of Soviet Jewry," in D. Sidorsky, ed., *Essays on Human Rights* (Philadelphia: JPS, 1971).

[163]See, for example, Howard Tolley, Jr., "Popular Sovereignty and International Law—I.C.J. Strategies for Human Rights Standard Setting," *Human Rights Quarterly* 11 (1989): 561–585; and Humphrey, 12–13.

"religion" provisions in the UN Charter and in the Universal Declaration of Human Rights, that ensured that Article 18 respecting freedom of religion was included in the ICCPR, that lobbied for and helped bring about the Genocide Convention, that made a substantial contribution to the provisions respecting discrimination in the Convention on the Elimination of All Forms of Discrimination and the UNESCO Convention, and that played a formative role in securing the provisions relating to religion in the Helsinki Final Act and the Declaration on the Elimination of All Forms of Religious Intolerance.

Indeed, the Copenhagen Conference on the Human Dimension is an excellent case study of the role and efficacy of Jewish NGOs. The National Conference on Soviet Jewry, the Union for the Councils for Soviet Jews, the World Jewish Congress and others, in concert with the American Delegation to the C.S.C.E. Conference, played an important role in the identification and drafting of "those principles of justice which form the basis of the rule of law . . . and which are essential to the full expression of the inherent dignity and of the equal and inalienable rights of all human beings."[164] Similarly, the Canadian Helsinki Watch Group, and the Canadian Committee on Soviet Jewry, working closely with both the Canadian and Soviet Delegations, contributed to the inclusion for the first time in a C.S.C.E. Concluding Document of a joint proposal by Canada and the USSR to combat racial incitement, including a specific condemnation of anti-Semitism itself. The proposal,[165] in part, reads as follows:

(40) The participating States clearly and unequivocally condemn totalitarianism, racial and ethnic hatred, anti-Semitism, xenophobia, and discrimination against anyone as well as prosecution on religious and ideological grounds.

They declare their firm intention to intensify the efforts to combat these phenomena in all their forms and therefore will:

---

[164]See C.S.C.E. Copenhagen Concluding Document on the Human Dimension, Article 2 (1990).

[165]Ibid., 42.

(40.1) take effective measures, including the adoption, in conformity with their constitutional systems and their international obligations, of such laws as may be necessary, to provide protection against any acts that constitute incitement to violence against persons or groups based on national, racial, ethnic or religious discrimination, hostility or hatred, including anti-Semitism.

Humanitarian Assistance to Victims of Human Rights Abuses

NGOs are playing an increasingly important, if not indispensable, role in rendering a variety of forms of humanitarian assistance to victims of human rights abuses and their families. Their activities include, for example, tracing disappeared persons, as in the case of the inquiry into the fate and whereabouts of Raoul Wallenberg;[166] visiting detainees in prison, as in the visits to the Chistopol prison by members of Helsinki Watch Groups;[167] securing humane conditions of confinement through representations made within the C.S.C.E. Conferences; and providing material and moral assistance to victims' families and the like. This humanitarian assistance may involve not only representations to the human rights violator government, but to the NGO's own government, to other governments, to inter-governmental bodies, and to international organizations.

Jewish NGOs are a dramatic example of this strategy, as they served as a vital lifeline for Jewish refuseniks, prisoners of con-

---

[166]In 1989, an NGO in the form of an International Commission of Inquiry into the Fate and Whereabouts of Raoul Wallenberg was formed. The Commission reported its findings in 1990. This led to the creation of the first Soviet-International Commission of Inquiry on the Fate and Whereabouts of Raoul Wallenberg in August 1990.

[167]For example, members of the U.S. Helsinki Watch Group and the Moscow Helsinki Group made visits to a number of Soviet prisons in 1989–90, including Perm Labor Camp #35. The writer became the first lawyer to visit Chistopol prison in September 1990, and was a member of the Soviet-International Commission of Inquiry on the Fate and Whereabouts of Raoul Wallenberg that spent a week in Vladimir Prison in September 1990.

science, and other victims of human rights violations in the Soviet Union. They saw to it that (1) every prisoner of conscience—indeed, every refusenik family—was adopted by some Jewish organization, synagogue, or family in the West; (2) children of prisoners or refuseniks were similarly "adopted"; (3) whole Jewish communities in the USSR were "twinned" with municipalities, provinces, or states in the United States, Canada, Europe, and elsewhere; (4) food parcels, mail, reading materials, and the like were sent to the "Sharanskys," "Nudels," and "Beguns" languishing in the Soviet Gulag; (5) prayer books, *matzos* on Passover, and other religious articles and necessities were delivered to synagogues in the Soviet Union; (6) regular visits to refuseniks and families of political prisoners would take place from their co-religionists abroad; (7) refusenik cancer patients were given special attention so that they might secure the best medical care that could be made available to them, and that, if they had to die, their dignity and religious sensibility would be protected as best it could. In a word, the work of Jewish NGOs in this area was a fulfillment of the principle that, as the Talmud instructs, and which is the guiding credo for Jewish NGOs engaged in humanitarian assistance, "all Jews are responsible one for another."[168]

Legal Representation to Victims of Human Rights Abuses

Providing legal representation to victims of human rights abuses is, admittedly, a difficult and somewhat complex role, but also a particularly compelling one. Legal representation not only helps to secure redress for victims of human rights violations, it serves a number of collateral functions at the same time. In many ways Jewish NGOs and the lawyers associated with them pioneered in the development of this legal strategy itself and the collateral benefits that attended it. In particular, Jewish NGOs and their respective attorneys inspired the mobilization of shame against the USSR rights violator regime through public legal petitions to the Procurator-

---

[168]*Shavuot* 39.

General of the USSR;[169] prepared a documented set of testimonies
to the innocence of the accused through the collection of witness
testimony and documentary evidence;[170] organized what was effectively a critical mass of human rights advocacy on behalf of refuseniks and political prisoners through petitions to inter-governmental
fora, including the UN Human Rights Committee (where appropriate), the ILO,[171] and UNESCO; utilized the complaints procedure and
"open forum" of the Helsinki process; used domestic courts to enforce international human rights norms; and exercised the UN 1503
procedure in cases of a "consistent pattern of gross violations of
human rights," such as in the denial of the right to emigrate to Soviet Jews. The advocacy work of the Jewish NGOs is a case study of
the use and efficiency of a myriad of procedures and remedies
under both domestic and international human rights law.

Human Rights Education

The educational process put into practice by Jewish NGOs involves
"conscientization," as some in the human rights movement call it—
or *"sensibiliser,"* as the French put it—in order to create a culture of
human rights, with particular respect for religious human rights. The
educational work of the American Jewish Committee is a case study
in the role of Jewish NGOs in the matter of education for tolerance—
or education against religious intolerance, in the promotion and
protection of religious human rights in general, and in the redress
of the violations of the human rights of Soviet Jews in particular.

---

[169]For example, the International Human Rights Law Group, a Wash-
ington-based NGO, organized a petition to the Procurator-General of the
USSR in the matter of prisoner of conscience Josef Begun in 1984. Petitions to the Procurator-General of the USSR by this writer on behalf of
Natan Sharansky, Ida Nudel, and the like were made more compelling
by reason of the NGO support and collateral advocacy.

[170]See, for example, "The Sharansky Case," an 800–page compendium
of witness testimony and documentary evidence.

[171]The International Human Rights Law Group and the Canadian Helsinki Watch Group submitted complaints to the ILO and UNESCO on
behalf of political prisoners in the Soviet Union.

Indeed, the American Jewish Committee's Jacob Blaustein Institute for the Advancement of Human Rights (JBI) has made the subject of religious intolerance—its dimensions, root causes, and possible remedial measures—a major focus of its activities,[172] while the international affirmation of "religious human rights" has been a focal point of its research and advocacy projects. JBI has worked to assure the adoption and later the implementation of the Declaration on the Elimination of All Forms of Religious Intolerance. It launched a series of colloquia in the 1970s and 1980s that brought together prominent international scholars and jurists to examine the central elements of religious freedom. The essays and publications that were produced helped equip scholars, international experts, diplomats, and practitioners, who in turn advocated, analyzed, and sought to implement "religious human rights," including, in particular, the characterization of the right to leave one's country as the most fundamental of rights.

Although the JBI, like the AJC itself, was particularly concerned with the fate of Soviet Jews who were barred from leaving their country, it perceived the problem of "the right to leave" as a far more universal one, affecting many people across the globe. A country's arbitrary refusal to permit its nationals to emigrate was seen as a standing violation of one of the most hallowed rights in international human rights law. Accordingly, from its earliest days, the JBI embarked upon a continuing educational effort to ensure the observance of this freedom in international law, while demonstrating how the denial of this freedom was tantamount to the denial of the right to liberty—including religious liberty—if not the right to life itself. In June 1972, the JBI, together with the International Institute of Human Rights in Strasbourg, France, and the Faculty of Law of the University of Uppsala, Sweden, convened some seventy scholars and human rights experts from twenty-five countries to discuss the right to freedom of movement throughout the world, in what has come to be known as the Uppsala Colloquium.

By exposing the devices some governments used to circumvent freedom of emigration and by setting out recommendations for international safeguards, the Uppsala Declaration adopted at the gathering focused world attention on this fundamental right. Widely

---

[172]Gaer, "The AJC and the Right to Freedom of Religion" (see note 77).

disseminated to scholars and practitioners in the human rights field, the Declaration was translated into several languages and published in numerous journals. It helped serve as a resource for the drafters of the Jackson Amendment to the Trade Reform Act of 1974, which linked most-favored-nation trade status with free emigration, and had an important impact on the Helsinki Conference on Security and Cooperation in Europe. Indeed, in the historic Final Act (Accord) of that Helsinki Conference in 1975, thirty-five nations, including the United States, Canada, and the Soviet Union, pledged to respect basic human rights and freedoms, including freedom of religion and belief and freedom to leave and to return. The colloquium proceedings, with background papers and recommendations, were published in a bilingual French and English volume titled *The Right to Leave and to Return,* which, with the Declaration, is still used as a basic educational resource—perhaps the most thorough on the subject—by scholars and officials.

The UN Subcommission on the Prevention of Discrimination and Protection of Minorities, which for years was prevented by the Soviet Bloc from dealing with the right to leave, finally initiated a study of the subject in 1982 and designated a special rapporteur to implement it. To provide guidance for the rapporteur, the JBI commissioned Hurst Hannum, Director of the Procedural Aspects of International Law Institute, to produce the widely used guidebook, *The Right to Leave and Return in International Law and Practice* (1987). The JBI then helped to arrange three conferences of experts on the subject. The special rapporteur's final draft declaration, issued in June 1988, was modeled on a proposed text developed at one of these conferences. The draft declaration was further considered at subsequent conferences in New York and Strasbourg in 1989, both arranged by the JBI, and it served in 1989 as the basis for the first declaration on the right to leave ever adopted in the USSR, at a conference in Moscow cosponsored by a group of Jewish NGOs.

Expressing Solidarity with Indigenous NGOs

This role involves providing not only a moral and physical lifeline to victims and their families, but also a juridical support system to indigenous human rights NGOs in the human rights violator countries, NGOs that may be putting not only their organizational status but the lives of their members on the line. While human rights struggles are fought and won for the most part in the national arenas, the international NGO support system provides not only promotion of, but protection for, these human rights struggles.

Again, the role of Jewish NGOs in the matter of the struggle for Soviet Jewry provides an illuminating case study of this basic strategy. For it was the international solidarity and support system developed by these Jewish NGOs that provided a protective umbrella for the Soviet Helsinki Watch Groups and the even more fledgling—and vulnerable—Jewish organizations and groupings in the USSR. In a word, the reality that "the whole world is watching" gave credence to the Camus pledge that "we cannot prevent children from being tortured—but we can prevent less children from being tortured." Jewish NGOs, like NGOs generally, could not prevent Helsinki Monitors from being arrested or Jewish refuseniks from being imprisoned, but they were able to prevent less Monitors from being arrested and less refuseniks from being imprisoned. The Concluding Document of the Copenhagen Conference on the Human Dimension gives expression and effect to this NGO support system within the Helsinki process. In Article 10 of the Concluding Document—which the Helsinki and Jewish NGOs themselves helped draft as part of their legislative role— the participating States reaffirm "their commitment to ensure effectively the rights of the individual to know and act upon human rights and fundamental freedoms, and to contribute actively, individually or in association with others, to their promotion and protection."[173]

Public Advocacy, "Shame," and the Role of the Media

While acting as Counsel to Soviet prisoners of conscience like Anatoly Sharansky, and to NGOs who had taken up their cause, I

---

[173]See Copenhagen Concluding Document (1990), 32–33.

had occasion to meet with Soviet dissident Andrei Sakharov in the Soviet Union in 1979. It turned out to be a fateful meeting, as I was expelled from the Soviet Union the next day—my meeting with Sakharov was described as one of my "criminal" activities—and Sakharov was himself forcibly exiled shortly thereafter to Gorky. But the words—the message of that encounter—were indelibly imprinted on my psyche, and advocacy, forever. As Sakharov put it, "I do not know what will help the cause of human rights—I do know that it will not be helped by silence." And as if to buttress his remarks and the need to combat the Soviet violations of religious human rights, he added the following: "Anti-Semitism in the Soviet Union has been raised to the level of a state religion in a Godless society." Public advocacy, then, for Sakharov, was an essential ingredient in the "mobilization of shame" against the Soviet Union. "Shame," as Sakharov put it, was the best sanction we had, for the Soviet Union was preoccupied with its legitimacy. And the media, as Sakharov concluded, was the carrier—the instrument —of this mobilization of shame. The Sakharov dictum was translated into Jewish NGO strategy, for whom public advocacy, the mobilization of shame, and the exposure by the media were guiding principles.

NGOs, Coalition Strategy, and the Internationalization of Advocacy: The Case of Josef Begun

The case of Soviet prisoner of conscience Josef Begun emerged as a *cause célèbre* for the cause of human rights in general and religious human rights in particular in the Soviet Union. Begun, one of the first to learn and to teach Hebrew in the USSR, also became an example of Catch-22 gulag justice in the matter of Jewish refuseniks in the Soviet Union. Fired from his job for desiring to emigrate, he was then charged with parasitism for not having a job and threatened with psychiatric confinement for the treatment of the condition of parasitism. Having served his sentence for parasitism, he was charged with unlawful residency upon his return to Moscow. Finally, he became the first refusenik ever to be subjected to "triple jeopardy" when he was charged and convicted for "anti-Soviet slander and agitation" for seeking nothing else but to exercise his right under Article 18 of the ICCPR—to which the USSR was a State Party—"individually or in community with others and in public or private, to manifest his religion or belief in worship, observance, practice, and teaching."

Accordingly, the Jacob Blaustein Institute for the Advancement of Human Rights, in concert with the International Human Rights Law Group, the International Human Rights Committee of the American Bar Association Section of International Law and Practice, and the American Association for the Advancement of Science, convened an international seminar of legal experts in early 1984 to discuss how to use existing UN procedures for the promotion and protection of the human rights of prisoners of conscience in general, and their religious human rights in particular. The legal scholars at the seminar drafted a memorandum to the Procurator-General of the Soviet Union seeking a reversal of Begun's conviction on the grounds that it violated both Soviet and international law.[174] This document was also forwarded to the UNESCO Director-General with the request that he intercede with the Soviet authorities (since the violations cited involved rights protected under the UNESCO Convention), to the UN Human Rights Committee, as it involved a direct violation of Article 18 of the CP Convention, and to the ILO as evidence of a policy and practice of discrimination in employment prohibited under the ILO Convention. Both the seminar and the memorandum attracted wide media coverage, heightening international awareness of the plight of Soviet Jews and the dismal state of human rights in the USSR. Indeed, it was one of the few instances in which the Soviet Union was called to account by the UN and its specialized agencies like UNESCO and the ILO and is a case study of the value of NGO coalition strategy and the efficacy of international advocacy.

------

[174]Ibid.

NGOs, Soviet Jewry, and the Parliamentary-Helsinki Connection

One of the most important and effective dimensions of NGO human rights strategy in general, and NGO public advocacy in particular, involved collaborative governmental and NGO work in the matter of Soviet Jewry. Indeed, it was this collaborative exercise that led to the enactment of the Jackson-Vanick amendment in 1974; to the coming into being of the Helsinki Final Act in 1975; to the first Congressional Public Hearings on Soviet violations of the Helsinki Final Act—including, in particular, violations of religious human rights—in 1978; to the first public rebuke in 1978 by the UN Human Rights Committee for Soviet violations of the ICCPR; and to the first public exposure of Soviet human rights violations in a Helsinki Forum in the Helsinki-Madrid Review of 1980.

Indeed, the 1980s witnessed a sustained and collaborative governmental-NGO campaign on behalf of Soviet Jewry, with Jewish NGOs at the forefront of this public advocacy campaign. More importantly, and of particular relevance to this study, it was this governmental-NGO collaborative involvement that led to elaborate protections of religious human rights within the Helsinki process and to the development of a Code of Conduct for the Rights of Minorities—including religious rights—that became a centerpiece of the Helsinki process.

THE ROLE OF INTERNATIONAL JEWISH NGOS IN THE PROMOTION AND PROTECTION OF RELIGIOUS HUMAN RIGHTS IN THE INTERNATIONAL ARENA: THREE CASE STUDIES

Religious Human Rights, the "Teaching of Contempt," and Inter-Faith Dialogue

Catholic–Jewish Dialogue

The birth of Christian anti-Semitism—the "teaching of contempt"—has long been regarded by Jews, and is now acknowledged by

Christians themselves,[175] as having been a major source of Jewish suffering through the ages. Indeed, the notion that anti-Semitism "had deep theological roots in Christianity"[176]—that the assault on the religious human rights of Jews was being made in the name of the Christian religion—began to be recognized by both Jewish and Christian NGOs as being as prejudicial to the cause of religious human rights in general as it was to Jewish human rights in particular. This recognition led to the founding in 1968 of a major international Jewish NGO, the International Jewish Committee for Inter-religious Consultations (IJCIC), on behalf of world Jewry, with representatives from the World Jewish Congress, the Synagogue Council of America, B'nai Brith/Anti-Defamation League, the American Jewish Committee, and the Israel Jewish Council for Interreligious Relations.

Since the mid-1960s and the founding of the ICJIC, Christian-Jewish relations in general, and Catholic–Jewish relations in particular, have evolved dramatically. The relations are no longer characterized by a tradition of mutual antagonism, exacerbated by an absence of dialogue, or a *dialogue des sourdes*. What follows is an enumeration of the dramatic developments in the past thirty years, where ICJIC has played an important participatory, deliberative, and at times initiatory role in a historic interfaith dialogue that has remained largely unknown, except to the cogniscenti.

The first step came in 1965 at the end of the Second Vatican Council with the repudiation of the traditional Catholic teaching of continuing Jewish guilt for the death of Jesus and a rejection of anti-Semitism. Following the Council, the Church began to speak of the Jews in completely new terms, recognizing Judaism as an ongoing, valid religion, as opposed to the former teaching of its dimunition and loss of validity since the coming of Jesus. Most important for Jews was the complete change concerning anti-Semitism: the Church, "instead of being part of the problem, became part of the answer."[177] Anti-Semitism was condemned, with the Church tak-

---

[175]Gaer.

[176]See G. Wigoder, *The Vatican-Israel Agreement: A Watershed in Christian–Jewish Relations* (Jerusalem: Institute of the World Jewish Congress, 1994).

[177]Ibid., 3.

ing an active role in combatting all instances of anti-Semitic manifestations and, for example, sending a joint Catholic-Jewish team
to Eastern Europe to examine the situation there and to decide
jointly how to fight it. At a joint conference held in 1990, the Vatican
representatives spoke of the need for the Church to do *teshuvah*—
repentance (the Church used the Hebrew word)—for the wrongs
it had committed against the Jewish people, and this statement was
subsequently repeated by the Pope.[178]

Moreover, shortly after the founding of the IJCIC, the Vatican
established a Commission for Relations with Judaism and since
1970 has maintained a dialogue with it. Two central documents,
published in 1974 and 1985, set down the new doctrines of the
Catholic Church toward Jews and Judaism. In particular, the documents—and doctrines—laid emphasis on the Jewish roots of Christianity, the Jewishness of its founders, and the statement that God's
Covenant with the People of Israel remained unbroken. The regular meetings between the Vatican Commission and the IJCIC suc-
ceeded in addressing—and for the most part resolving—a host of
contentious issues. By the 1980's the major divisive item remaining on the agenda was the relationship between the Vatican and
the State of Israel. Edgar Bronfman, President of the World Jewish
Congress and elected Chairman of IJCIC, affirmed and reaffirmed
the shared consensus of all Jewish NGOs that "there can be no
normalization of relations between the Catholic Church and the
Jewish people, as long as the Church refuses to recognize and
establish diplomatic relations with the State of Israel,"[179] making it
clear that Israel was central to the Jewish people, and normalization, therefore, of Catholic–Jewish relations depended upon normalization of relations between the Catholic Church and Israel. In
1994, with the Vatican-Israel Agreement, that normalization was
achieved.

According to the Agreement,[180] which includes a preamble and
15 Articles, the Vatican and the State of Israel agreed to normalize
relations fully, including the exchange of ambassadors within four

---

[178]Ibid., 6.

[179]Ibid.

[180]Ibid.

months of the signing of the agreement. Among the Articles was a joint commitment to cooperate in combatting all forms of anti-Semitism, and in promoting mutual understanding among nations, tolerance among communities, and respect for human life and dignity. In particular, the Holy See reiterated its condemnation of hatred, persecution, and all other manifestations of anti-Semitism directed against the Jewish people. As well, it expressed its condemnation of attacks on Jews and desecration of Jewish synagogues and cemeteries, which offend the memory of victims of the Holocaust. These undertakings toward protecting the religious rights of Jews, set down in an agreement with Israel, thereby constituted an acknowledgement by the Holy See of the centrality of Israel for the Jewish people. As well, the State of Israel recognized the right of the Catholic Church to carry out its religious, moral, educational, and charitable functions and to have its own institutions. Both parties to the Agreement recognized the need for dialogue and cooperation, while the State of Israel guaranteed the freedom of Catholic worship and affirmed its continuing commitment to maintain and respect the status quo in the Christian holy places.

The signing of the Agreement, the recognition of the State of Israel by the Vatican, as well as the establishment of diplomatic relations, symbolize, according to former President of Israel Chaim Herzog, "an historic Jewish victory against an institution that has shown extreme hostility toward the Jewish people throughout the generations. . . . We are speaking about historic recognition from the spiritual leadership of the Christian world, a recognition that the State of Israel, the state of the Jews, is an accomplished fact, a country with standing and value in the community of nations."[181]

In 1992, the Catholic Church issued a new Universal Catechism, which appeared in English two years later. As the catechism is an authoritative doctrinal Church document, Jews examined it with interest for its teachings relating to Jews and Judaism. Most of the progressive steps that had been stated in Church documents over the past thirty years were integrated, including the rejection of collective Jewish guilt for the death of Jesus, the Jewish roots of Christianity and of its founders, and the Jewish roots of the Catho-

---

[181]Ibid., 8

lic liturgy. In particular, genocide, persecution, and discrimination "by race or religion" are condemned, and the document incorporates the Pope's statement, which is revolutionary in the light of previous teaching, that the covenant between God and the Jews has not been broken and retains its validity. At the same time, however, the new catechism affirms the belief that the importance of the Hebrew Scriptures is that they prefigure the events of the New Testament, a teaching that is obviously objectionable to Jews.

Protestant–Jewish Dialogue

The IJCIC has not only been engaged in a dialogue with the Catholic Church in general and the Vatican Commission on Catholic–Jewish relations in particular; it has also been involved in a dialogue with the Protestant world. In that context, an imporant declaration was issued in 1994 by the Evangelical Lutheran Church in America. This is a sequel to the declaration adopted at a meeting between IJCIC and representatives of the World Lutheran Federation in Sweden in 1983, wherein the Lutheran participants repudiated the anti-Jewish teachings of Luther—a declaration endorsed in 1984 by the Assembly of the Lutheran World Federation. Similarly, the new American Lutheran Church declaration, addressed to the Jewish community, "rejects Luther's violent invective against the Jews and expresses deep and abiding sorrow over its tragic effects on subsequent generations."[182] In particular, it deplores the appropriation of Luther's words by modern anti-Semitism and undertakes increasing cooperation and understanding between Lutheran Christians and the Jewish community, with IJCIC playing an increasing role in this interfaith dialogue.

Restitution of Jewish Property and the Reclamation of Jewish Religious Patrimony: Birth of an International Jewish NGO

The Holocaust—the genocidal murder of six million Jewish men, women, and children simply because they were Jews—is clearly

---

[182]Ibid.

the greatest tragedy to have befallen the Jewish people, if not the cause of religious human rights, in this century. What may not be so well known—and which constitutes a continuing violation of religious human rights and unrequited war crime—has been the "despoliation of victims of mass murder, or their heirs"[183] through the seizure of Jewish property, much of it communal religious property. For, in addition to the murder of the six million, the murderers and their accomplices helped themselves to vast amounts of Jewish property, public and private, movable and immovable. In fact, the prospect of seizing that property was often a tempting incentive for local people to assist in, or even orchestrate, the murder of their Jewish neighbors. During the war certain states retained nominal independence and allied themselves with Germany. Others were directly occupied or annexed. But irrespective of who was responsible for the actual seizure, the bulk of stolen property devolved to the State, or to the entities or persons occupying the assets.

Even before the end of the hostilities in Europe, the World Jewish Congress (WJC) had initiated activity aimed at the recovery of Jewish property and had published an extensive study on the subject by Dr. Nehemiah Robinson. Nahum Goldmann, cofounder of the WJC, raised the issue at the War Emergency Conference in Atlantic City, in November 1944, when he declared: "The principle that Jewish assets must be given back to their legitimate holders wherever possible must be regarded as inviolable."[184] However, in the period immediately following the Second World War, survivors who attempted personally to secure the return of their property were sometimes killed by those who had enriched themselves, and these deaths intimidated others from making such claims. At the same time, new legislation passed at the time made it exceedingly difficult to recover plundered property. In some countries inheritance was limited to lineal relatives, and very short claims deadlines were imposed. Still others, like Hungary and Rumania, which, by virtue of the peace treaties they had signed

---

[183]World Jewish Congress, *Restitution of Jewish Property in Central and Eastern Europe* (Jerusalem: Institute of World Jewish Congress, 1994), 4.
    [184]Ibid., 2.

with the Allied and associated powers, were compelled to turn over heirless Jewish property to organizations working toward the rehabilitation of Jewish survivors, refused to do so.

The collapse of Communism and the "defrosting" of history[185] have now presented Jews with an opportunity to renew efforts to reclaim Jewish property in Central and Eastern Europe. In 1992, leading Jewish NGOs, including the World Jewish Congress, B'nai Brith, Joint Distribution Committee, the Jewish Agency, and survivors' groups created the World Jewish Restitution Organization (WJRO). WJRO activities are focused on the coordination of claims for the return of communal property and the transfer to the Jewish people of heirless holdings. The organization also aims to secure for individual Jews, whether resident in the countries in question or not, the same rights as those of local citizens.

In November 1992, WJC President and WJRO Chariman Edgar Bronfman and Israeli Minister of Finance Avraham Shohat signed a memorandum in which the State of Israel's special interest in the restitution of Jewish property was established. The memorandum recognized that "the State considers itself to be the natural and principal heir to Jewish public property and where there is no other heir, to Jewish private property, together with local Jewish communities and the Jewish people."[186] Similarly, the WJRO has concluded agreements with Jewish communities in order to coordinate restitution efforts.

Regrettably, the emerging democracies of Eastern Europe continue to block restitution of Jewish property to their rightful owners just as their predecessor regimes had done at the end of the Second World War. While the situation varies from country to country, a disturbing pattern of state-sanctioned discrimination can be discerned. The discrimination may not be apparent on its face, as the governments have seemingly enacted "neutral" legislation providing for the restoration of property seized by post-Second World War communist regimes. However, the legislation has an adverse impact upon Jewish claimants, who are effectively barred from having their property restored, for the following reasons:

---

[185]Ibid., 1.

[186]Ibid., 2.

First, according to the legislation, foreign citizens not domiciled in the country are ineligible to reclaim their assets. This provision would effectively extinguish any Jewish claim, as most survivors left their countries of origin (in part due to the prevalent atmosphere of anti-Semitism in those countries after the war) before they could reclaim their assets. Second, and having regard to communal religious property, the legislation limits its restitution only to communities and churches that have enjoyed an uninterrupted existence since the war. For Jewish communities, this constitutes a "double killing": first they were murdered, and their property plundered; now they are to be punished because they were murdered. Indeed, many of those who directly and indirectly benefitted from plundered Jewish property have expressed opposition to the restitution of this property to Jews. Third, while the governments of the Eastern European emerging democracies have been disposed to return communal religious property to churches, they have refused to return Jewish communal religious property to the Jews. This discrimination is particularly disturbing in a country like Poland, where the government has enacted legislation providing for the restitution of property to the Roman Catholic Church and other Christian churches, but has refused to do so in the case of the Jewish community. Yet the pre-war Jewish community in Poland numbered 3,300,000 Jews—85 percent of whom were murdered—with the magnitude of their holdings valued in billions of dollars. Fourth, in many countries the disposition of Jewish property has been left in the hands of the local authorities to whom it devolved. These authorities have shown little inclination to returning the property. Indeed, they often have a vested interest in blocking the restitution or in attaching conditions that would make it impossible (or unattractive) for the Jewish community to repossess it. In the Czech Republic, for example, local authorites have displayed a tendency to return to Jewish communities neglected burial grounds and synagogues that require a significant Jewish investment (and even those concessions were only granted after local authorities were subjected to pressure from the Czech government), but are not prepared to return potentially lucrative income-producing properties such as buildings in the center of Prague.

Accordingly, representatives of the WJRO have met with leaders of East European governments with a view to securing agreements with them on restitution, have worked to implement the agreements so secured, and have enlisted the support of the U.S. Congress and government in their efforts. In a letter of April 10, 1995, Congressional leaders urged U.S. Secretary of State Warren Christopher to take action in this matter:

> It should be made clear to the countries involved . . . that their response on this matter will be seen as a test of their respect for basic human rights and the rule of law, and could have practical consequences on their relations with our country. It is the clear policy of the United States that each should expeditiously enact appropriate legislation providing for the prompt restitution and/or compensation for property and assets seized by the former Nazi and/or Communist regimes. We believe it is a matter of both law and justice.[187]

The UN, Religious Human Rights, and the New Anti-Semitism: Founding a New International NGO

In July 1992, the World Jewish Congress convened an International Conference in Brussels on "Racism, Anti-Semitism, Xenophobia and Other Forms of Intolerance." The Conference brought together an unusual international consortium of political leaders, scholars, and NGO activists to consider the explosive question of the racial and religious hatred stalking across Europe and other global stages. One of the panels[188] addressed the question of the development of a "new anti-Semitism," and the anchorage of that anti-Semitism in the United Nations itself. As one of the participants put it:

> What Jewish NGOs are witnessing today—and which has been developing incrementally, almost imperceptively, for some 25 years now—is a new anti-Semitism—grounded in classical anti-Semitism, but distinguishable from it; anchored in the "Zionism is Racism" Resolution but going beyond it; a new anti-Semitism which almost requires a new vocabulary to define it—but which can best be de-

---

[187]Ibid., 3.

[188]This panel recommended the establishment of an international NGO to monitor, inter alia, anti-Semitism at the United Nations.

fined as the discrimination against, or denial of, national particularity anywhere, whenever that national particularity happens to be
Jewish.

In a word, classical anti-Semitism is the discrimination against,
or denial of, the right of individual Jews to live as equal members of
a free society; the new anti-Semitism involves the discrimination
against, or denial of, the right of the Jewish people to live as an equal
member of the family of nations. What is indigenous to each form of
anti-Semitism—and common to both—is discrimination. All that has
happened is that it has moved from discrimination against Jews as
individuals—a classical anti-Semitism for which there are indices
of measurement—to discrimination against Jews as a People—the
new anti-Semitism—for which one has yet to develop indices of
measurement.[189]

It is not surprising therefore, that if classical anti-Semitism, anchored in religious discrimination against Jews, has been a centerpiece of Jewish NGO concern, then the new anti-Semitism—or
discrimination against Jews as a people—should emerge as a priority on the Jewish NGO agenda. As the Conference panelists
demonstrated, "the most distinguishing feature of this new anti-
Semitism has been its anchorage in the very body created to combat racial and religious discrimination—the United Nations."[190] In
a word, as the witness testimony and documentary evidence reveals,[191] the UN, founded as an alliance against racism and anti-
Semitism, has been converted into a forum for the dissemination
of hatred. Jewish NGOs, for whom the United Nations was sword
and shield against religious discrimination, have found themselves
having to challenge the very integrity of the UN itself.

Accordingly, the Brussels Conference recommended the establishment of a new NGO—to be called "United Nations Watch"—
whose mandate would be to "monitor the United Nations and to

---

[189]Excerpt from paper by I. Cotler, "U.N. and the New Anti-Semitism,"
presented at the 1992 WJC Brussels Conference on Racism, Xenophobia, Anti-Semitism and Other Forms of Intolerance.

[190]Ibid.

[191]Ibid.

measure that organization's performance by the yardstick of the UN Charter."[192] In particular, UN Watch would investigate the "new anti-Semitism"—the singling out of Israel for differential and discriminatory treatment by the UN—as a case study of UN compliance with its own Charter. As UN Watch's founding statement put it, "We believe that the UN's treatment of Israel is an important test of how the UN is complying with its Charter."[193] It might be useful, therefore, to identify the several varieties, or indices, of this new anti-Semitism as described at the WJC Conference, in order to appreciate better the mandate of this new NGO, as well as to appraise the UN not only as a case study of this new anti-Semitism but as repository and instrument for its expression.

First, there is political anti-Semitism, involving the discrimination against, or denial of, the legitimacy, if not the existence, of the State of Israel. This is the contemporary analogue of classical or theological anti-Semitism, which discriminated against, or denied the very legitimacy of, the Jewish religion. In each instance the essence of anti-Semitism is the same—an assault upon whatever is the core of Jewish self-definition at any given moment in time, be it the Jewish religion at the time of classical anti-Semitism, or the State of Israel as the "civil religion" of the Jewish people under the new anti-Semitism. Indeed, to the extent that Israel has emerged as the "civil religion" of world Jewry—the organizing idiom of Jewish self-determination, as Schlomo Avineri has put it—this new anti-Semitism is an assault on the religious sensibility of the Jewish people.

There is a second variant of political anti-Semitism—the "demonizing" of Israel—the attribution to Israel of all the evils of the world, and the portrayal of Israel as the enemy of all that is good and the repository of all that is evil, not unlike the medieval indictment of the Jew as the "poisoner of the wells." In other words, in a world in which human rights has emerged as the new secular religion, the portrayal of Israel as the metaphor for a human rights violator in our time exposes Israel as the "new anti-Christ," with

---

[192]Mission Statement of UN Watch (Geneva, 1995), 1.
[193]Ibid.

all the "teaching of contempt" for this "Jew among the Nations" that this new anti-Semitism implies.

There are a number of additional indices by which this new anti-Semitism can be identified and measured. These include: (1) ideological anti-Semitism, in the form of the "Zionism is Racism" indictment, and the singling out of Israel's ideological *raison d'être* for discriminatory treatment; (2) the denial to Israel of "international due process" in the international arena, as in the singling out of Israel for differential if not discriminatory treatment amongst the family of nations, and where Israel emerges, as it were, as "the Jew among the Nations"; (3) the international "legal" character of this anti-Semitism, where, in a kind of Orwellian inversion of law and language, human rights becomes the mask under which this "teaching of contempt" is carried out; (4) the economic coercion and discrimination practiced through the Arab boycott, which emerges as the contemporary economic analogue of classical economic anti-Semitism: classical economic anti-Semitism involved discrimination against Jews in housing, education, and employment; the new economic anti-Semitism involves the extra-territorial application of an international restrictive covenant against Jews wherever they may be, with a "chilling" effect against persons who would seek to do business with them; (5) the cutting edge of this new anti-Semitism in the form of Holocaust-denial, which moves inexorably from denying the Holocaust, to accusing Jews of fabricating the "hoax" of the Holocaust, to indicting Jews for extorting false reparations from the innocent German people in order to build their "illegal" State of Israel on the backs of the real indigenous owners, the Palestinians; and (6) the clear incitement to violence against Jews, including the singling out of Israelis and Jewish nationals as targets of international terrorism.

This is not to suggest, nor would the Jewish NGOs who have addressed this phenomenon wish to have it inferred, that Israel is somehow above the law, or that Israel is not to be held accountable for any violations of law. On the contrary, Israel is accountable for any violations of international law or human rights like any other State, and the Jewish people are not entitled to any privileged protection or preference because of the particularity of Jewish suffering. The problem, as UN Watch has put it, is not that Israel as the "Jew among Nations" seeks to be above the law, but that it has been systematically denied equality before the law; not that Israel must respect human rights—which it should—but that the human rights of Israel have not been respected; not that human rights standards should not be applied to Israel—which they must—but that these standards have not been applied equally to anyone else. What follows is an examination of this new anti-Semitism, using, ironically enough, the repository of international law and human rights—the United Nations—as a case study. As Ambassador Morris Abram, the President of UN Watch, has put it, it is under the protective cover of the United Nations and its specialized agencies that this new anti-Semitism has found sanction and sustenance.[194]

Political Anti-Semitism

UN Watch and Jewish NGOs are here referring to the spate of UN resolutions, declarations, statements, and other actions that involve the discrimination against, or denial of, the legitimacy, if not the existence, of the State of Israel. The NGOs see this as the contemporary analogue to classical or theological anti-Semitism that discriminated against, or denied the legitimacy of, the Jewish religion; or, where UN actions attribute to Israel responsibility for all the evils of the world—the contemporary analogue to the medieval indictment of the Jews as the "Poisoner of the Wells"—so that Israel now stands accused of "poisoning the international wells."

Ideological Anti-Semitism

The reference here is to resolutions, declarations, and statements that purport to, or have the effect of, denying the legitimacy of Zionism or the Jewish people's right to self-determination, for example, the UN "Zionism is Racism" Resolution and related indictments that, as Sakharov put it, "gave the abomination of anti-Semitism the appearance of international sanction."[195] Indeed, it

---

[194]Statement at founding meeting of UN Watch (Geneva, October 1993).

[195]Quoted in D. Moynihan, "The Significance of the Zionism is Racism Resolution for International Human Rights," in D. Sidorsky, ed., *Essays on Human Rights* (Philadelphia: JPS, 1977), 40.

was the UN giving its imprimatur to the "Zionism is Racism" Resolution that gave "legitimation" to this discriminatory and scurrilous indictment of the Jewish people, and which galvanized Jewish NGOs into making the combatting of the "Zionism is Racism" Resolution a priority on the Jewish NGO agenda. As David Moynihan put it, "The prior UN commitment to a Decade of Action to combat racism was now, through the ploy of defining Zionism-as-racism, to be rededicated to propagating anti-Semitism—one of the oldest and most virulent forms of racism."[196]

The Promotion of Hatred and Contempt against Israel

Jewish NGOs, as we have seen, have been at the forefront of combatting discrimination against Jews, particularly that involved in racist hate speech—the willful promotion of hatred and contempt against Jews as an identifiable group. Indeed, Canadian Jewish NGOs invoked the UN Convention on the Elimination of All Forms of Racial Discrimination, and its prohibition of hate speech as a discriminatory practice, to help secure the enactment of anti-hate legislation in Canada. Yet, as the WJC World Conference on Racism and Anti-Semitism demonstrated, the UN, and particularly its specialized agencies, have served as a forum for the very "teaching of contempt"—including the most aggressive expressions of classical anti-Semitism, such as the infamous "blood libel" of the Jews[197]—that the UN Treaties themselves condemn, thereby bringing the UN justice system itself into disrepute.

Israel as the Embodiment of Evil:
The UN "Legitimization" of Anti-Semitism

Human rights having emerged as the new "secular religion of our time," to describe—or indict—Israel as the embodiment of all evil is to say that Israel has become the "new anti-Christ" of our time,

---

[196]Ibid., 89.

[197]See, for example, submission by Syrian delegate to the UN Commission on Human Rights in February 1991, affirming the infamous "blood libel."

with all the attending discriminatory fallout from such indictments. As UN Watch has put it, what is involved here is the use and abuse of human rights as a cover for the continuing delegitimization of Israel. "The UN Department of Public Information and the UN Commission on Human Rights have produced thousands of documents over the years where [human rights] sentiments have masked anti-Semitism."[198]

Denial to Israel of International Due Process— or the Denial to Israel of Equality before the Law in the International Arena

The first of the UN Watch founding principles is "the balanced, fair, and nondiscriminatory application of the UN Charter to all UN member states." Accordingly, the continued singling out of Israel for discriminatory and differential treatment in the decision-making by UN bodies is regarded by UN Watch as tantamount to a standing denial of international due process. Moreover, this obsessive, unidimensional preoccupation with Israel has resulted in exculpatory immunity being granted at the same time to the real violators of religious human rights—including even the perpetrators of genocide—thereby prejudicing the peace and security of humankind as a whole. For instance, from 1980 to 1990 some 30 percent of the indictments of the UN Human Rights Commission were registered against Israel; yet during this same period not one resolution was ever registered against Iraq, notwithstanding the fact that the evidence was clear that Iraq was using poison gas not only in the Iran-Iraq war, but against its own Kurdish civilians. The result was not only the singling out of Israel for differential and discriminatory treatment, but the licensing of Iraq to continue to act with impunity.

The Pursuit of the Arab Boycott through the UN and Its Agencies

As UN Watch has put it, "Israel is kept from membership within the United Nations system in any of [its] meaningful bodies, such

---

[198]Mission Statement, UN Watch, 3.

as the UN Human Rights Commission, where the real work of the United Nations is conducted."[199] As well, the United Nations has systematically refused to "let" any contracts to Israel, thereby acquiescing in the application of the Arab boycott to Israel through the United Nations system. As Per Ahlmark, a member of the Board of UN Watch, concluded,[200] and which aptly summarizes this part, the emergence of the United Nations as a case study of anti-Semitism—old and new—demonstrates, once again, the historical adage that "while it may begin with Jews, it doesn't end with Jews." The use of the UN as a cover under which the new anti-Semitism is carried out and legitimized ends up being an assault upon the very integrity, and legitimacy, of the UN itself and its specialized agencies.

DISTINCTIVE FEATURES OF THE GENERAL PANOPLY OF RELIGIOUS HUMAN RIGHTS PROTECTIONS WITH WHICH JEWISH NGOS ARE ESPECIALLY CONCERNED

A distillation of the foregoing discussions in this paper—having regard to the Jewish NGO agenda in the matter of the promotion and protection of religious human rights, and the strategies developed to secure that protection—suggests the following distinctive features of the general panoply of religious human rights as being the particular concern of Jewish NGOs:

Religious Liberty as "First Liberty"

If there is one right or freedom that is regarded by Jewish NGOs—no less than by their non-Jewish counterparts—as the basis for all other freedoms, it is that of religious liberty. Indeed, the characterization of religious liberty as the "first liberty" and the "first freedom" underlay the founding of the major and mainstream Jewish

---

[199]Ibid.

[200]Supra note 196.

NGOs. It is this generic and fundamental right of religious liberty that was at the heart of "a number of enduring and interlocking principles which found widespread support in the early [American] republic, many of which were included in the constitutions— liberty of conscience, free exercise of religion, pluralism, equality, separationism, local regulation of religion, and disestablishment of religion. Such principles remain at the heart of the American experiment still today."[201]

Liberty of Conscience and the Free Exercise of Religion as Grundnorm Principles

The cardinal principle in the panoply of religious human rights for Jewish NGOs is the free exercise of religion, which is inextricably bound up with the principle of liberty of conscience. John Witte has aptly summarized this relationship—this "organic linkage [between] religious belief and religious action"—as follows: "Liberty of conscience was a passive guarantee: the right to be left alone to choose one's beliefs. Free exercise of religion was an active guarantee: the right to act publicly on the choices of conscience once made."[202] Indeed, the free exercise of religion is not only a *grundnorm* principle of religious liberty for Jewish NGOs, it is the defining principle for the work of all Jewish NGOs—sectarian and secular, conservative and liberal. It is not only a "first freedom" for Jewish NGOs, but a unifying principle; and it inspired Jewish NGO advocacy, designed to protect the panoply of essential rights and freedoms bound up with this cardinal principle.

Accordingly, as set forth earlier in this paper, Jewish NGOs filed *amicus* briefs in support of the principle of equality, as in their support of the religious activities of groups singled out for discriminatory treatment by municipal and state ordinances; in support of the principle of liberty of conscience, as when Jewish NGOs sup-

---

[201]J. Witte Jr., and M. Christian Green, "The American Constitutional Experiment in Religious Rights: The Perennial Search for Principles," in J.D., van der Vyver and John Witte, Jr., eds. *Religious Human Rights in Global Perspectives: Legal Perspectives* (Martinus Nijhoff, 1996), 497, 514.
[202]Ibid.

ported the right of children of Jehovah's Witnesses, in accordance with their parents' religious convictions, to refuse to salute the flag in public school; in support of the principle of pluralism, as in the *amicus* brief supporting the right of Amish parents to limit their children's education to the eighth grade; and, most notably, perhaps, in the landmark case of *Sherbert v. Verner*, in support of what came to be known as the principle of strict scrutiny, or the "compelling state interest" test, and which, as Witte put it, "drew together the classic principles of liberty of conscience, free exercise, equality, pluralism, and localism, and accorded free exercise protection to both religious individuals and the religious groups."[203]

Indeed, when the use of the compelling state interest test in the adjudication of free exercise claims was subsequently undermined in the *Employment Division v. Smith*[204] case, a "wall-to-wall" consortium of Jewish NGOs supported—and, indeed, were legally instrumental in the drafting and enactment of—the 1993 *Religious Freedom Restoration Act*. It marked one of the few occasions in recent years when the secular and liberal NGOs, such as the American Jewish Congress and the American Jewish Committee, joined together with sectarian and conservative NGOs such as Agudath Israel and its Commission on Law and Public Affairs—and when the principal draftspeople of the Act were representatives from both sets of NGOs.

The Free Exercise of Religion, Disestablishment Law, and the Principle of Separationism

If Jewish NGOs, regardless of religious and political ideology, have been united in their support for the "free exercise of religion" principle and clause—and the multiple and related principles bound up with it—they have increasingly been divided in the United States with respect to the establishment clause and its single underlying principle of separationism, or a "wall of separation between Church and State." Accordingly, when the secular and liberal American Jewish NGOs join other American Christian

---

[203]Ibid.
[204]494 U.S. 872 (1990).

groups in filing *amicus* briefs opposing government sanctioned religious symbols on public property, the sectarian and conservative American Jewish NGOs file *amicus* briefs in support of the government. When secular and liberal American Jewish NGOs file *amicus* briefs in opposition to a rabbi leading prayers at a school graduation ceremony,[205] American Orthodox Jewish NGOs like Adgudath Israel support the clergy-led prayer. And when the secular and liberal American Jewish NGOs file *amicus* briefs opposing aid to religiously related schools, including voucher systems and other "choice" programs, the American sectarian and conservative NGOs support "properly drawn education choice programs [that] can constitutionally and equitably provide funds for non-public school students."[206] In Canada, conversely, government sanctioned religious symbols on public property is a non-issue, while all Canadian Jewish NGOs support government aid to Jewish parochial schools, and, as we have seen, are going to the Supreme Court of Canada to seek its validation.

Perhaps the most divisive, and dramatic, expression of the opposing positions in the United States on the separationism principle occurred with the *Kiryas Joel* case. The NJCRAC participated in an *amicus* brief filed by the American Jewish NGOs urging the U.S. Supreme Court to uphold the decision of the New York State Court of Appeals, which invalidated a state statute establishing a separate public school district in and for Kiryas Joel, a Satmar hasidic Village in Orange County, for the purpose of providing remedial education only to the children of the Satmar hasidic group. As well, the American Jewish Committee, the ADL, and the National Council of Jewish Women participated in a brief prepared by Americans United for the Separation of Church and State, which, like the American Jewish Congress brief, claimed that the legislation violated the Establishment Clause of the First Amendment.

The legislation was supported by the conservative and sectarian Jewish NGOs, such as the Union of Orthodox Jewish Congregations, on the grounds that "religious observance is not so disfavored by the Constitution that those who practice it devoutly and

---

[205]*Lee v. Weisman*, 112 S.Ct. 2649 (1992).

[206]Orthodox Union, *Leadership Briefing* (Spring 1995), 3.

distinctly must forfeit the opportunity, available to everyone else, to provide and administer secular public services."[207] Indeed, their brief added, "no one seems to question the power of the present Village, acting through duly elected officials (all of whom are necessarily Satmar *hasidim*), to provide police services, fire protection, trash disposal, or any other standard municipal service to a Village population consisting entirely of Satmar *hasidim*; the provision of remedial public education is no different; and the legislation designed to accommodate the observances of a religious group and promote the free exercise of religion is constitutionally valid so long as it does not pay with public funds for any religious activity and does not coerce religious observance or nonobservance."[208]

The Supreme Court rejected these arguments, saying that the legislation had crossed the line from "permissible accommodation to impermissible establishment," that the state had delegated civic authority on the basis of religious belief rather than neutral principles, and that it had thereby brought about an impermissible "fusion" of governmental and religious functions. In a scathing dissent, Justice Scalia characterized the majority opinion as "astounding . . . unprecedented . . . except that it continues, and takes to new extremes, a recent tendency in the opinions of this Court to turn the Establishment Clause into a repealer of our nation's tradition of religious tolerance."[209] Accordingly, what was for the majority, and the liberal and secular Jewish NGOs in support, an issue of the Establishment Clause and the principle of separationism, was for the minority, and the conservative and secular Jewish NGOs in support, an issue of the free exercise of religion and the principle of toleration. The division amongst the Jewish NGOs mirrored the division in the Court; or perhaps, one might say, the division in the Court was not unrelated to the division amongst Jewish NGOs.

----

[207]*Amicus* brief, Union of Orthodox Jewish Congregations, in *Kiryas Joel v. Grumet.*

[208]Ibid.

[209]Scalia, J. dissenting in *Kiryas Joel v. Grumet.*

Jewish NGOs and the Religious Freedom Restoration Act: The Free Exercise of Religion as an Underlying Principle

In consequence of the jurisprudence eroding the compelling state interest test in matters relating to the adjudication of the free exercise of religion, Jewish NGOs joined together to draft and help secure the enactment of the Religious Freedom Restoration Act. The Congressional findings and declaration of purposes of the legislation not only represent the principles of religious liberty—principles around which Jewish NGOs could agree—but the efficacy of that Jewish NGO unity in giving legislative expression to those principles. The principles, as contained respectively in the findings and purposes of the legislation, are as follows:

The Congress finds that:
1. the framers of the Constitution, recognizing free exercise of religion as an inalienable right, secured its protection in the First Amendment to the Constitution;
2. laws "neutral" toward religion may burden religious exercise as surely as laws intended to interfere with religious exercise;
3. governments should not substantially burden religious exercise without compelling justification;
4. in *Employment Division v. Smith*, 494 U.S. 872 (1990), the Supreme Court virtually eliminated the requirement that the government justify burdens on religious exercise imposed by laws neutral toward religion; and
5. the compelling interest test as set forth in prior court rulings is a workable test for striking sensible balances between religious liberty and competing prior governmental interests.

The purposes of this chapter are:

1. to restore the compelling interest test as set forth in *Sherbert v. Verner*, 374 U.S. 398 (1963), and *Wisconsin v. Yoder*, 406 U.S. 205 (1972), and to guarantee its application in all cases where free exercise of religion is substantially burdened; and

2. to provide a claim of defense to persons whose religious exercise is substantially burdened by government.

The Religious Freedom Restoration Act, Disestablishment, and the Principle of Separationism

As the Religious Freedom Restoration Act demonstrated, if the religious human rights at issue are or can be characterized as related to the free exercise of religion—including such associated rights as liberty of conscience, equality, or pluralism—it will secure the endorsement of all Jewish NGOs regardless of whether they are liberal and secular or conservative and sectarian. If, however, the issue is characterized as one of disestablishment and separationism, the Jewish NGOs find themselves on opposing sides of the issue. This litigious adversarialness amongst Jewish NGOs may influence thereby the division in the courts themselves, particularly where, as in the Kiryas Joel case, they are the primary *amici* in the case. Moreover, these opposing divides among the Jewish NGOs can be expected not only to continue, but perhaps to be exacerbated. For the Republican "Contract with America" is organized around a legislative program that mandates prayer in schools, support for religious education, religious symbols on public property, and the like. While the "Contract with America" is fiercely opposed by the liberal and secular coalitions of Jewish NGOs, parts of it are supported by the coalition of conservative and sectarian Jewish NGOs. Accordingly, the divisions may become not only more dramatic, but also more political, thereby fusing not only church and state, but church and politics.

Jewish NGOs and the "Report Card" on Religious Freedom: Separation as a Dividing Principle

In 1987 the American Jewish Congress established the Kahn Religious Liberty Resource Center to evaluate the status of religious liberty in the United States. In 1992 it began to publish the *Report Card on Religious Freedom*—an annual report on judicial trends in interpreting the Free Exercise Clause and Establishment Clause of the First Amendment. Religious liberty experts from across the country have been asked to evaluate judicial trends in five areas— corresponding to the five principles respecting religious human rights: (1) freedom from explicit government discrimination against individuals due to their religious beliefs, such as rules prohibiting people of a certain religion from holding public office; (2) freedom from indirect government burdens or restrictions on religious practices, including laws that impinge upon an individual's religious practices or beliefs; (3) freedom from government promotion of religion—government-sponsored religious services, the display of religious symbols at government sites, and so forth; (4) freedom from government inculcation of religion in public schools, including organized prayer, religious pageants, and religious songs at public schools; and (5) freedom from government financial entanglements with religious institutions, including financial aid (particularly in the form of direct payments), grants, tax credits, and vouchers.

While the first two principles involve the free exercise of religion and therefore represent features or principles of religious human rights that would be supported by all Jewish NGOs, the last three—organized around the principle of separationism—enjoy the support only of the liberal and secular NGOs and not of the conservative and sectarian ones.

Protection against Discrimination
on Grounds of Religion

This principle—which enjoys support amongst all Jewish NGOs—is based on the following principle: "Discrimination shall mean any distinction, exclusion, restriction, or preference based on race, colour, religion or belief, descent, ethnic origin, language, or sex, which has the purpose or effect of nullifying or impairing the recognition, enjoyment, or exercise, on an equal footing of human rights and fundamental freedoms in the political, economic, social, cultural, or any other field of life."[210] In particular, it protects against

---

[210]See texts of the UN Convention on the Elimination of All Forms of Racial Discrimination, the ILO Convention on Discrimination in Employment and Occupation (No. 111), the UNESCO Convention against Discrimination in Education, and the UN Declaration on the Elimination of All Forms of Intolerance and of Discrimination Based on Religion and Belief. For these texts, see *Human Rights*.

"classical anti-Semitism," that is, explicit government or private discrimination against Jews on grounds of their religion, such as rules prohibiting people of a certain religion from holding office, or renting an apartment, or securing employment, or serving in the military and the like, whether the rules be explicitly discriminatory, or fairly neutral but with an adverse impact on Jews. As well, Jewish NGOs have invoked this principle to protect against the "new anti-Semitism," which involves the discrimination against, or denial of, national particularity anywhere whenever that national particularity is Jewish, be it in the extraterritorial and discriminatory provisions of the Arab boycott; or the "Zionism is Racism" Resolution; or the singling out of Israel or the Jewish people for differential and discriminatory treatment in the international arena; or the persecution and denial of religious human rights of oppressed Jewish minorities; or the seizure and plunder and non-restitution of Jewish religious property.

Protection against Hate Speech and Hate Crimes That Are Motivated by Bias against the Religion of the Target Group

The 1990s have witnessed an explosion of religious and racial incitement—and bias-motivated hate crimes—in democratic societies against vulnerable minorities, including Jews in their midst. The result has been that the issues of hate speech (in Canada) and hate crimes (in both Canada and the United States) have emerged as salient religious rights issues for Jewish NGOs concerned with protection and discrimination on grounds of religion. In Canada, racist hate propaganda, including Holocaust-denial, has targeted members of the country's Jewish community in particular, resulting in Canadian Jewish NGO support for the enactment of anti-hate legislation. In the U.S., bias-motivated crimes have resulted in American Jewish NGO support for hate crimes legislation, but American Jewish NGOs have rejected all suggestions to characterize hate speech as unprotected speech. Indeed, American Jewish NGOs have yet to appreciate that for Jewish NGOs anywhere else in the world, hate speech is characterized as a discriminatory practice, and anti-hate legislation, both domestically and internationally, is regarded as a matter of religious human rights, of the protection of minorities from discrimination on grounds of religion.

Interestingly enough, not only have Canadian Jewish NGOs taken a position in support of anti-hate legislation distinguishable from their American Jewish counterparts who eschew such legislation, but the involvement of Canadian Jewish NGOs as intervenors in support of the constitutionality of such legislation in hate speech cases has been much more pervasive and sustained than in cases involving church–state issues, further indicating the priority that is attached to protection from discrimination. The role of American Jewish NGOs has been exactly the opposite. Not only have they opposed any anti-hate speech legislation, but they have involved themselves in all major church–state cases. Admittedly, the ADL and other Jewish NGOs have supported the enactment of "hate crimes" legislation, but they have made it clear that the core of the legislation is "penalty enhancement" of an existing crime. Hate speech, however, is characterized as protected speech under the First Amendment and is not viewed as a discriminatory practice.

Tolerance and Intolerance:
The Assault on Religious Pluralism

It is ironic that while the United Nations has proclaimed 1995 the UN Year of Tolerance, a religious rights movement—the "religious right"—has mounted a crusade in the United States against "separationism," as it seeks to unite its version of Christianity with state power. This is not to say that some of the concerns of the religious right about a cultural breakdown—buttressed by grievous statistics about family breakdown, crime, health, and the like—are not without merit; or that members of the religious right do not have the right to advocate, organize, lobby, demonstrate, or exercise any other First Amendment right of expression. Indeed, religion anchored in a certain moral authority that challenges the power of the state—or secularism—can help keep the state accountable as it keeps secularism, or pluralism, from being consigned to the "friendly face of nihilism."

The problem is not just that the religious right seeks to mandate the state to legislate religious values, but that it seeks to clothe the state with its own religious, or "Christian," identity. In a word, it seeks to replace the "wall of separation"—where, arguably, the "separationism" may be too exclusivist of religion—with a citadel of Christianity, which is religiously exclusivist. Moreover, its rhetoric—no less than its policies—is increasingly incendiary in its assault on, and scapegoating of, pluralism. It suggests that the defenders of the separationist wall are "enemies of God," or proponents of "religious cleansing," and that the original "Christian" America has been expropriated by an anti-Christian elite, including feminists who "kill their children, practice witchcraft, destroy capitalism, and become lesbians—itself the most pernicious evil today."[211]

Perhaps most dangerous of all—and of particular concern to the liberal and secular Jewish NGOs, if not also the conservative and sectarian ones—the religious right's crusade has been supported, and at times inspired by, figures who have expressed anti-Jewish, extremist, and conspiratorial sentiments, or have demonstrated an insensitivity, if not hostility, to Jews and Jewish concerns. This mounting intolerance can expect increasingly to engage Jewish NGOs committed to the principles of pluralism, tolerance, and equality, and, as the American Jewish Committee has put it, to "make the subject of religious intolerance—its dimensions, root causes, and possibly remedial measures—a major focus of its work."

Restitution of Jewish Religious Communal Property: The Reclamation of Jewish Heritage

If actions intended to damage, profane, or destroy objects of religious worship are prohibited as a matter of domestic criminal law, the seizure and plunder of both individual and Jewish religious communal property during World War II was a clear violation of the "laws and customs of war"—a clear "war crime" in the context of the crime of genocide. The restitution of that religious communal property—whose seizure and plunder constituted a mas-

---

[211]Anti-Defamation League, *The Assault on Religious Pluralism* (New York: Anti-Defamation League, 1994).

sive violation of religious human rights—is regarded by Jewish NGOs entrusted with their restitution not only as the protection of religious human rights, but as tantamount almost to a religious duty. Accordingly, one can expect the issue of this reclamation of Jewish heritage—of the protection of memory—to be a priority issue for international Jewish NGOs in the protection of religious human rights.

Religious Rights of Jewish Women

The notion of *agunot* ("chained women") may not yet be a household word among Jewish NGOs, let alone in the Jewish community in general. But it has inspired the creation of a newly formed international Jewish women's rights NGO—the International Coalition for *Agunot* Rights (ICAR)—whose *raison d'être* is the plight of these "forgotten" women and which declared 1994 to be "the Year of Freedom for *Agunot*." If nothing else, it has been the year when the issue finally made it onto the Jewish religious and human rights agenda, though it has yet to become a priority for the mainstream Jewish "human rights" NGOs in Canada, the United States, or Israel, the country constituencies of ICAR.

Briefly put, the problem or plight of these *agunot* is inextricably bound up with Jewish law, or *halachah*, where Jewish women face particular hardship and discrimination by reason of the *get*, or bill of divorce.[212] If the husband refuses to give a *get*, the wife cannot remarry according to Jewish law. If she remarries in a civil ceremony, her children wil be labeled *mamzerim*, or illegitimate, and they, too, will be denied the opportunity of marriage within the precepts of Jewish law. In Canada, this problem is not restricted to the Orthodox Jewish community. Rather, it has repercussions for all Jews who might wish to follow the traditional procedure, and who want their children to be recognized as legitimate members of the Orthodox Jewish community should they so desire.

Interestingly enough, if the woman refuses to receive the *get*, the husband can still appeal for a type of rabbinical dispensation

---

[212]S. Van Praagh, book review of *Religion and Culture in Canada in Family Law*, by John Tibor Syrtach, *McGill Law Journal* 38 (1993): 243.

so that he can remarry; and even if he fails to do so, any children of such a second marriage will nonetheless follow the religion of the mother and therefore will not be subject to the stigma of being *mamzerim*, so that the *get*, even if facially neutral, impacts adversely on Jewish women.

"Regrettably," as Shauna van Praagh has put it, "the importance of the *get* to Jewish women has made it an ideal tool for blackmail."[213] For the "recalcitrant spouse," usually the husband, may refuse to grant a *get* until serious concessions on issues of property division, custody, and support are made by the "victimized spouse," usually the wife, with the "non-gender-neutral character of the problem" reflected in the power and leverage that husbands enjoy in the *get* encounter. Concludes van Praagh: "Wives who fail to receive a *get* are fittingly referred to as *agunot* or 'chained women'."[214]

Examples of such *agunot* abound, of which but a few are the following[215]: (1) A *bet din* in the United States told one woman to drop charges that her husband sexually molested their daughter, in exchange for his issuing the *get*. When she told the rabbis she feared that he might abuse other children, they said the next mother can press charges. (2) In another American case, a woman who had been beaten by her recalcitrant husband with a baseball bat was advised by the rabbis to go on a vacation with him to try and save the marriage. (3) In Canada, a woman mortgaged her house for $120,000 to pay the ransom her husband demanded for a *get*. Another Canadian woman handed over the business she had built to her husband in order to receive a *get*. These practices are now prohibited under the 1990 amendments to the Canadian *Divorce Act* that prevents using a *get* as a bargaining tool to extract concessions in civil matters, such as access to children. (4) In Israel, the rabbinical courts did nothing for a woman who was infected with venereal disease by her recalcitrant husband, who openly lived with a mistress. (5) In one international case, ICAR was able

---

[213]Ibid.

[214]Ibid.

[215]Most of these examples were provided by Norma Baumel Joseph, President of the International Coalition of Agunah Rights (ICAR).

to convince the rabbis to reverse a decision in favor of an abusive husband. When a battered Israeli woman fled to Montreal, rabbis judged her a "rebellious wife" and awarded custody of their children to the father. Through ICAR's intervention, custody eventually went to the mother.

A series of possible solutions may be gleaned from the *get* laws passed by the state of New York in 1984 and 1992,[216] the *get* law passed by the Canadian Parliament in 1990,[217] the representations from a delegation of Jewish women "from across the religious and political spectrum"[218] who met with the two Chief Rabbis of Israel in September 1993, and the *get* law passed by the Israeli Knesset in 1994. These recommendations include the following: (1) prenuptial agreements in which both partners agree to a *get* transaction if the marriage fails; (2) refusal of rabbis to perform marriages in the absence of such prenuptial agreements; (3) "conditional" or "constructive" *gets*, whereby the recalcitrant husband is deemed to have undertaken to divorce his wife in the same way that a husband going to war signs a document that he will be deemed to have divorced his wife if he disappears for a certain number of years; (4) a civil remedy, such as that now provided for in section 21.1 of the Canadian *Divorce Act*, itself the result of effective lobbying by Jewish women NGOs and such mainstream Jewish NGOs as B'nai Brith. This remedy allows the "victimized spouse" to file an affadavit stating that the "recalcitrant spouse" has failed to remove all the barriers to remarriage under his or her control. If the barrier is not removed within fifteen days, the court may dismiss any proceeding or claim filed by the recalcitrant spouse. A similar civil remedy exists under the first *get* law passed by New York State in 1984, which mandates that in order to be granted a civil divorce, the parties must affirm that there is no barrier to remarriage; (5) taking into account a party's refusal to give or receive a *get* when dividing up the assets of a marriage, as provided for in the second *get* law passed by New York State. The law further requires

---

[216]*New York Domestic Relations Law*, s.253 (Consol. 1990).

[217]*An Act to Amend the Divorce Act (Barriers to Religious Remarriage)*, S.C. 1990, c.18, amending R.S.C. 1985 (2d Supp.), c.3, s.21.1.

[218]Joseph (see note 215).

courts to consider the effects of a "barrier" to remarriage on awards of maintenance; (6) annulment of the marriage, which is possible in Judaism; (7) increasing the number of sanctions that rabbinical courts may impose on husbands who refuse to grant their wives a *get*, as provided for in a recent law passed by the Knesset. Hitherto, the only mode of coercion available was imprisonment. Because the *dayanim* (judges on rabbinical courts) were reluctant to avail themselves of so severe a measure, there have been only fourteen cases of imprisonment since the founding of Israel in 1948. In all but one of the cases, the measure proved effective. As a result of the new law, rabbinical courts will be able to limit a recalcitrant husband's right to leave the country, to receive or hold an Israeli passport, to hold a driver's licence, to engage in any employment that requires a bank account, or (if he is in prison) to be released from his imprisonment.

However, if the husband gives a *get* as a result of communal pressure or under threat of fine or imprisonment by a secular court, such pressure may be deemed coercive and therefore invalid according to Jewish law, or invalid as an unconstitutional breach of section 2(a) of the Charter respecting freedom of conscience and religion. Accordingly, any remedy by the state and its courts to aid a wife who has not been granted a *get* must be carefully crafted so that it does not contravene religious law, or does not "fetter" or burden the free exercise of religion, or does not recognize or "further" one particular religion. Both mainstream Jewish NGOs and Jewish women's rights organizations may yet find themselves having to defend remedial measures against the recalcitrant husband and against constitutional challenge on grounds of freedom of religion.[219]

CONCLUSIONS

What has the role of Jewish NGOs in the promotion and protection of religious human rights taught us about the importance of reli-

---

[219]Van Praagh, book review, 245–46.

gious human rights in the panoply of human rights and about the importance of religious human rights to the agenda of Jewish NGOs?

First, the foregoing analysis of the role of Jewish NGOs not only confirms the anchorage of religious human rights in the pantheon of international human rights law—which cynics and skeptics alike will regard as trite law and trite observation—but it demonstrates the persuasive authority of international law in the matter of religious human rights and the efficacy that can be made of it. Whether it be the struggle for the religious human rights of oppressed Jewry abroad, or for the constitutionality of anti-hate legislation at home, international human rights law in the matter of religious human rights has had a significant impact. For example, in the case of the former Soviet Union, preoccupied as it was with law and legitimacy, the invocation of international law and remedy by Jewish NGOs was crucial in the "mobilization of shame against the Achilles heel of the human rights violator," as Sakharov put it, while in the matter of upholding the constitutionality of antidiscrimination and anti-hate legislation, the Supreme Court of Canada invoked international law adduced by Jewish intervenor NGOs as a "'relevant and persuasive authority.'" On both the level of principle and precedent, as well as that of tactics and strategy, the observation may be trite, but the law is not.

Second, religious human rights are not only bound up with the protection of all other rights—and are often the condition for their enjoyment—but they are an indispensible part of the Jewish NGO agenda. Indeed, the major national and international Jewish NGOs not only have the protection of religious human rights as a priority on their agenda, but they have actually been founded for that purpose, as their respective mission statements reveal.

Third, for both national and international Jewish NGOs, the adjectival "Jewish" referent is to be construed broadly as containing not only Jewish concerns of a sectarian character, but ethnic, cultural, national, indeed, existential concerns of a "people." Jewish NGOs regard themselves—though they may not always be so regarded by others—as representing and advocating on behalf of a "people," not just a religion, or a religion that must be construed as being bound up with the identity of a people. Accordingly, the broad construction that is to be put on both the terms

"Jewish" and "religious" in the discussion of "Jewish NGOs and religious human rights" ensures that religious human rights will be at the core not only of the struggle for human rights, but of the Jewish NGO agenda.

Fourth, as the three case studies of the role of international Jewish NGOs in the protection of religious human rights in the international arena demonstrate, the protection of religious human rights is not only part of the larger agenda of human rights, but it is at the core of the Jewish NGO agenda—and Israel, as the "civil religion" of the Jewish people, is central to both. Accordingly, the restitution of Jewish property seized and plundered in the Second World War is not only a question of an unrequited war crime—and therefore central to both the general human rights and Jewish NGO agenda—but the memorandum of agreement between the WJRO and the State of Israel in the matter of the restitution of Jewish religious communal property recognized the State of Israel as "the natural and principal heir to Jewish public property. . . ." Similarly, the agreement between the Vatican and Israel not only recognized the struggle against anti-Semitism as part of the larger struggle for human rights, and central therefore to Jewish NGOs like the World Jewish Congress, but WJC President Edgar Bronfman continuously emphasized that "there can be no normalization of relations between the Catholic Church and the Jewish people, as long as the Church refuses to recognize and establish diplomatic relations with the State of Israel." And the emergence of the new anti-Semitism at the United Nations—where the United Nations, founded as an alliance against racism, was converted into a forum for the dissemination of racism itself—spawns UN Watch, concerned as much with the integrity of the United Nations and the principle of nondiscrimination as with Israel as the pariah "Jew among the Nations." For both national and international Jewish NGOs, Israel is central to Jewish identity, to the Jewish people, to the Jewish NGO agenda. It is inextricably bound up with the promotion and protection of religious human rights as part of the larger agenda for human rights.

Fifth, the principle of separationism—or the "wall of separation" between church and state—is as much culture-bound as it is rights-based. How else to explain that American and Canadian Jewish NGOs have come down on opposite sides of church–state issues in the matter of state aid to religious education, or religious symbols on public property? For the Canadian Jewish NGOs, it is a matter of both the free exercise of religion and the equality of all religions and should be supported; for the American Jewish NGOs, it is a matter of the establishment of religion and should be rejected. One thing, however, is clear: For both sets of NGOs, church–state issues are part of the larger struggle for human rights and central to their respective agendas. It may well be, however, that the opposing views are rooted more in different "rights-based" views of church–state issues and in whether one is speaking of the free exercise of religion or the principle of separationism, rather than whether one is for or against the principle of separationism itself. One equally wonders whether the different rights-based views are not themselves an expression of the legal culture from which they spring, rather than of any "wall of separation" to which they cling. The rights-based perspective itself may not be unrelated to the different Jewish sensibility of American and Canadian NGOs.

Sixth, the contrasting Canadian and American Jewish NGO approaches to the constitutionality of anti-hate legislation—reflected in the earlier snapshot of the syntax of opposing legal arguments—represent not only "two views of liberty," but different views of equality. Indeed, the American perspective is different not only from the Canadian, but from that of the European, Asian, African, and Latin American Jewish NGOs, whose views on hate speech are more communitarian than individualistic, more egalitarian than libertarian, and more inclusive than exclusive. In a word, for all Jewish NGOs except for American ones, combatting racist hate propaganda is not only a compelling issue of combatting discrimination on grounds of religion, but a priority on the Jewish NGO agenda.

Seventh, one of the more interesting findings of this inquiry is that the articulated major premise for Jewish NGO advocacy in the matter of religious human rights reposes in the teachings of the Jewish religion itself. The teachings of the Jewish religion find expression in the very mission statements of the Jewish NGOs, which speak of the responsibility that Jews have for the mending of the world. Moreover, Jewish NGOs have increasingly taken to explaining, or validating, their human rights advocacy with a *Dvar Torah*— a religious teaching grounded in the Torah, Talmud, or rabbinical teaching—thereby emphasizing the importance to Jewish NGOs of religious teachings for the promotion and protection of religious human rights.

Eighth, one of the most encouraging outcomes of this inquiry is the appreciation of the importance that each of the major religions attaches to religious human rights, and the principle of universality that finds expression in the teachings of each of the major religions—the notion that all human beings have been created in the image of God. This holds out much promise and hope not only for the value and validity of interfaith dialogue, but also for joint "trans-religious" NGO advocacy in the promotion and protection of religious human rights. Such "trans-religious" and, where appropriate, transnational advocacy organized around a universalist perspective and principle can be an enormously powerful and effective voice in the struggle for human rights and human dignity in our time.

Ninth, the advocacy and litigation strategy of the major Jewish human rights NGOs in the matter of religious human rights proceeds from the assumption that the "human rights of Jews would be respected and secured to the degree that the rights of all people were safeguarded and respected." Again, this not only reaffirms the importance of religious human rights to the larger agenda of human rights but the importance of religious human rights to the Jewish NGO agenda. Accordingly, most of the cases in which Jewish NGOs filed *amicus* briefs were on behalf of non-Jews. Yet, while this principle is to be welcomed, it can also be a double-edged sword. To the extent that the Jewish NGO intervenes to challenge the constitutionality of policies and practices that are part of the mainstream Christian sensibility, they run the risk not of being respected for their intervention, but of being resented for it.

Tenth, anti-Semitism continues to be history's "longest hatred," as it is history's first "hate crime." But anti-Semitism, as Per Ahlmark has continuously emphasized, is not so much a Jewish problem as a non-Jewish responsibility. As Jean-Paul Sartre put it, "If the Jew did not exist, the anti-Semite would create him." But if a struggle against anti-Semitism must be seen as part of the larger agenda of human rights, so must any religious or racial hatred be seen as a universal responsibility and as part of the Jewish NGO agenda.

Eleventh, the internationalization of human rights—or humanization of international law—has been paralleled by the internationalization of Jewish NGO advocacy. Indeed, it is arguable that it was the early internationalization of Jewish NGO advocacy around religious human rights that may have inspired the Jewish contribution to the development of international human rights law as a whole. As well, in an increasingly interdependent universe, transnational public advocacy may be the defining characteristic of the human rights NGO of the twenty-first century. Accordingly, transnational Jewish NGO advocacy in the promotion and protection of religious human rights may serve as both case study and model for strategic advocacy by human rights NGOs in the matter of the promotion and protection of human rights generally.

Finally, the struggle for Jewish religious rights in the decade ahead will contain its own internal struggle for gender equality. Indeed, while the plight of *agunot* is more a struggle for equality than it is for religion, this denial of equality is rooted in religion itself—a matter that may presage the struggle for equality in all religions as part of the larger struggle for human rights itself and central to the NGO role in the promotion and protection of religious human rights.

EPILOGUE
Human Rights and Human Duties in the Jewish Tradition
Michael J. Broyde
Emory University

The Jewish tradition, as each of the chapters in this book has observed, is a duty-based legal system; rights are not the fundamental coin in the realm of Jewish law. While it is true that almost all "rights" can be expressed as "duties," and the reverse as well, it is equally clear that legal systems make statements about their core values when they express legal norms in one form or another. In Jewish law, the core value is a legal "duty."

Thus, at some level, were this work to be exclusively grounded in the linguistic norms of the Jewish tradition and system, the term "human rights" would be replaced throughout by "human duties." This is not merely a linguistic slight-of-hand maneuver; rather, the substantive rules are expressed as individual and personal obligations. Thus, there is no "right to an education," but rather a "duty to educate"; there is no "right to be fed," but rather a "duty to feed." Indeed, even such commonplace phrases as the "right to divorce" is expressed in the Jewish tradition as a "duty to divorce." Within the Jewish tradition, the expression of legal norms as duties almost inevitably creates a specific duty imposed on a person or group of people obligated to act to fulfill this duty. It is rare that one finds generalized societal obligations in the Jewish tradition—the imposition of a duty requires that one answer the question "Whose duty?" In rights-based systems, frequently this question goes unanswered, and thus rights go unfulfilled.

RIGHTS AND DUTIES IN THE JEWISH TRADITION: THE EXAMPLE OF EDUCATION

Professor Robert Cover of Yale Law School noted the crucial difference between the rights-based approach of common law countries and the duties-based approach of Jewish law:

> [In the United States] [w]hen there is some urgently felt need to change the law or keep it in one way or another, a "Rights" movement is started. Civil Rights, the right to life, welfare rights, and so on. The premium that is to be put upon an entitlement is so coded. When we "take rights seriously," we understand them to be trumps in the legal game. In Jewish law, an entitlement without an obligation is a sad, almost pathetic thing.[1]

Cover's insight is worthy of exploration, since—while the Jewish tradition clearly has a notion of human rights[2]—they are much more clearly expressed as a human duty to act to help others than as a right to be helped.

A classical example of how the rights–duties dichotomy affects how rights and duties actually are implemented can be found in a comparison of the modern human right to an education with the ancient Jewish version of the parent's and society's duty to educate children. Jewish law mandates that a parent—and if a parent cannot, then society—must provide for the religious and moral education of children, and in addition that each person is under a duty to be educated. This obligation is as much a part of the parental duty as is the obligation to feed and clothe. The classical code of Jewish law, the *Shulchan Aruch*, written by Rabbi Joseph Caro, codified the rule: "There is an obligation upon each person to teach his son Jewish law; if the father does not teach him, the son is obligated to teach himself . . . . One is obligated to hire a teacher to teach one's children . . . ."[3] In the Jewish tradition, the duty to pro-

---

[1]Robert M. Cover, "Obligation: A Jewish Jurisprudence of the Social Order," *Journal of Law & Religion* 5:65 (1987): 67 (footnotes omitted).

[2]See, for example, Haim Cohn, *Human Rights in Jewish Law* (1984).

[3]*Shulchan Aruch, Yoreh Deah* 245:1.

vide for the education of children is discussed in considerable detail. Jewish law explains that the obligation to "teach" a child is not limited to reading and text skills, but includes rudimentary Jewish philosophy and theology:

> When does one begin to teach a child? When he begins to speak, one teaches him that God commanded Moses on the Mount with the Law (*Torah*) and the principle of the unity of God. Afterwards, one teaches him a little bit until he is six or seven, at which point one sends him to elementary school.[4]

The Code also mandates that a Jewish school system be established in every community: "Every community is obligated to have an elementary school, and every community that does not have an elementary school should be shunned [until one is established] . . . since the world only exists out of the merit of the discourse found when small children study."[5]

Indeed, that broad mandate to educate is not the end of the discussion. The Code addresses the details of classroom management also. For example, it states: "Twenty-five children to a teacher. If there are more than twenty-five students and less than forty, one must provide a teacher's aide; when there are more than forty students, a second teacher must be provided."[6]

The purpose of this duty to educate is not merely an abstract commitment to aid in the acquisition of knowledge. Rather, as one recent article noted:

> Jewish law imposed a duty to educate a child in those duties [and laws] that he will be obligated in as an adult, in order that he should be prepared and familiar with the commandments. . . . Even though a minor is not obligated to observe the law, he should do so as a form of preparation for adulthood. . . . The same is true for the study of religious texts. The early authorities note that the biblical verse "and you should teach your children to speak about

---

[4]*Shulchan Aruch, Yoreh Deah* 245:5.
[5]*Shulchan Aruch, Yoreh Deah* 245:7.
[6]*Shulchan Aruch, Yoreh Deah* 245:15.

[Jewish law]"[7] requires that one familiarize one's children with the study of Jewish law.[8]

Jewish law does not confine the duty to receive an education to children only. In the chapter immediately following the rules related to teaching children, the *Shulchan Aruch* states: "Every Jew is obligated to study Judaism whether he be rich or poor, healthy or sick, single or married. . . . All are obligated to set aside a time for study every day and night."[9]

Adults, like children, have a duty to spend time educating themselves and have the right to receive an education. When a Jewish society allocates resources to education, adult education is no less a priority than children's education.[10] Indeed, it is an open issue how, in the Jewish tradition, parents are supposed to balance their own needs to study with the needs of their children. A person who cannot afford for himself to study and also to pay for the education of his child is only supposed to assign a higher priority to his child's education if he feels that the child will derive more benefit from that education than he will.[11]

In sum, the Jewish tradition mandates a duty to educate oneself and one's children. This creates first and foremost a duty to educate, and then a resulting right to education. The emphasis, however, remains on the duty. There is well nigh no discussion of the "right" in the Jewish tradition.

---

[7]Deuteronomy 11:19.

[8]"Chinuch," *Encyclopedia Talmudica*, pp. 161–162, note 5. Indeed, the Hebrew term used to discuss children's education reflects this notion. The term used (*chinuch*) means "beginning" or "preparation," as the focus of Jewish law's educational policies is to prepare children for their roles as adults. For more on this, see Maimonides, *Commentary on the Mishnah, Minachot* 4:5.

[9]*Shulchan Aruch, Yoreh Deah* 246:1.

[10]Indeed, when the *Shulchan Aruch* discusses the laws of education, it has some sections that discuss the problems of educating adults (*Yoreh Deah* 246:7–17) and some sections discussing the problems of educating children (*Yoreh Deah* 245:9–20).

[11]*Shulchan Aruch, Yoreh Deah* 245:2.

Given this parental duty to educate, it is not surprising to discover that the abandonment of this duty affects many other parental rights. One of the classical examples of this is in the area of child custody law. Rabbi Asher ben Yecheil, one of the premier medieval commentators on Jewish law, in the course of discussing the custody of children, asserts the theory that the right of parents to custody of their children appears to be a manifestation solely of the duty to educate one's children.[12] Rabbi Asher states that since the Talmud ruled that one must educate children, it is intuitive and obvious that this "duty" to educate gives rise to a "right" of custody, which is necessary to fulfill the duty to educate. He then asserts that one should use this obligation to educate to determine which parent should receive custody in cases where the marriage has ended. In those cases where the mother bears the primary duty to educate, the mother has the right of custody; when the father bears the duty, he has the right.

The Jewish duty-based approach stands in contrast to the rights-based approach of modern legal theory. There is little doubt that modern international law recognizes the right of children to an education. For example, Article 28 of the United Nations Convention on the Rights of the Child declares:

> States' parties recognize the right of the child to education, and with a view to achieving this right progressively and on the basis of equal opportunity, they shall, in particular:
>
>   (a) Make primary education compulsory and available free to all;
>
>   (b) Encourage the development of different forms of secondary education, including general and vocational education;[13]

So too, Article 29 of this same convention tells us the purpose of this right to an education:

> States' parties agree that the education of the child shall be directed to:

---

[12]Rabbi R. Asher ben Yecheil, *Responsa of Asher (Rosh)* 17:7; *Responsa of Asher* 82:2.

[13]United Nations Convention on the Rights of the Child, Article 28, U.N. Doc. A/Res/44/23 (1989).

(a) The development of the child's personality, talents, and mental and physical abilities to their fullest potential;[14]

However, international law imposes no duty on a child to be educated, and certainly imposes no duty on adults to continue their education. Indeed, it is unclear whether parents have any duty to educate their children at all. While there has been a vast expansion of the rights of a child to an education in the last decade in America, this has been nearly exclusively limited to the redefining of the child's *right to an education.*[15] When the requirement of society to fulfill children's rights to education ceases, the obligations of education cease, as the young adult is under no obligation to self-educate. Indeed, while a child has a "right to an education," he does not have a duty to receive that education, either as an adult or a child.

Thus, the secular human rights tradition has created a right without a duty, and the Jewish tradition has come close to creating a duty without a right.

RIGHTS, DUTIES, AND RELIGIOUS OBLIGATIONS

A focus on duty alone as the Jewish form of rights, however, risks the loss of the essentially religious character of the Jewish tradition. People were "created in the image of God" (Genesis 1:27); an innate conceptualization of humanity that focuses merely on the technical legal rules—whether they be rights or duties—misses one of the fundamental purposes of the Jewish tradition: to provide a sense of the Divine in the lives of people. In this regard the essential characteristics of Jewish law differ from those of any secular legal tradition, as Jewish law is predicated on the duty to imitate the Divine. As one of the essays in this book puts it so well, Jewish law provides a medium in which the top of Jacob's ladder, which

---

[14]United Nations Convention on the Rights of the Child, Article 29.

[15]See, for example, Alexandra Natapoff, "1993: The Year of Living Dangerously: State Courts Expand the Right to Education," *Education Law Reporter* 92 (1994): 755–787, which documents the vast increase in the right to education given to children within the last ten years.

reached into the heavens, interacts with our daily life on the bottom of the ladder.[16]

Indeed, one can point to a variety of doctrines that are part of the Jewish tradition, whose purpose is to facilitate the moral development of people. Thus, the prophet Isaiah (Isaiah 42:6) directs that the Jewish people should be a "light onto the nations of the world." As noted by Rabbi David Kimchi in his classical commentary, "because of the influence of the Jews, the Gentiles will observe the laws they are directed to observe and follow the right path."[17] So, too, the mandate to correct the failures of the world (*tikkun olam*) provides clear evidence that the Jewish tradition recognizes a place beyond the technical legal formulations found in Jewish law and instead directs the Jewish tradition to participate in the world around it.

Indeed, this spirit imbues even legal issues that are central to the Jewish tradition and clearly demonstrates that the outer parameters of that which Jewish law dictates as permissible do *not* establish that which is morally laudatory or preferred. For example, it seems well established that, for a variety of reasons, the Jewish tradition averred that one was under no legal obligation to stop a gentile from violating even basic tenets of morality.[18] But yet, the

---

[16]See chapter by Berger and Lipstadt herein.

[17]For other examples of this phrase in rabbinic literature, see *Bava Batra* 75a; *Midrash Rabbah Esther* 7:11; *Midrash Berashit* 59:7; and *Midrash Tehilim* (Bubar) 36:6. For a sample of its use in the responsa literature, see Tzitz Eliezer 10:1(74); Yavetz 1:168; and particularly Chatam Sofer 6:84; see also Responsa of Rosh 4:40, which is also cited in Tur OC 59. This concept plays yet a more prominent note in kabbalistic literature; see *Sefer Rasesai Layla*, §57, *s.v. techlat* and *vezehu.* For a defense of this beacon-like (i.e., Jews behave properly and this illuminates the world) understanding of the verse as the proper understanding of the literal meaning of the Bible itself, see Harry Orlinsky, "A Light onto the Nations: A Problem in Biblical Theology," in Neuman & Zeitlin, *The Seventy-Fifth Anniversary Volume of the Jewish Quarterly Review* (1967): 409–428.

[18]See my "Public Policy and Religious Law: Assisting in a Deliberate Violation of Noahide Law That Is Permitted by Secular Law," *Jewish Law Association Studies 8: The Jerusalem 1994 Conference*, vols. 11–20 (Scholars Press, 1996).

Jewish tradition is replete with moralistic dicta encouraging one to engage in this conduct. Thus, Rabbi Judah the Pious, writing in the middle of the Crusades, states: "When one sees a gentile erring, if one can correct him, one should, since God sent Jonah to Nineveh to return them to his path."[19] Indeed, Rabbi Joseph B. Soloveitchik continues the theme of Rabbi Judah the Pious when he states:

> There may be an additional reason for [the prophet] Jonah's association with Yom Kippur . . . Nineveh was the capital city of pagan Assyria . . . It was a country which would later, under Sennacherib in 722 B.C.E., besiege Jerusalem and exile the ten tribes. Yet God's compassion embraces all of humanity . . . It is, therefore, characteristic of the universal embrace of our faith that as the shadows of dusk descend on Yom Kippur day . . . the Jew is alerted . . . that all of humanity are God's children. We need to restate the Universal dimension of our faith, especially when we are sorely persecuted and are apt to regard the world in purely confrontational terms.[20]

In short, the Jewish tradition has a clear religious model for involving itself in the broader community for the betterment of the whole community—which is the fundamental concept of human rights.

THE TASK AHEAD

On July 4, 1994, on receiving the Liberty Medal in Philadelphia, President Vaclav Havel of the Czech Republic noted—with the flair of the dramatic poet that he is—the challenge for human rights in the world today. He stated:

> [T]he only real hope of people today is probably a renewal of our certainty that we are rooted in the Earth and, at the same time, the

---

[19]Rabbi Judah the Pious, *Sefer HaChasidim* (Jerusalem, 1964), 1124.

[20]*Reflections of the Rav: Man of Faith in the Modern World* (adaptations of the lectures of Rabbi Joseph B. Soloveitchik), by Abraham Besdin (New York, 1984), 142–144.

cosmos. This awareness endows us with the capacity for self-transcendence. Politicians at international forums may reiterate a thousand times that the basis of the new world order must be universal respect for human rights, but it will mean nothing as long as this imperative does not derive from the respect of the miracle of being, the miracle of the universe, the miracle of nature, the miracle of our own existence. Only someone who submits in the authority of the universal order and of creation, who values the right to be a part of it, and a participant in it, can genuinely value himself and his neighbors, and thus honor their rights as well.[21]

The essays in this book have each attempted to provide a uniquely Jewish answer to this challenge. Together they paint a picture that outlines much about how the Jewish tradition views human rights, both on a political level and on a religious one. As *Ethics of the Sages* (2:16) recounts, "It is not your job to finish the task; however, you are not free to abandon the task (merely because you cannot complete it)." Yet many other essays remain to be written in the field, and may it be that the field of religious human rights generally, and Jewish human rights specifically, continues to grow and blossom—so that we may all eat from the fruits of its accomplishments.

---

[21]V. Havel, "Speech on July 4, 1994, in Philadelphia, on Receipt of the Liberty Medal," reported and excerpted in *Philadelphia Inquirer* (July 5, 1994): A08; *Buffalo News* (July 10, 1994): F8; and *Newsweek* (July 18, 1994): 66.

NOTES ON CONTRIBUTORS

Michael S. Berger, Ph.D. (Columbia), is Assistant Professor of Religious Authority and Ethics in Judaism at Emory University. He has received a number of distinguished awards and fellowships at Columbia, Princeton, and the Hebrew University, including the Memorial Foundation for Jewish Culture Award. He has published a number of articles and book chapters on the Jewish legal and moral tradition and has a book forthcoming on *The Authority of the Babylonian Talmud*.

Michael J. Broyde, J.D. (New York University), is Senior Lecturer in Law and Director of the Project on Law, Religion, and the Family at Emory University. He serves on the Executive Board of the Jewish Law Association and edits its journal. Professor Broyde received his Advanced Ordination at the Rabbi Isaac Elchanan Theological Seminary of Yeshiva University and is a widely recognized authority in Jewish law. He has published some fifty articles in both English and Hebrew on comparative law and contemporary halakhic approaches to technology, ethics, and public policy issues and is the author of a new volume, *The Pursuit of Justice and Jewish Law*.

Irwin Cotler, LL.D. (York University), is a Professor of Law and Member of the Institute of Comparative Law at McGill University in Montreal and a regular visiting professor at Harvard Law School and the Hebrew University of Jerusalem. Professor Cotler is a distinguished authority and advocate of international human rights and constitutional protections and has led a number of celebrated campaigns to free prisoners of conscience in the former Soviet bloc, including Natan Sharansky and Andrei Sakharov. He has lectured frequently and testified in human rights cases in North America, Latin America, Europe, Russia, and the Middle East. His recent publications include *The Sharansky Case*, *International Human Rights Law: Theory and Practice*, and *Nuremberg, Forty-Five Years Later*.

Deborah E. Lipstadt, Ph.D. (Brandeis), is Dorot Professor of Modern Jewish History and Holocaust Studies at Emory University, Director of Research at the Skirball Institute on American Values, and Consultant on America and the Holocaust at the United States Holocaust Memorial Museum in Washington, D.C. Professor Lipstadt is also a Member of the Board of Directors of the Association for Jewish Studies and Senior Contributing Editor of the *Jewish Spectator*. She is a widely respected authority on Holocaust studies and American Jewish History and has received numerous grants and awards for her work. Her publications include *Beyond Belief: The American Press and the Coming of the Holocaust, 1933–1945*, and *Denying the Holocaust: The Growing Assault on Truth and Memory*.

Asher Maoz, LL.B. and LL.M. (Hebrew University, Israel), M. Comp. Lit. (Chicago), J.S.D. (Tel-Aviv), is Senior Lecturer of Law at Tel-Aviv University, member of The Institute for Research of Family Law, and co-director of the Temple-Tel-Aviv summer law program. Professor Maoz is an expert in Israeli law, human rights, and family law and has received numerous scholarships and awards for his work, which is regularly cited by the Israeli Supreme Court and other Israeli tribunals. He has published more than three dozen articles and book chapters in both Hebrew and English and is co-author of *The Law of Succession*.

David Novak, Ph.D. (Georgetown), is the Director of the Programme in Jewish Studies at the University of Toronto, Vice President of the Institute on Religion and Public Life, and founder and Vice President of the Union for Traditional Judaism. Dr. Novak is an internationally acclaimed scholar in the field of Jewish law, ethics, and theology and has lectured throughout the world. Among his books are *Jewish*

Social Ethics, The Theology of Nahmanides, Jewish–Christian Dialogue, and *The Image of the Non-Jew in Judaism.*

John Witte, Jr., J.D. (Harvard), is the Jonas Robitscher Professor of Law and Director of the Law and Religion Program at Emory University, and a member of the Project on Religion, Culture, and the Family at the University of Chicago. A specialist in legal history, church–state relations, and law and religion, he has published some seventy professional articles and book chapters, has edited amid eight books, *Christianity and Democracy in Global Context, A Christian Theory of Social Institutions,* and *The Weightier Matters of the Law: Essays on Law and Religion,* and is the author of three forthcoming volumes, *From Sacrament to Contract: Religion, Marriage and Law in the West; Law and the Protestants: The Lutheran Reformation;* and *The American Experiment in Religious Rights and Liberties.*

INDEX

About the Editors

Michael J. Broyde is a senior lecturer at Emory Law School and the Associate Director of the Law and Religion Program at Emory University. His primary areas of interest are Jewish law and ethics, law and religion, and comparative religious law. He received a *juris doctor* from New York University and is an ordained rabbi by Yeshiva University. He currently serves as the rabbi of the Young Israel Synagogue in Toco Hills, Atlanta. Michael J. Broyde has published nearly 50 articles in various aspects of Jewish law, and a number of articles in other areas of law and religion. His first book is entitled *The Pursuit of Justice and Jewish Law*.

John Witte, Jr. is the Jonas Robitscher Professor of Law and Ethics and is Director of the Law and Religion Program at Emory University in Atlanta. An authority on legal history, marriage law, and religious liberty, he has published 65 professional articles and eight books, including *Religious Human Rights in Global Perspective* (*Volumes 1 & 2*), *Christianity and Democracy in Global Context*, and *From Sacrament to Contract: Marriage, Religion, and Law in the West*. Mr. Witte has lectured throughout North America, Western Europe, Israel, and South Africa.